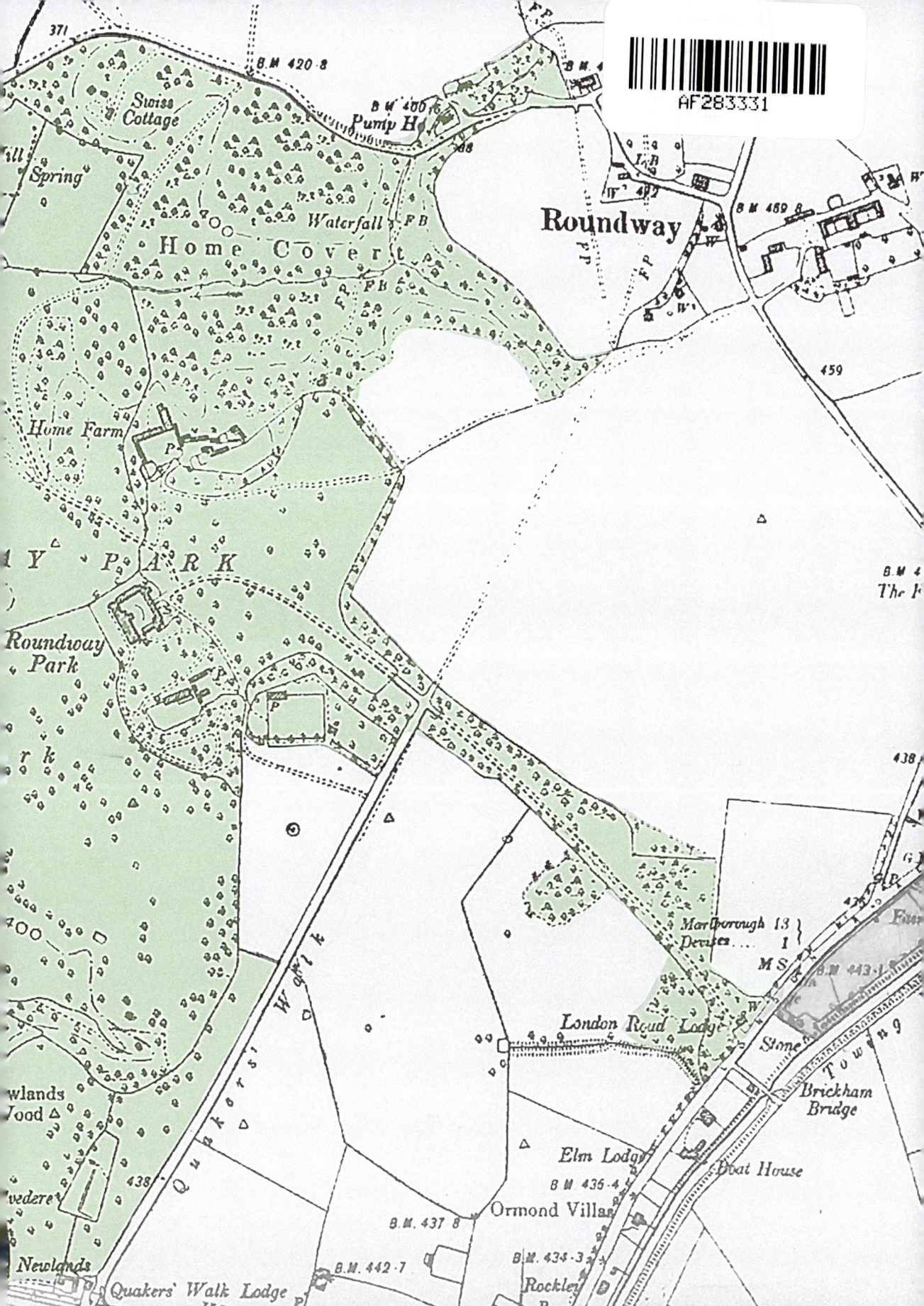

THE
FORGOTTEN
COUNTRY HOUSE

THE
FORGOTTEN
COUNTRY
HOUSE

The Rise and Fall of Roundway Park

Simon Baynes

Quiller

First published in the UK in 2019 by Quiller,
an imprint of Quiller Publishing Ltd.

British Library Cataloguing-in-Publication Data
A catalogue record for this book is available from
the British Library.

ISBN 978 1 84689 3063

Printed in Great Britain by Bell and Bain Ltd, Glasgow

Quiller
An imprint of Quiller Publishing Ltd
Wykey House, Wykey, Shrewsbury, SY4 1JA
Tel: 01939 261616
Email: info@quillerbooks.com
Website: www.quillerpublishing.com

To

*my mother Shirley, Lady Baynes, and
my late father, Lt Col Sir John Baynes, Bt,
for all their love and encouragement.*

Contents

Preface   ix

PART 1: RISE   1

  1   The High Summer of Georgian Devizes   3
  2   James Wyatt and Humphry Repton at New Park   13
  3   The Suttons, Addingtons and Estcourts   27
  4   The Colstons: Honeymoon and Grand Tour   37
  5   The Colstons at Roundway Park   45
  6   Lives Cut Short   53
  7   Love and Marriage   61
  8   Family Life   69

PART 2: HEYDAY   81

  9   Roundway Park's Victorian Heyday   83
 10   A Day in the Life of Roundway Park   101
 11   Henry Robinson: Butler Extraordinaire   111
 12   The New Century   121
 13   The World at their Feet   131
 14   The Great War   139

PART 3: DECLINE   151

 15   'Never Glad Confident Morning Again!'   153
 16   The Inter-war Years   161
 17   Loyal Service   171
 18   The Beginning of the End   179
 19   Sounding the Last Post   187
 20   The Sale of Roundway Park   193
 21   White Knight   201

EPILOGUE   213

Left: The west front of Roundway Park in the 1870s.

Appendix I: Key Dates   221
Appendix II: A Brief History of the Ownership of New/Roundway Park   226
Appendix III: Slavery and Philanthropy – the Life of Edward Colston   227
Appendix IV: A Portrait of Dorothy Colston-Baynes   235

Endnotes   248
Acknowledgements   267
Index   269

Preface

IN 1974, when I was aged 14, a battered tin trunk arrived at our home containing papers and correspondence relating to the historical biographer Dormer Creston, the pen-name of my cousin Dorothy Colston-Baynes, who had died the previous year. Reading through the contents, I found a wealth of information about Roundway Park, the estate in Wiltshire which had belonged to Dorothy's mother's family, the Colstons, and about which she had written glowingly in her autobiography *Enter a Child*. I became fascinated and determined to find out more about this now largely demolished and forgotten country house.

The house, designed in the Palladian style by James Wyatt, was built between 1777 and 1783 and had grounds and parkland landscaped by Humphry Repton. It was closely linked to the town of Devizes by its history, as well as by a magnificent tree-lined avenue called Quakers Walk.

After the death in 1944 of Dorothy's first cousin Edward Colston, the 2nd and last Lord Roundway, whose only child, Betty, had tragically died at the age of 14, the mansion at Roundway was sold in 1947 to the local education authority. A year later the surrounding estate of 1,584 acres was acquired by the Society of Merchant Venturers of Bristol with which the Colston family had been closely connected since the 17th century.

Within a very few years of its sale, it became apparent that the house was completely unsuited to its new proposed use as a teacher training college and the cost of its upkeep unsustainable for the local education authority. After questions were asked in the House of Commons in April 1953 to the Education Minister, who said her Department had no further use for Roundway, the local council quickly declared it to be of no particular architectural merit and put it up for sale, in the full knowledge that the house would most likely be demolished.

By November of the same year, it had indeed been sold for demolition to a London firm called Griffiths for £6,000. By good fortune, a Devizes building contractor, Peter White, heard about the sale and managed to buy it from Griffiths in time to save the house from being condemned in its entirety. In a manner later praised by John Betjeman and the Georgian Group, Mr White reduced it to a manageable size in 1954 and lived there with his family until the early 1960s.

The smoothly synchronised way in which Roundway Park was despatched for demolition by central and local government seems shocking to us now but was not unusual in the very straitened times following the Second World War, when many such houses met with the same or worse fates. In many ways, the history of Roundway Park epitomises the rise and fall of the

English country house, which thrived in the Georgian and Victorian eras but in many cases collapsed under the weight of social and economic change in the 20th century.

Shortly after the arrival of Dorothy's letters and papers at my childhood home, the seminal exhibition *The Destruction of the Country House 1875–1975* took place at the Victoria & Albert Museum, and did so much to heighten public awareness of the fate of the country house. My father and I saw the exhibition, in which a photograph of Roundway was included, when it travelled to Bristol. Roundway was just one of 1,116 houses listed which had been destroyed since 1875, with over half having perished after 1945. Since then the figure for the total number destroyed between 1880 and 2014 has been revised upwards to 1,921.[1]

Decaying greenhouse at Roundway House in 1978.

I visited Roundway for the first time in 1978, when I stayed with Eileen Thomas, the widow of Lord Roundway's last estate manager, in the Swiss Cottage on the estate, and saw the remains of the mansion, gardens and home farm. Since then, I have discovered many letters, journals, interviews and published memoirs which provide precious details of the Colstons and their predecessors, the Suttons and Estcourts, and country-house life at Roundway over the best part of two centuries.

Roundway Park's owners played an active role in the town of Devizes and the county of Wiltshire for more than two centuries and also distinguished themselves on the national stage, in politics, business and literature. Generations of staff worked at Roundway, none more so than the remarkable butler Henry Robinson (1874–1959) who was a leading authority on breeding hounds. This book also gives voice to their lives and recognises the vital contribution that they made.

There are aspects of the story that are troubling to us today, particularly that part of the Colstons' wealth which originated from the slave trade. Compared to many landed families, however, the Suttons, Estcourts and Colstons were enlightened landowners and employers who loved their corner of Wiltshire and the community in which they lived.

Much that is written about country houses in Britain focuses on well-known aristocratic families whereas this book, drawing on a large amount of new research, provides a picture of the lives of the gentry who far outnumbered their aristocratic counterparts and played a central role in the rural communities which characterised much of Britain up until the First World War.

Above all, this book has been a personal pilgrimage, inspired by my late father John Baynes (1928–2005), a noted military historian, who used to tell my brothers, Christopher, Tim and William and me stories about the lost inheritance of Roundway Park. Writing about your own family is problematic: I feel a loyalty to them regardless of whether I knew them or they died many years ago and I appreciate that this story will affect people's view of my family, not always favourably.

I am also aware of being mercenary in my analysis but I do not believe that you can understand the rise and fall of any country house unless you comprehend the ebb and flow of the family's finances. The book also carries the risk of implying that I think the gilded past it depicts was better, which I certainly do not: our own times, with all their faults and inequalities, are immeasurably better and fairer for the vast majority of people.

Despite these reservations, my father and I felt that the story of Roundway Park should be told because of the rich detail that exists in our family papers and because history comes alive when illustrated by real people with all their eccentricities and often strange experiences. My father had a relatively modest upbringing in comparison to the senior branch of our family which features in this book; he was the son of a professional soldier, and worked hard throughout his career in the army, running Lake Vyrnwy Hotel in Mid-Wales and writing 11 books. My discovery of the Roundway papers was made in the 1970s when Britain's decline was all too clear to see, so it is not surprising that we both looked back in our own family history to a wealthier age and wanted to describe it and then analyse how it changed.

I am very sorry that my father's untimely death some years ago means that he will not see the final version of our joint enterprise but I hope he would have approved and that this book ensures the remarkable story of Roundway Park is no longer forgotten, but instead is celebrated and enjoyed.

Simon Baynes, September 2019

PART 1

RISE

Left: New Park, Wiltshire from *The Beauties of England and Wales* by John Britton (1814).

Map of Wiltshire by M. F. Peck (©The Salmon Picture Library).

1

The High Summer of Georgian Devizes

THE BUILDING of Roundway Park in the last quarter of the 18th century, or New Park as it was then known, was a celebration of the dynamism and success of Georgian Devizes. The fine Palladian house was built by a local family, the Suttons, who had made their money as cloth merchants, a business that had flourished on the back of the rich wool trade of the West Country.

Devizes itself was in historical terms a relatively modern creation. The first castle was built around 1080 by Osmund, Bishop of Salisbury, and was known as 'castrum ad divisas', the castle of the boundaries, from which the town derives its name. Over time, a small town developed outside the castle's boundaries to supply the castle. In the 14th century the cloth trade gradually became the most important local industry, overtaking the leather trade, and the medieval street pattern from that time has lasted to this day. The town continued to prosper, which resulted in many fine buildings, particularly in the Georgian period in which the story of our house begins.

James Sutton (1733–1801) epitomised both this prosperity and the propensity to use cloth trade wealth for ambitious building projects. As neoclassicism became the defining style for the late 18th century English country house, the design of New Park perfectly represented this affinity with the classical age. James set his sights at the highest level in his choice of architect, James Wyatt, and landscape designer, Humphry Repton, both of whom were the leading practitioners in their fields at the time. New Park was built between 1777 and 1783 and Repton made his Red Book of landscaping designs for the house and estate a little later in 1794.

This fascinating time in Devizes' history is chronicled in the work of the historian Dr Lorna Haycock:

> The fine Georgian architecture of Devizes fossilises a provincial community at the height of its prosperity as a commercial, social and service centre in its regional hinterland. Lying in the centre of the county, it became the secondary capital of Wiltshire after Salisbury. As a Quarter Sessions town and a political and administrative

centre, it attracted gentry and professionals. Behind the brick facades and the medieval street pattern, a hierarchical society developed, based on trade, business and manufactures. But although there was a marked social pyramid in the town, a web of contacts linked traders, professionals and gentry, who contributed to its economic and cultural life by taking the lead in the administration of borough and social affairs. The presence of this elite provided the ethos and dynamics of Devizes society ...

Devizes Town Hall designed by Thomas Baldwin in 1806 (©Wiltshire Museum, Devizes).

This stable core of local gentry, business and professional families, forming some 4% of the population, and becoming more outward-looking through their national investments and connections and their ownership of lucrative property, assisted the integration of rural and urban society, while their life styles generated greater economic growth. It was no accident that the finest houses in town were occupied by the Garths, Heathcotes, Lockes, Salmons and Suttons. They played an important role in establishing the conditions in which trade could flourish and helped to create the high summer of the Devizes economy.[2]

The Suttons had been based in Devizes since the 16th century and had risen in wealth and influence to become one of the richest clothier families in Wiltshire and the dominant political force in Devizes in the second half of the 18th century.[3] James Sutton's ancestor Edward Sutton had been elected MP for Devizes in 1656 and his grandfather, also James (1678–1740), had been Mayor of Devizes several times. This political strength brought many benefits to the family, not only in terms of local prestige but also in influencing national policy, such as the protection of cloth manufacture and agriculture, the two main sources of income for the Suttons and, indeed, for the whole country before the Industrial Revolution.

The Suttons married well. James's father, Prince Sutton (1701–79), married Mary Willy in c1730[4] thereby unifying two leading families of the town which had been linked by business

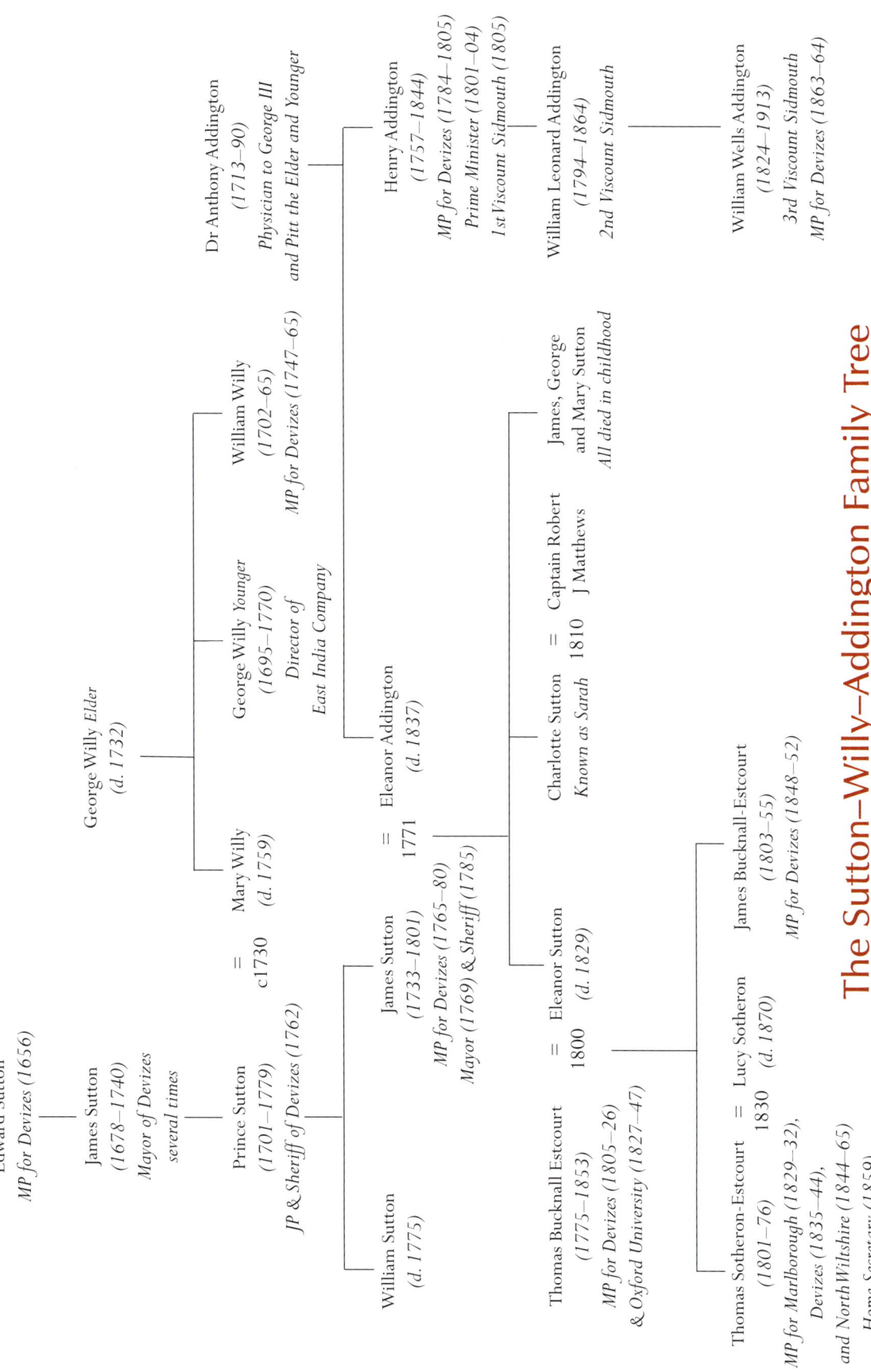

The Sutton–Willy–Addington Family Tree

Edward Sutton
MP for Devizes (1656)

James Sutton
(1678–1740)
Mayor of Devizes
several times

George Willy *Elder*
(d. 1732)

Prince Sutton
(1701–1779)
JP & Sheriff of Devizes (1762)

=
c1730

Mary Willy
(d. 1759)

George Willy *Younger*
(1695–1770)
Director of
East India Company

William Willy
(1702–65)
MP for Devizes (1747–65)

Dr Anthony Addington
(1713–90)
Physician to George III
and Pitt the Elder and Younger

William Sutton
(d. 1775)

James Sutton
(1733–1801)
MP for Devizes (1765–80)
Mayor (1769) & Sheriff (1785)

=
1771

Eleanor Addington
(d. 1837)

Henry Addington
(1757–1844)
MP for Devizes (1784–1805)
Prime Minister (1801–04)
1st Viscount Sidmouth (1805)

William Leonard Addington
(1794–1864)
2nd Viscount Sidmouth

Thomas Bucknall Estcourt
(1775–1853)
MP for Devizes (1805–26)
& Oxford University (1827–47)

=
1800

Eleanor Sutton
(d. 1829)

Charlotte Sutton
Known as Sarah

=
1810

Captain Robert
J Matthews

James, George
and Mary Sutton
All died in childhood

William Wells Addington
(1824–1913)
3rd Viscount Sidmouth
MP for Devizes (1863–64)

Thomas Sotheron-Estcourt
(1801–76)
MP for Marlborough (1829–32),
Devizes (1835–44),
and North Wiltshire (1844–65)
Home Secretary (1859)

=
1830

Lucy Sotheron
(d. 1870)

James Bucknall-Estcourt
(1803–55)
MP for Devizes (1848–52)

interests from the late 17th century.[5] Mary's father, George Willy the elder, left property to his Sutton relations in his will of 1732,[6] a process that would be repeated by the next generation.

Between 1759 and 1762 members of the two families held between them the principal offices in Devizes: George Willy the younger (1695–1770) as Mayor, and his brother-in-law Prince Sutton as Sheriff (1762) and Justice of the Peace.[7] In the absence of bureaucratic control from central government, a Justice of the Peace at that time wielded great power and influence locally, being in a sense a 'one man local authority' who administered local justice, maintained the roads, bridges, prisons and workhouses, licensed public houses and levied a public rate if required.

The families also retained their parliamentary influence. Between 1747 and 1832, one of the two Devizes parliamentary seats was held by a member or associate of the New Park family, while the other one was held by a local merchant or someone with strong local connections, rather than being controlled by a wealthy aristocrat. George Willy the younger's brother, William (1702–65),[8] was MP between 1747 and 1765; after his death the seat was inherited by James Sutton himself. James held the position of MP from 1768 until 1780 and was also Mayor of Devizes in 1769 and Sheriff in 1785. Records show that he never spoke in debates in the House of Commons and generally supported the government.

Up until the 1832 Reform Act,[9] the electorate consisted of the burgesses of the town and the highest number who voted was 30 in 1830. Parliamentary elections in Devizes were not contested between 1785 and 1818; little wonder that 'Orator' Henry Hunt, the radical campaigner for parliamentary reform, described Devizes as 'a corrupt and vile rotten borough'. James Sutton viewed his position as an MP as a civic duty: 'unfit as I am for a public life, I should have thought it criminal to have disturbed the unanimity of the Borough, which by declining I should inevitably have occasioned'.[10]

Apart from political influence, James owed a great deal to his maternal uncles, George Willy the younger and William Willy, for two other reasons. It was through George that he inherited the New Park estate, which included a Queen Anne house; George had originally left the estate to James's elder brother, William, who died unmarried aged 43 in 1775.[11] From William Willy, a Director of the East India Company, a highly lucrative position at the time, James also inherited in 1765 a mercantile clothing business in London.

James, like his father, married well. In 1771 he wed Eleanor Addington at the City church of St Stephen Walbrook in London.[12] She was the daughter of Dr Anthony Addington of Reading who was physician to George III (he was consulted on the monarch's 'madness') and to both Pitt the Elder and Younger. Eleanor's brother Henry went on to be Prime Minister between 1801 and 1804.

Two years after James and Eleanor's marriage, Dr Addington was called upon by Pitt the Elder in 1773 to see his 14-year-old son, William, who had been taken seriously ill while at

Cambridge. He recommended that the younger Pitt should go to bed early, follow a specific diet, take regular exercise on horseback and should 'drink a daily quantity of port wine, variously recollected down the generations as "a bottle a day" or "liberal potations" …' This famous piece of medical advice may have influenced, in the words of his biographer William Hague, Pitt's 'social habits throughout the rest of his life and quite possibly contributed, three decades later, to his early death'.[13]

Eleanor and James had five children of whom only two, Eleanor and Charlotte (also known as Sarah), survived to adulthood. Their London base was a house in Southampton Street, between the Strand and Covent Garden, where expenses for furnishings were recorded in 1774–76.[14] Their growing family was probably an important factor in leading James, now in his mid-forties, to start work on New Park to Wyatt's designs in 1777.

James was also in a strong financial position. The late 18th century was a period of economic expansion, fuelled by population growth at home (the population of England and Wales grew by about two thirds in the 18th century) and a significant expansion in Britain's overseas territories and, therefore, access to export markets abroad. In addition to his inheritance of New Park, and his uncle's business, James also stood to inherit his father Prince Sutton's extensive property at Manningford Bruce and Beckhampton. It was, no doubt, helpful that his cousin, also named James Sutton, co-founded the first Devizes bank in 1775, which became necessary due to the confluence of expanding commerce and more productive agriculture at this time. The number of country banks expanded rapidly over the next years, rising nationally from 119 in 1784 to 800 by 1809,[15] which meant that the Suttons had done well to establish their bank early on.

The area covered by the New Park estate had formed part of one of two parks around Devizes that belonged to the Earls of Pembroke and was known as the 'new' or 'little' park. The 'old' or 'great' park, which lay south-west of Devizes Castle, was a heavily wooded deer park of about 600 acres, surrounded by a 15ft rampart to protect the hunting, which had been created by Roger of Caen, Bishop of Salisbury, who rebuilt Devizes Castle after it burnt down in 1113.[16] The new park, first recorded in 1157, was mainly pastureland, probably surrounded by a bank and ditch. Both parks and Devizes Castle had previously been part of the dowry of the queens of England. Katherine Parr (1512–48), the sixth wife of Henry VIII, was the last queen to hold the dowry.[17]

The Pembrokes sold the parks in the early 17th century at which point they were split up under several ownerships,[18] including Sir Peter Vanlore (father and son), the Earl of Stirling and Edmund Hope,[19] until the Willy and Sutton families effectively stitched 'new' park back together again through their various land purchases.

The Willy family and, to a lesser extent, the Suttons had started to acquire land in the area in the late 17th century, thereby increasing their status and local influence. These acquisitions were typical of the period when merchants as well as large landowners started to buy out struggling small squires who lacked capital to invest in new methods of land improvement and were hard hit by the land tax which was introduced to fund the wars of William and Mary. The acquisitive landowners were also driven by the need to convert their mercantile wealth into real estate in the absence of alternative investments due to the lack of a regular stock market or, until the end of the 18th century, a well-developed banking sector.

James's uncle William Willy is shown as the owner of a patchwork of landholdings on Edward Nicholas's plan of Roundway Farm (undated but probably drawn up in the mid-18th century), which adjoin smaller plots of land and a road marked as belonging to James Sutton.[20] The Nicholas land holdings at Roundway passed by sale to the Willy family sometime after 1770.[21] The Nicholases had held land here since the end of the 13th century and lived at Nicholas Place, at the end of Quakers Walk on the footpath to the west of the town where earthworks can be found today.[22]

Quakers Walk in Victorian times.

The Queen Anne house, built between 1700 and 1720, most likely by George Willy the elder, provided the ideal site for James Sutton's new house and it was incorporated into Wyatt's house as the north side of the quadrangle behind the new west front. As a result, it effectively survived until demolition in 1954 and so there is a significant amount of photographic and documentary evidence for its original appearance.[23]

The Queen Anne house was probably built on the site of the old keeper's lodge from the time when it was a Royal Park.[24] It was brick-built and orientated to face north–south. It is

1773 Map of Roundway by Andrews and Dury (©Wiltshire Museum).

Queen Anne house as modified by James Wyatt (Historic England Archive 1954).

thought to have consisted of a five-bay centre block of two storeys with an attic, with stone dressings and rusticated corner quoins, finished off with a balustraded parapet and flanked by wings of two storeys, the whole over a basement with a light well. It may have begun as a single rectangular block containing small rooms, to which two larger rooms, the drawing and dining rooms, were added later as the flanking wings. A lower, irregular block at its western end, which contained a single room and passage and was retained by Wyatt to provide a link with his west front, may have represented part of the offices of this house, or the remains of an even earlier dwelling on this site.

A mid-20th century photograph of the north facade shows the scar of the centrally sited door formerly reached by steps over the basement well and afterwards replaced by Wyatt by a long sash window. There are also markings in the brickwork under the large sashes of the end pavilions, indicating that these may have replaced an earlier arrangement of doors and fenestration.

The entrance hall opened onto a fine oak staircase panelled to dado-height with plain and spindle carved balusters with open strings decorated with acanthus ornament. The staircase had 22 treads, three half landings and a gallery.[25] Above it the ornate plasterwork ceiling of recessed panels and a central semi-dome with foliate roses was after designs by Inigo Jones.

Some of the rooms contained decorative pine panelling, with oak or deal floors. Three

Clockwise from top left
(Historic England Archive 1954):
Staircase in Queen Anne wing.
Ceiling above the staircase.
First floor panelled room.
First floor panelled room with fireplace.

panelled rooms and a panelled passage appear to have survived into the 20th century. The panelling of one first-floor room was later described as being 'carved with fluted pilasters carrying up a deep trabeated frieze and with carved figurative overdoors'.[26]

James Sutton was thus fortunate in not only having the Queen Anne house and its grounds as the basis for his new house but also in the magnificent views that it commanded to the west, of which both Wyatt and Repton would take full advantage in their design.

The Changing Face of the House

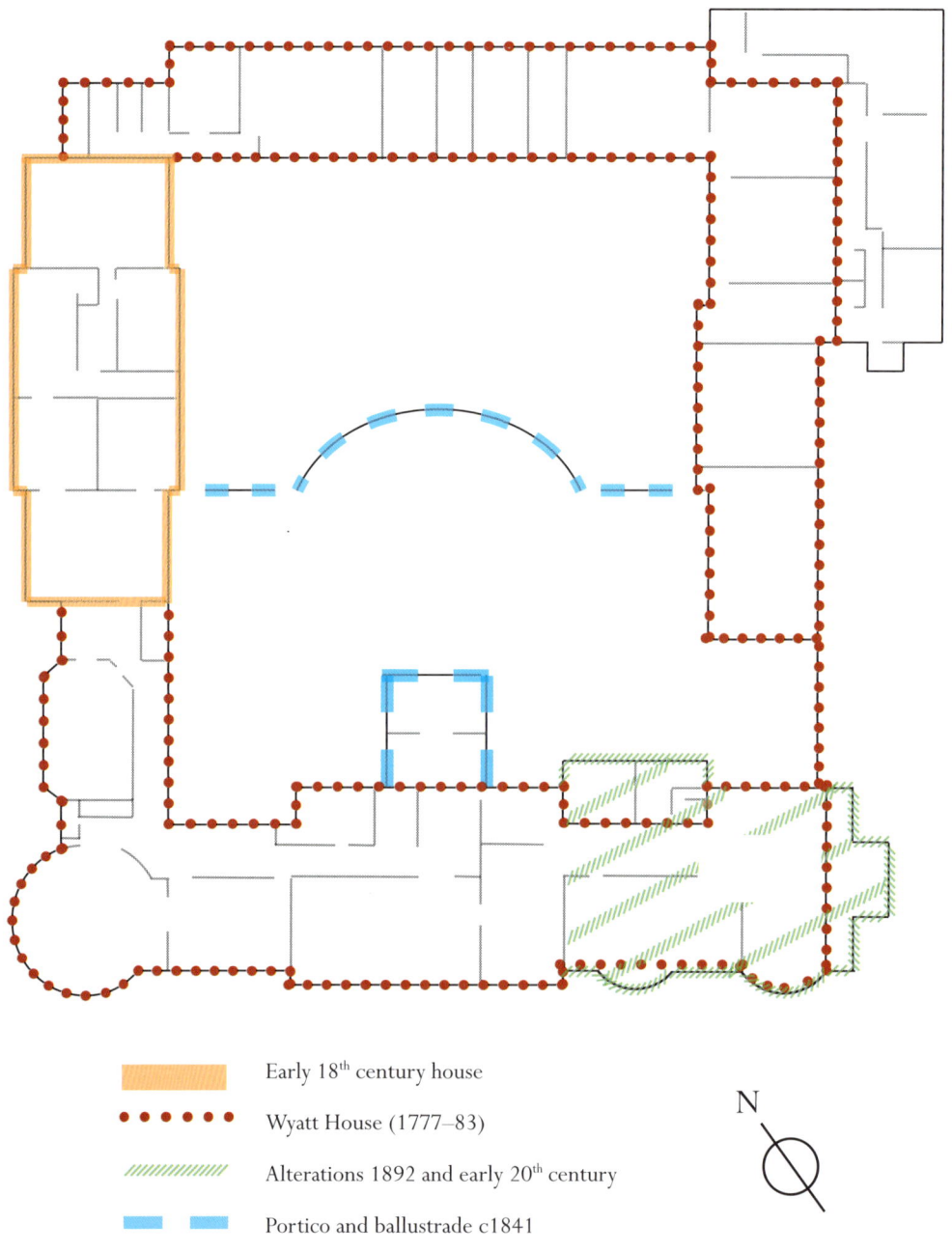

Early 18th century house

Wyatt House (1777–83)

Alterations 1892 and early 20th century

Portico and ballustrade c1841

N

2

James Wyatt and Humphry Repton at New Park

THE OVERALL DESIGN for New Park by James Wyatt was based upon the Palladian plan for a great house, with a central block and lower flanking wings, also found at other Wyatt houses such as Heaton Hall, Lancashire (1772–89), and Castle Coole, County Fermanagh (1790–97).[27] As at Heaton, the flanking wings at New Park terminated in projecting bays with a shallow bow, introducing variety and movement into what might otherwise be a rather rigid design. The wings also served to aggrandise what was a comparatively small house, relying on the superb physical topography of its site and the strength of its architecture to create visual impact.

New Park, Wiltshire, from *The Beauties of England and Wales* by John Britton (1801).

The new house was built around a central courtyard, with its main facade facing west, orientated to take advantage of extensive views across the park and landscape. The west facade consisted of three bays, three storeys high, framed by giant Ionic columns. These bays had

Venetian windows in tabernacle frames on the ground floor surmounted by shallow pediments, three plain sash windows in the upper storey, and an attic concealed by a balustraded parapet with a central Diocletian window. The flanking single-storey wings were symmetrical, each with three semi-circular headed windows framed by Tuscan pilaster-strips and blank niches. Each wing terminated in a shallow bow with tripartite windows, surmounted by a balustraded parapet.[28]

Prestigious as Wyatt's appointment as architect was for the Sutton family, it may well be that James Sutton knew of Wyatt's reputation as a wasteful and economically chaotic building contractor,[29] and so decided not to award him the building contract. James Sutton's account book for 1765–91 includes payments to Wyatt 'for improvements at New Park, 1779–80'. Numerous payments for brick-makers (who made the bricks on the estate), labourers and carpenters were also recorded between 1777 and 1782.[30] Bath stone was transported on the River Kennet, which was made navigable for cargo between Bristol and the Thames at Reading in 1727.[31]

Sutton's account book also records payments for a stable in 1777 and for 'raising garden walls' and labouring in the gardens in 1778.[32] Payments for 'preventing smoking chimneys' in 1781 indicate that the carcass of the house was complete. In the same year the kitchen gardens were being improved, with payments for trees and melon pits.[33] Payments of £30 and £20 are recorded to Mr Wyatt in 1779, and £100 in 1780,[34] the year in which he must have been most frequently on site, as his fees were in the region of ten guineas a day.[35] Approximately £2,400 (£423,000 today) was expended on building over this period.[36]

The entrance arch to the courtyard – the curved balustrade was added in 1841 (Historic England).

The core of the Queen Anne house was retained on the north side of the courtyard but had its attic storey removed and was stuccoed and re-fenestrated on the courtyard side in order to harmonise with Wyatt's work. A new stable block on the east side was constructed of brick and faced with Bath stone. Its shallow hipped slate roofs were concealed behind a parapet and, in the centre, the entrance arch, through which carriages passed into the courtyard, was surmounted by a pediment with a clock.[37] The south range contained a coach house and service accommodation, with a gateway giving access into the gardens.

Wyatt's west range contained the principal accommodation. A square-shaped central entrance hall led into an enfilade of six reception rooms and a conservatory, which opened out for a length of about 70 yards. To the north of the entrance hall a breakfast room or parlour led into a rectangular drawing room with the enfilade terminating in an oval dining room. To the south of the hall, the enfilade continued with a library and a picture gallery or music room, and terminated in a conservatory. Glazed bookcases lined the walls of the oval-shaped library and a marble fireplace ornamented with a portrait medallion, probably representing Homer, was built into one of the curved walls.

Just as Wyatt's ground-floor reception rooms reflected the fashion to connect directly with the outdoors by floor-length windows (and by allowing the garden to enter the house in the conservatory),[38] so the inter-linking reception rooms reflected the change in social gatherings in the late 18th and early 19th century. Humphry Repton referred to this in verse in his 1816 book *Fragments on the Theory and Practice of Landscape Gardening* in which he described an old-fashioned 'Cedar Parlour' and a contemporary 'Living Room', the latter being representative of life at New Park:

> *No more the cedar parlour's formal gloom*
> *With dullness chills, 'tis now the living room,*
> *Where guests to whim, to task or fancy true*
> *Scatter'd in groups, their different plans pursue.*
> *Here politicians eagerly relate*
> *The last day's news, or the last night's debate.*
> *Here books of poetry and books of prints*
> *Furnish aspiring artists with new hints.*

The most elaborate decorative treatment in the house was given to the drawing and dining rooms. Joseph Rose worked on the plasterwork to Wyatt's designs. A letter containing the estimate for this work reveals that Rose had called on Wyatt to acquaint him with 'the absolute necessity of their being done immediately':

1782 Estimate of Stucco Work in Oval Dining Room in New Park, the seat of James Sutton Esq. Made from Mr Wyatts [sic] designs … To execute in the best manner the plain Ceiling with Sixteen garlands composed of Wheat, and Vines, with Honeysuckles and Husks running through the centre. Enriched oval frame with ruffled leaf Rose in centre of Ceiling, with Entablature round the Room, and plain Stucco in Niches and Spherical heads, and on walls in many small parts. The whole agreeable to the design given, Amounts to Seventy-Six pounds.

Estimated 19th June 1782 Jos. Rose.

Estimate of Drawing Room Ceiling, Cornice and Frieze
VIZ

To execute in the best manner the plain ceiling, with several sunk pannels [panels], Elliptic spherical to Dome in centre, plain fillets with edges on each side large border. Cast ornaments in Border. Elliptical and circular reeds and ribbon. Plain and enriched mouldings to Lozenge pannel, plain and enriched mouldings to Elliptical Dome, plain avised fan with Waterleaf Flower in centre, four trophies to spandrels. Four enriched frames to circles for paintings. Festoons and drops of small husks with ties of ribbon round large oval, with cornice and frieze round the room. The whole agreeable to the design given Amounts to Eighty-two pounds five shillings.

Estimated 2nd Septem 1782 Jos. Rose.[39]

Wyatt ceiling in the drawing room (Historic England).

The four paintings in the ceiling roundels in the drawing room, for which Mr Rose executed the plaster frames mentioned above, represented night and day, and the elements of earth and water. They have been variously attributed to three of the most fashionable decorative artists of the day, namely Biagio Rebecca,[40] Giovanni Battista Cipriani and Antonio Zucchi.[41]

Wyatt converted the dining room of the old Queen Anne house into a kitchen. In the 19th century it occupied a double-height space with an ornate trabeated plaster ceiling which was probably original to the Queen Anne house. The Queen Anne drawing room became the laundry. As Henry Robinson, the last butler at Roundway, was to observe many years later, they must have been the finest servants' quarters of any English country house.

The main staircase in the west front led to the first floor with six bedrooms and a further five or six bedrooms on the attic floor above. Bedrooms in the Queen Anne section of the house were used by household staff. There was a tunnel under the courtyard from the east block to the west front so that the servants were hidden from view when going from ancillary buildings to the main part of the house. The cellars under the west front were built on a grand scale with a vaulted dome chamber as shown in a photograph and scale drawing by Devizes historian John Girvan.

The building works were completed in 1783 and in the following year the design for New Park was exhibited at the Royal Academy by Wyatt's draughtsman, Mr Dixon, with the description: 'lately built by Mr Wyatt'.[42]

The Red Book for New Park was made by Humphry Repton (1752–1818) in May 1794, just over ten years after the house had been completed to Wyatt's designs. By the time Repton arrived at New Park to undertake the relatively modest

Detail of trabeated kitchen ceiling in Queen Anne wing (Historic England).

Above and below: Photograph and plan of dome chamber in cellars (*Under Devizes* by John Girvan).

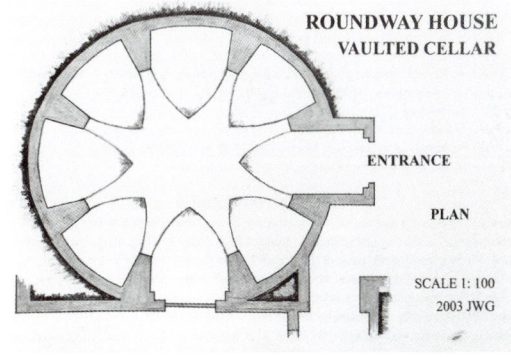

commission of landscaping the former deer park in which it stood, he had already produced more than 100 of his famous Red Books for his clients, many of whom were or had been MPs like James Sutton.[43] It is possible that Repton's work for William Pitt, which started at the end of 1791 at Holwood House near Keston in Kent, led to James Sutton's commission, particularly given their connection through Henry Addington. The commissions that Repton received between 1792 and 1794 in areas where he had not worked before most likely arose from Pitt's patronage.[44]

A draft bill for enclosure of land, including some in the vicinity of Roundway, dating from 1793,[45] may have been intended to enable Repton's plans for distant views and vistas from New Park to be carried out. A view of the house was included in an entry in *Peacock's Polite Repository*, published in 1795.[46]

The Red Book which survives for New Park, held in the Gloucestershire Record Office, lacking its original text and disbound, is annotated: 'belonged to James Sutton and then T.G. Estcourt 1823'.[47] Recently scholars have argued that few of the schemes in the Red Books were ever fully executed; many of Repton's clients carried out parts of schemes with their own labourers as their funds and inclinations directed.[48] Similarly, James Sutton does not appear to have carried out all the alterations which Repton recommended, although those that were executed were apparently complete by 1801 when John Britton published a description of New Park, quoted at the end of this chapter.

Repton's work at New Park reflected his theories that the landscape should present an aspect of variety and cheerfulness, reflecting the natural landscape while also offering selected views beyond the boundary, carefully filtered to take in distant vistas while maintaining the social exclusivity appropriate to a gentleman's seat.[49] This close connection with nature expressed in the work of both Wyatt and Repton at Roundway and many other country houses built at this time was part of a new social and ideological development that valued nature as a positive force which engendered spiritual renewal.

In general, Repton's plans involved rerouting carriage drives and garden walks to take in old and new landscape features as well as new planting, clearing and possibly some earth removal in order to open up views otherwise partially or completely hidden.[50] The plan which Repton produced, presented as Plate No. I in the Red Book for New Park, encompassed the parkland to the west of the house and immediately to the north and south (excluding the land south of Quakers Walk and the fields to the east below Roundway Village). Repton's plan provided for landscape improvement and areas of cultivation contrasted with wilderness.

From the evidence of the surviving landscape it seems likely that Repton's plans for planting around the house and walled gardens were executed, and that he created some of the vistas across and out of the park as well as introducing landmarks within it. The exact timing of these works is not clear and it is probable that James Sutton's son-in-law Thomas Estcourt (whose name is also inscribed in the Red Book) executed some of the works himself after he inherited the estate in the early 19th century. Repton's plans for rerouting the drives across the park, however, may not have been carried out, perhaps because of the worsening economic climate after the outbreak of war with France in 1793 or an unconnected decline in James Sutton's fortunes, or simply because the utility of the existing roads militated against change.

Repton's Plan No. I delineated a large walled garden directly to the south of the new house, encircled by a dense plantation of trees and shrubberies. Another sliver of planting runs due north of the house and a thick broken band of planting flanks Quakers Walk on its north side, both of which are characteristic of his approach. These plantings conform to his theory that a mansion needed a mass of wood next to it so that plantations framed the house but screened its offices.[51]

Repton Red Book for New Park (Gloucestershire Archives D1571/E396)[52] – Plan I.

The original formal garden to the north-west of the Queen Anne house shown on 18th-century maps, such as that of Andrews & Dury on page 9, were obliterated by the building of the new house, and Repton designed new formal gardens and a pleasure ground close by.[53] Walks were cut through the plantation surrounding the kitchen garden,[54] a characteristic of Repton's practice by the 1790s, creating a sheltered circular walk from the house, converging upon a small building sited where Repton's proposed new drive crossed Quakers Walk, probably a lodge and temple combined, which was designed to provide a resting point.

Cedar of Lebanon, 1978.

The mixed planting, particularly the Wellingtonia and other evergreens on the north, south and east side of the house, are typical of early 19th-century planting schemes. The large cedar of Lebanon on the south side was planted in 1805 to mark the fifth anniversary of the marriage of Eleanor Sutton to Thomas Estcourt. The terrace in front of the house is shown unplanted (Plate No. VI), and in 19th-century photographs it remains in this state, ornamented with stone urns and bounded by a ha-ha and a paling.

Repton Red Book – Plate No. VI.

Thatched cottage in the 19th century.

Repton was also probably responsible for the rustic thatched Bailiff's House which is visible from the carriage approach to the west of the Home Farm. This cottage has been attributed to John Nash with whom Repton was in partnership at the time.[55]

Repton also retained the Quakers Walk avenue (so named either as a corruption of Keepers Walk or after the Quaker fraternity) but broke across the planting along its north side to provide views into the park and towards the house. Other than planting, Repton's main proposal for New Park seems to have been reordering the drives across the park so that they took in his new picturesque planting and views over the surrounding countryside. Repton defined a 'drive' as an extended route around the park for admiring scenery from a carriage which often followed a more intricate route than a ride where exercise was the pre-eminent concern.[56] The main drive to the house in 1794 was from Conscience Lane to the west. Repton's plans provided for a lodge at the gates in the temple style, which it is thought would have involved replacing an older building marking the drive which served the Queen Anne house, but the plan was never executed.

Many of the plates for the New Park Red Book fulfilled these criteria. For instance, Plate Nos. VII & VIII and XII show the view from the north-west corner of the Wyatt house looking down through the fields towards Bath and Warminster Downs. In Plates Nos. VII–VIII, shown below, a flap or slide shows the view before, and afterwards, revealed by cutting away earth between two natural hillocks, with a far off cottage on the site of the lodge in Conscience Lane improved as a temple.

Red Book – Plate Nos. VII & VIII – Before.

Red Book – Plate Nos. VII & VIII – After.

Plate Nos. XII show the same view before and after from lower down the slope, once again providing evidence of some earth removal, and the improved view with the existing waterway rerouted to describe a meandering curve across the middle ground, as proposed in Plate No. I. This view, now rather obscured by scrub, can be identified today.

Red Book – Plate No. XII – Before.

Red Book – Plate No. XII – After.

With regard to other plates, No. IX, with a slide marked B and C, apparently corresponds to these letters as they appear on Plan No. I, on the north end of Quakers Walk, showing two vistas which Repton proposed to open across the landscape to the north to be glimpsed from the Walk.

Red Book – Plate No. IX B.

Red Book – Plate No. IX C.

In Plate Nos. X, a rough quarry bank in a forest glade (in the middle of a plantation in the centre of the park known as Sunset Copse) is transformed, by the removal of a slide, into a rustic grotto with the straightforward type of rockwork which Repton avowedly preferred to shellwork or spas.

Red Book – Plate No. X – Before.

Red Book – Plate No. X – After.

In Plate Nos. XIII, the house is shown in the distance from the north-west corner of the park, with the foreground improved by the re-routing of a water course.

Red Book – Plate No. XIII – Before.

Red Book – Plate No. XIII – After.

A distant vista of the house, set against its new plantations from the high ground of Roundway Down to the north, is shown in Plate No. XI. The other plates do not survive.

Red Book – Plate No. XI.

When the following description of New Park was published in 1801 by John Britton in *The Beauties of Wiltshire*, it is clear that James Sutton was the owner of a highly regarded new country house:

A seat of James Sutton, Esq. is about one mile from Devizes, to describe which I shall avail myself of an extract from Mr Repton's Red Book, wherein he has particularised the beauties and 'capabilities' of this place. 'All the materials of natural landscape seem to be collected, if not actually displayed, within the very pale of this park. It presents every possible variety of shape in the ground, from the cheerful and extended plain, to the steep hill and abrupt precipice. The surface is every where enriched by wood of various growth and species, either collected in ample masses, or lightly scattered in groups and single trees. Such are the natural advantages of the fore ground, to which must be added the richest prospects of distant country; and while nature has been thus bountiful, Art has also lent assistance, under the direction of Mr. James Wyatt, to decorate the scene with a building of the most elegant form. The house at New Park is a lasting monument of the contrivance and good taste of that ingenious architect.'

3

The Suttons, Addingtons and Estcourts

JAMES SUTTON had some 20 years in which to enjoy his new house before his death in 1801 at the age of 68. The end of the 18th century ushered in a golden age of the country house. During this time landowners such as James Sutton benefited financially from greater agricultural returns while improvements in transport meant that they could take a full part in political life in London as well as enjoying the social advantages of entertaining on a grand scale in their country houses.[57]

In keeping with the general trend towards land consolidation, James continued to be active in buying and exchanging land holdings, as shown in his agent's memorandum book.[58] Richard Richardson's survey in 1784 of James's property calculated that the annual value of the land was £1,923 16s 6d and that the total annual property income was over £5,000 (£730,000 today[59]). James continued to acquire property throughout his life, his last purchase being Bishops Cannings Parsonage for £24,000 (£1.77m today) in 1801, the year of his death, by which time he held 4,000 acres in Wiltshire. In addition to New Park he also owned the manor of Manningford Bruce and land at Marden, Heddington, Bromham, Bulkington, Chittoe, Horton, Melksham, Potterne, Nursteed, Stert, Wick and Welsford.[60]

James was a respected landowner, contributing annually to poor relief and providing a *Twelfth Night* entertainment at Potterne costing £14 18s 6d in 1784. John Ward, writing to the Earl of Ailesbury on 30 September 1793, after a Kennet and Avon Canal meeting, referred to 'Mr Sutton's gentlemanly conduct' winning 'the esteem of those who were strangers to him'.[61] This compliment is not to be underestimated as the building of the 57-mile canal section, which was carried out between 1794 and 1810 and created part of the southern

Towpath and bridge to the Quakers Walk lodge over the Kennet and Avon Canal.

Henry Addington as Speaker by John Singleton Copley which used to hang at New Park.

border of the Roundway estate with the town of Devizes, initially caused considerable controversy locally.

Mid-way through the building of the house, in 1780, James stepped down as one of the two MPs for Devizes, although he retained political influence locally.[62] In 1784 he used this influence to ensure that his brother-in-law Henry Addington became MP and Recorder for Devizes. (The banker John Lubbock who was planning to stand against Addington decided against it 'for the sake of peace'.)[63] Henry Addington was a childhood friend of Pitt the Younger, who had become Prime Minister in 1783 and instigated Addington's election as Speaker of the House of Commons in 1789, an event that was celebrated in Devizes, as James observed in a letter to Addington: 'You have thrown both Town and Country into a state of excess and riot.'[64]

In 1799, the year of the resumption of war against France, Addington gave the colours to the Devizes Loyal Volunteers, the presentation being made by his sister, Mrs Sutton, on Roundway Hill, with much ceremony and the afternoon being spent 'with the utmost conviviality'.[65] Pitt the Younger, when Prime Minister, was a regular visitor with Addington to New Park. George Sloper in 1798 reported 'the famous Mr Pitt came through Devizes', an

Cartoon by James Gillray of Pitt kicking out Addington.

occasion which James marked by paying £2 12s 6d for the church bells to be rung.[66]

A few months before James's death, Addington succeeded Pitt as Prime Minister on 5 February 1801. He held the position until 1804 when Pitt manoeuvred him out of office and resumed the role of Prime Minister. Addington's authority had been severely weakened as Prime Minister by a widespread perception of his administration's incompetence, leading Lord Canning to make his famous jibe in 1803: 'Pitt is to Addington as London is to Paddington.'

After being raised to the peerage as Viscount Sidmouth in 1805, Addington occupied several Cabinet positions, including Home Secretary in Lord Liverpool's administrations 1812–22. These years were marked by considerable social unrest (ranging from the demands of the Luddites to the Peterloo massacre in 1819), not least due to economic recession and chronic unemployment after the Napoleonic Wars. Addington, however, continued to take an interest in Devizes. In 1791 he had made a gift of £500 to rebuild the Shambles and in 1814 he donated the new market cross, which replaced the 16th-century statue of the black bear on four columns (subsequently incorporated into the Bear Hotel opposite).[67] In 1826 Leg o' Mutton Street was renamed Sidmouth Street in his honour.[68] He died in London on 15 February 1844 at the age of 86.

Left: Market cross in Devizes.
Above: Corn Exchange and The Bear Hotel in Devizes (photographs from 1920s ©Wiltshire Museum, Devizes).

By the time of James Sutton's death in 1801, the work of Wyatt and Repton, his continuing acquisition of land and the economic disruption created by the war with France had taken its toll on his finances. The year 1799 proved particularly difficult, with income tax being introduced in January and bad weather leading to a very poor harvest. This period also saw increased competition in the worsted and wool industries from Yorkshire, which overtook the West Country and East Anglia in terms of output. Mechanised spinning was starting to edge out the home-based spinning that characterised areas such as Devizes, which lacked the north's water-power to drive the mills.[69]

Although James Sutton's estate was valued at £52,483 10s 10d on his death (£3.9m today),[70] his will took a year to prove;[71] he died leaving business debts and had taken out various loans which were accruing large sums of interest, all of which took more than a decade to disentangle and settle. James's business partner had committed suicide in 1799, an event possibly connected with these debts.[72] Papers of 1801 itemising rents, debts and charges on the estate show that debts of £54,025 had accrued by the time of his death. Of this, it was estimated that £44,000 could be raised to pay off loans through the sale of land and the collection of rent in arrears.[73] In 1811 there was still about £8,000 owing against the estate. Under the terms of the will, household goods and furniture at New Park were valued at £5,000.

After James's death, his daughter Eleanor and her husband Thomas Grimston Bucknall Estcourt (1775–1853) and their family lived at New Park[74] as tenants of her mother. Three of Eleanor's siblings (James, George and Mary) had died in childhood. Her surviving sibling, Charlotte (known as Sarah), later eloped with Capt. Robert J. Matthews and was married to him in May 1810.

Eleanor and Thomas Estcourt had been married in 1800 at St George's Church, Hanover Square, in London, a year before her father died.[75] Their marriage settlement was dated 10 May 1800, by which Eleanor's jointure was £1,000 provision and £1,000 secured against her father's estates. The rents of the manor of Bishops Cannings were also settled upon the couple, producing a substantial net income of £3,200 annually (£265,000 today).[76] The Estcourt family had lived at Shipton on the borders of Wiltshire and Gloucestershire since about 1300.[77] They were also substantial landowners in both counties with Estcourt Park, Tetbury, in Gloucestershire, and landholdings to the south of the New Park estate in Wiltshire.[78]

Thomas Estcourt was a barrister and became MP for Devizes between 1805 and 1826, having succeeded Henry Addington, and for Oxford University from 1827 until 1847. He always refused to take office but was active on several parliamentary committees.[79] In Devizes, Thomas took a prominent role with the militia and presided over the local courts. He planted the Leipzig Plantation near Devizes after the defeat of Napoleon at the battle of the same name in 1813.[80]

Thomas and Eleanor continued to invest in new land and the development of New Park. In 1812 they leased 704 acres of park from the diocese of Salisbury.[81] In 1817 they received permission from Justices of the Peace Wadham Locke (a cousin-in-law on the Sutton side of the family) and Henry Bayntun to divert the 'public footway', Quakers Walk, from passing close to New Park by straightening it out so that it ran directly north-east to Roundway village. Thomas Estcourt later made reference to his planting of this new path: 'New path from the Quaker Walk to Roundway village marked out. Since planted by me, and now a beautiful avenue.'[82]

It is highly likely that the walled garden and pleasure gardens that Repton designed in 1794 were not implemented until this time.[83] They are not marked on the 1817 map which accompanies the JPs' order allowing the diversion of Quakers Walk but are marked on an estate map of 1838. The Repton Red Book of 1794, annotated as it is with: 'belonged to James Sutton and then T.G. Estcourt 1823', also suggests that the gardens were established at this later date.

Path to Roundway village from Quakers Walk.

A further indication comes from the brick and stone archway in the walled garden, surmounted by an eagle. The Estcourt family crest features an eagle (one of the lodges to Estcourt Park, Gloucestershire, is called Eagle Lodge); it may be that the eagle at New Park was a celebration of Thomas's realisation of his father-in-law's and Repton's plans.[84] At the main drive entrance on Conscience Lane, the Estcourts are believed to have rebuilt or re-faced the existing lodge in red brick with ornamental barge-boarding. Repton's plans for a temple design were never carried out.

Left: Stone eagle above gateway to walled garden (Devizes Heritage).
Right: Victorian photograph of Conscience Lane Lodge.

In January 1824, New Park featured in Volume V of Jones's *View of the Seats of Noblemen and Gentlemen in England, Wales, Scotland and Ireland*, as illustrated below.

New Park in Jones's *View of the Seats of Noblemen and Gentlemen* 1824.

Thomas and Eleanor's eldest son, Thomas Henry Sutton Estcourt (1801–76), or Thomas Jnr, was educated at Harrow and Oriel College, Oxford, where he took a First in Classics. He followed in his father's footsteps by becoming an MP, initially for Marlborough (1829–32) and then for Devizes (1835–44) and North Wiltshire (1844–65). Although Thomas Jnr established a reputation early on in parliament as one of the most promising Tory members, he inherited his father's disinclination for office and felt that he served the cause best by speaking regularly in the House from the backbenches. He eventually consented to take office as President of the Poor Law Board at the behest of his friend the Prime Minister Lord Derby in 1858. He was a competent minister and succeeded Spencer Percival as Home Secretary for four months in 1859.[85]

In 1830 Thomas Jnr married a wealthy heiress, Lucy, daughter of Admiral Frank Sotheron of Kirklington, Nottinghamshire (assuming the name of Sotheron in conjunction with Estcourt in 1839 but reverting to Estcourt in 1855). In the same year the couple took over New Park from his parents and lived there until 1839. His mother, Eleanor, had died in 1829 after an operation for a strangulated hernia[86] while his father, Thomas Snr, moved in 1831 to Estcourt

Park (built at the same time as New Park in 1776–79) which he described as 'my permanent residence' although he continued to visit New Park about three times a year.[87]

Just before Thomas Jnr took over New Park from his father, it may have gone through a period of neglect, and in 1829 a 'little garden' was planted or replanted there, with lilacs, phlox, lobelias, violets and several other species, 'bought by Miss Bathurst'.[88] Inside the house, notable pictures included the portrait by John Singleton Copley of Henry Addington in his robes as Speaker of the House of Commons (now in the Saint Louis Art Museum in Missouri). There was also a painting by George Morland of rustic figures in a landscape and another one by Thomas Gainsborough of a landscape with figures.[89]

At this time the New Park estate was valued at £55,410 (£6.2m today), the details of which were as follows:

Particulars and valuation of the New Park Mansion and Estate part situate in the Tything of Roundway in the parish of Bishops Cannings and part in the parish of Rowde in the county of Wilts, belonging to Mrs Sutton …

T.G.B. Estcourt Esq. Tenant	
New Park Mansion Offices	
Pleasure Grounds Gardens and Deer Park,	125 acres
Woods and Plantations,	65 acres
Home Close or Cow Leaze,	16 acres
Arable Piece adjoining,	6 acres
Cow Yard, Rack, Bartons, Timber Yard and Small Paddocks,	2 acres
Land occupied by William Cook,	54 acres
Ditto Taylor,	25 acres
[… there follows a list of further tenants]	
Summary	
Tenants	
T.G.B. Estcourt,	295 acres
William Cook,	372 acres
Taylor,	76 acres
Other tenants, a further	72 acres
£1,397 per annum at 30 years purchase	£41,910
Add for Mansion House and Timber	£13,500
	£55,410

Memo – This estate is free of Great Tythes and is from land tax excepting a trifling payment of 5 or 6 pr annum. There are seven cottages forming part of the property, five situate at Roundway and two at Bedbro' Lane for which no addition is made in consideration that the annual value calculated at thirty years purchase embraces a Mill and Cottages occupied by Smith and by Pearse and Whitelock which would otherwise call for a deduction equivalent to the difference between the value in years purchase of Land and perishable property.

20th July 1830 , Signed John Hayward[90]

There was a break in the Estcourt family's representation of Devizes in parliament between 1826, when Thomas Snr ceased to be MP, and 1835 when Thomas Jnr became one of the two MPs, retaining the seat until 1844. The local government of Devizes had been described in 1805 as being 'in the hands of a self-perpetuating body of two dozen burgesses, dominated by the influence of the owners of New Park'.[91] In the 1820s there was considerable agitation for electoral reform in Devizes, particularly among Nonconformists, tradesmen and professionals, as there was elsewhere across Britain. This culminated in the 1832 Reform Act, which was marked in Devizes by a celebration on the Green with 1,600 people processioning to a dinner and fireworks. Devizes retained its two MPs but the electorate was increased by over 400 people (from about 30 before) with male householders paying £10 rent being enfranchised.[92]

The Estcourts sold New Park in 1839 for two main reasons: firstly, Lucy's father died in that year leaving them a large inheritance, including Darrington Hall in Yorkshire, on condition that Thomas Jnr assumed the surname Sotheron. Secondly, following the death of Thomas Jnr's grandmother Eleanor in 1837, New Park had become the joint property of Thomas Jnr and his aunt, Sarah (Thomas Jnr inheriting by right of his mother who, in 1829, had predeceased his grandmother).[93] A sale was therefore the simplest way of resolving the issue of the shared ownership.

George Charles Holford of Westonbirt bought New Park that October.[94] It is likely that the Estcourt and Holford families knew each other from their shared roots in Gloucestershire. The Holfords were in the process of rising from the ranks of Gloucestershire squires to great wealth, going on to build not only Westonbirt itself but also Dorchester House in Park Lane.[95]

Thomas and Lucy moved to Bowden Park in Wiltshire, a house owned by the Estcourt family and, like New Park, designed by James Wyatt. Thomas retired from public life in 1863 after a paralytic seizure. He continued to be held in high regard in Devizes and after his death in 1876 his statue, designed by James Wyatt's son Benjamin, was erected by public subscription

Statue of Thomas Estcourt and fountain in the Devizes town square in the 1920s
(©Wiltshire Museum, Devizes).

(a tribute to his founding of the Wiltshire Friendly Society in 1828) on top of the fountain in the Market Place, where he presides over Devizes to this day.[96]

The parliamentary connection between Devizes and the Estcourt and Addington families was to continue: James Bucknall-Estcourt was one of the two MPs between 1848 and 1852 and William Wells Addington (later 2nd Viscount Sidmouth) was MP between 1863 and 1864.

Holford carried out improvements to the house at New Park and furnished it elegantly but was forced to sell because he found that the climate of the Devizes neighbourhood was bad for his health.[97] The house and estate were bought by Edward Francis Colston in 1840, who renamed it Roundway Park and whose family went on to own it for over a century, presiding over its continued rise and then hastening its fall.

Roundway Estate Map, 1841 (Wiltshire & Swindon History Centre).

4

The Colstons: Honeymoon and Grand Tour

EDWARD FRANCIS COLSTON (1795–1847) of Filkins Hall in Oxfordshire bought New Park from Holford in 1840. He had inherited a great fortune established by his ancestral namesake Edward Colston (1636–1721), known as 'the Philanthropist' for his charitable donations and commemorated by a statue in Bristol and numerous charitable endowments such as the Colston School.

The Colston name today in Bristol is also known for its association with the slave trade. In 1680 Edward became a member of the Royal African Company, based in London, which had the monopoly between 1672 and 1698 of slave trading between the west coast of Africa and the Americas. He took an active part in the planning and financing of slave trading ventures to Africa. His name was present in the company's records for 11 years and he was the company's Deputy Governor in 1689–90. His life and the history of the Colston family by descent to Edward Francis is covered in detail in Appendix III. As with many landed families in Britain, the Colstons' involvement with the slave trade casts a long shadow over succeeding generations and estates like Roundway.

Edward Francis Colston owned over 4,000 acres, including Roundway, having derived his wealth not only from the Colston family but also from his marriage in 1819 to the 27-year-old heiress Marianne Jenkins (1792–1865).[98] Born in Bath, she was the only daughter and heir of Somerset landowner William Jenkins (c1751–1837) of Shepton Mallett and Sarah Jenkins (née Watkin), whom it is reasonable to assume Edward met when visiting the Colston estate at nearby West Lydford.[99]

Portrait of Marianne Colston (c1830) by James Godsell Middleton (reproduced by kind permission of Heather McOmie).

Edward and Marianne's honeymoon and Grand Tour took them through France, Switzerland and Italy between 1819 and 1821. Thanks to Marianne's diligence as a diarist and her considerable artistic skills, we have a vivid record of their journey in the three-volume book that she later published, entitled *Journal of a Tour in France, Switzerland, and Italy, during the years 1819, 20, and 21: illustrated by fifty lithographic prints, from original drawings, taken in Italy, the Alps and the Pyrenees.*[100] It is a testament to Marianne's skill as a diarist and artist that her journal remains in print to this day in a facsimile edition and that there is an active international market in her lithographs.

Marianne's journal captures the great energy and aspirational nature of this well-educated and intrepid young couple, as well as their shared love of the arts and the classical world, facilitated by their command of French and Italian. The young couple had grown up immediately after the French Revolution in 1789 and during the wars with France between 1793 and 1815. They were therefore in the vanguard of British travellers returning to the continent after Waterloo, resuming the long-standing tradition of the Grand Tour.

In her preface, Marianne light-heartedly downplays the significance of her journal, claiming that it was 'written originally for her own amusement, and for the eye of partial friends' while demonstrating her literary knowledge by quoting from Jonathan Swift and Madame de Staël when she claims to be resigned 'to send her quires to line a trunk' or to 'make use of it for her own bonnet boxes'. Marianne comes across as a forthright, down-to-earth person with a natural curiosity about people and the world around her, as well as progressive views on subjects such as education. She was also driven by a desire to record accurately their remarkable journey, so she 'wrote her memorandums, in presence of the objects, and as they were passing before her eyes en route'. Her mother Sarah contributed verses to the journal and shared Marianne's interest in drawing.

The journal also marks the start of her new life as a married woman:[101]

> On the 1st November, 1819, I quitted my beloved parents, having that morning tied that awfully important Gordion knot, which the hand of death can alone untie, and from which the thread of life becomes either much more or much less happy than before.

The Colstons were accompanied by a servant and a coachman. They brought with them their own carriage and hired horses at each stage of their journey through Europe. Marianne described in detail one of the postillions at Le Havre who harnessed the horses to their carriage and demonstrates that the truthfulness of her acute powers of observation transcended her prejudice:

A night-cap, that had once been white, covered his curly locks and weather-beaten face, surmounted by a cap in shape like that of Don Quixote's helmet, and appearing as if composed of the skin of hedge-hog; a sort of mock military jacket, bedizened round the waist and flaps with metal buttons, bearing fleurs-de-lis on them … Farcical, however, as is their appearance, their skill and care, I am inclined to believe, exceed those of our smart English drivers.

They travelled to Paris passing through Normandy, where the 'apple trees planted in straight rows all over the country, appear defects to an eye accustomed to English scenery', and stayed in Rouen. They usually started travelling each day at 6am and considered their carriage 'to be far more our home than the inns at which we dined or slept'. They carried spare parts in case the carriage was damaged, which

The castle of Henry IV and part of the town of Pau, Pyrenees
by Marianne Colston from her Journal.

was a constant danger given 'the extreme roughness and badness' of some of the roads. When they stopped, they had to watch out for blacksmiths who would surreptitiously remove a nut from a traveller's coach wheel and then kindly offer to sort out the resulting problem. If they were crossing a river, they opened the doors of the carriage to let the water pass through and thereby reduce its resistance and the risk of it being washed down river. On a particularly uneven and bumpy road, they would move around in the carriage to counterbalance and maintain its stability.

They reached Paris on 6 November, five days after embarking from Southampton. Marianne was dazzled by the city: 'We were at once struck with surprise and delight at the magnificence of the architecture, the extent of the buildings and gardens, forming together a coup-d'oeil worthy of the entrance of a great capital.' Later, on leaving Fontainebleau, Marianne observed 'the politeness of the French nation, and contrasts strongly with the haughty reserve with which our countrymen and countrywomen behave to each other, until the important ceremony of an introduction has passed between them … The gentleman we met was elderly, and, I should suspect, belonged to the ancien regime, who far surpass in refinement the class of people who sprang up under Bonaparte's government.'

Whenever possible, the Colstons did not travel on Sundays in order to 'keep the Sabbath day holy to the Lord our God' and Edward would read the 'church service' if they could not attend church in person. They also tried not to travel in the dark in case they had an accident or were attacked and this next excerpt from late November 1819 brings home the dangers of this long journey to Italy:

> We set out on the 23rd, at ten o'clock, to pass the Jura Mountains, and began to ascend with four horses; one of those unfortunately had a propensity for kicking, and we had gone but a very short way before he kicked his two hind legs over the pole of the carriage. Soon after, the cord traces (which were rotten) of the two leaders gave way, and the horses ran off from the carriage. A very considerable quantity of snow had already fallen, and the passage of the Juras at such a season, with the accompaniments of a kicking horse, and rotten tackle, were too much for my courage …

Marianne quickly regained her composure and the ascent was completed safely, although this was by no means the last of the hazards on their way.

Like many modern travellers, they risked being over-charged: 'For a little bread and cheese in the evening, and a cup of coffee each the next morning, with our bed, she demanded fifteen francs; we gave her nine, and escaped from her clamour into our carriage just after seven o'clock.' The snow was now four feet deep so the carriage was put on a sledge 'drawn by three horses, harnessed one before the other, and a second sledge was employed to convey the wheels. One man guided our horses, and two walked on each side, to support the carriage whenever it inclined violently to the ground.' Inside the carriage, Marianne was comfortable 'wrapped in warm clothing, and my feet heated by a chaudpied …' Later that day, they reached the Hotel d'Angleterre at Sécheron, near Geneva. 'We here met the gentleman who had travelled on the Juras so short a time before us; he told us, that he had not only been upset three times, but had also been obliged to be dug out of the snow five or six times.'

On the morning of 27 November they experienced what would be a constant problem throughout their journey: '… we rose at five o'clock, having ordered the horses to be ready exactly at six; but to our great disappointment, we found that two couriers, who had passed in the night, had taken all the horses, and we were obliged to wait an hour until those returned had been refreshed.' The same problem affected them in the evening: 'Dr. W., an English General, and the Duchess of Narbonne, all reached Chambery on the evening of the 27th, and continued their journey during the whole of the night. We had great cause to lament our being preceded by so many fellow-travellers, as arriving a few hours after them at each post, we got such tired horses, that they could scarcely move, and were often obliged to wait a long time to procure even these.'

The night of 28 November 1819 was spent travelling through the Alps and Marianne slept fitfully, badly affected by the intense cold and fears of black wolves: 'the most savage of their species, and when the snow lies deep on the ground, so that they can get no food in the woods, hunger drives them to the road-side'. The Colstons carried pistols but no harm came to them. Their journey continued across the Alps with the snow in many places forming 'a wall of seven feet high on each side of the road, and was level with the *top* of the carriage!' and their passing 'many waterfalls frozen in their descent: one of these presented a mass of icicles, from eighteen to twenty feet long ...'

By 1 December they reached Turin but set off again the following day: '... we seemed to verify the frequent observation of our continental neighbours, that the English travel through foreign countries as if they were pursued by an enemy ...' On 4 December, for instance, they travelled 90 miles, reaching Modena at nightfall. By 8 December they reached Florence, where they stayed until 21 February 1820, enjoying the cultural and social life of the great city to the full.

On the next leg of their journey they were accompanied by the 'agreeable addition of Miss A' (we know no more about her identity) and it is significant that Marianne complained of a 'severe sick headache' on the first day of their travels to Siena where they stayed until 23 February. A constant concern was the threat of highwaymen as is illustrated by this incident near Radicofani:

> Ascending one of these steep acclivities, we met eight of the most desperate, blackguard-looking fellows I ever saw in my life; they were all armed with bludgeons, and, as they approached the carriage, they divided into two ranks, taking different sides of the road, and changed their bludgeons from the left to the right hand, as if shouldering arms. They assaulted us however only with their looks; indeed our pistols were prepared to give them a proper return if they had attempted to stop us, and they probably thought that we were too well guarded to be attacked with impunity.

Just after Radicofani, Marianne recorded a gruesome sight: 'A little beyond this town, we saw suspended to a wooden cross the bones of thieves, and murderers, who had been executed, turned perfectly black by exposure to the elements. A sight how horrible to an English traveller!'

On 3 March they arrived in Rome where they stayed, or in the environs, until 9 May and undertook a very energetic programme of visits to all the famous sights and also artists' studios such as that of Antonio Canova 'the Michel Angelo of the 19th century; at once sculptor, painter and architect'. Marianne mentions sketching periodically in the journal but does not dwell upon it, although she produced 50 pictures of high quality and charm during her travels. This is a typical entry, recorded at the Velino falls after they had left Rome: 'The lake offers a highly picturesque subject for the pencil; the ancient castle of Labro crowns the highest mountain, and a small town is situated underneath it. Miss A. and myself delayed, to take sketches, and Mr C. made some attempts at fishing …' Later the same day, even Edward was inspired to pick up a pencil and join the two ladies sketching.

The Bridge over the Adour at Bayonne by Marianne Colston from her Journal.

Marianne was clearly devoted to Edward but this does not prevent her from commenting on good-looking men whom she encounters on their travels: after passing Mount Soracte, they dine 'at the same table with a young and very handsome Italian Marchese, whom the waiter informed us had been a short time ago staying under the same roof, in the suite of our Queen'.

After travelling across the plains of Lombardy, regaled with the song of nightingales, they stayed briefly in Bologna before moving on to Padua. Then came Venice from 1 to 12 June, visiting the many sights and enjoying trips by gondola, and Lodi, Verona, Mantua and Cremona. Marianne recounts a visit to a girls' school, made possible by a letter of introduction from Maria Cosway, the Italian-English artist and educationalist, which illustrates how progressive her views were about the education of women:

> An Italian nobleman had the public spirit and philanthropy to endow the institution, and Maria Cosway was the person whom he chose to commence and bring it into order. She has likewise founded a similar institution in Lyons. It is gratifying to an English female to reflect, that a countrywoman should be instrumental in beginning this useful undertaking. The abilities of the Italian ladies appear so good, that if they obtain universally similar means of improvement, the English fair must be careful that they are not left behind in the intellectual race.

Milan was reached on 26 June and there they stayed until 5 July. They explored the city and saw 'some of the improvements which Bonaparte made … and which in a considerable measure, atone for the injury that the city previously suffered from his arms'. This reluctant admiration for Napoleon is a recurrent theme throughout the journal (Napoleon was then in exile on Saint Helena and would die a year later in 1821).

On leaving Milan they drove to Lake Como where they stayed in a lakeside villa. There is a gap of two months in the journal between 19 July and 18 September, which is explained in the diary entry for the latter date in a playful manner: 'This town is celebrated for having given birth to Pliny the younger; to Paolo Giovio, who was successively physician, bishop and historian; to Pope Innocent XI … and to the physician Volta. But it possesses a higher interest in my breast, as having been the birthplace of my little darling Arabella, who here first saw the light of day, at half after eleven o'clock, on the 29th of July.'

On 18 September, the Colstons resumed their travels accompanied by their baby with Miss A. occupying a vehicle by herself and headed to Lake Maggiore and then to the Simplon. On 21 September they took advantage of meeting with Mr F., 'a very agreeable English clergyman', to have Arabella baptised, probably the 'first English child who has been baptized on the summits of the Simplon'.

Shortly afterwards, the Colstons crossed the border into Switzerland and spent their first night in Glis. Their subsequent travels through the Rhone valley delighted Marianne; she was a devotee of Byron and the Colstons visited Chillon Castle, 'which has of late years acquired a new interest, from the beautiful poem of Lord Byron, "The Prisoner of Chillon"'.

After staying in Berne, the Colstons visited the waterfalls at Giessbach near Interlaken in early October where they were welcomed by 'a worthy old Swiss peasant' in a hut by the waterfalls: 'He kept a book, in which the visitors to this delightful spot inserted their names, and we recognised the signatures of many of our English friends … He lit a fire to warm us … and regaled us with a little *Kerswasher*, a Swiss spirit distilled from cherries, a little resembling whiskey … little darling Arabella had likewise been comfortably housed here, during the whole time of our stay at the cascade.'

Arabella was a stoical baby who tolerated tough travelling conditions with good humour, protected by her devoted parents. This next diary entry about their arrival at their lodgings in Brienz reminds us how remarkable it was for a baby to be transported in this way with such little fuss: 'The landlady of the inn (who spoke only German), seemed very curious to discover what we had with us, so carefully wrapped up in a shawl; she approached it, and very gently opening the folds, found to her great astonishment, that the treasure contained in it was a baby! She expressed her surprise that so young a traveller could bear so arduous a journey …'

In Geneva, Marianne bought 'a few trifles' of jewellery, one of the few times that she refers to shopping. On 4 November their companion Miss A. departed and their vetturino mistook his way for the first time on their travels. The customs officers at Bellegarde-sur-Valserine searched all their cases for contraband on their entry into France. They reached Montpellier where they remained for three months until 19 March, enjoying the Carnival and being 'invited to a great many private dances, called *Soirées priées* which were brilliant, and agreeable'. Married ladies could waltz but the unmarried ones were not allowed to do so, reflecting that it was a relatively new dance with a greater degree of intimacy than its predecessors. Marianne refers to the 'indecorum' of the waltz but observed that at least the French version was slower than the Russian.

When they resumed their travels, they crossed the river Lot by boat: 'Our boatman had been taken prisoner at Trafalgar; and, during his eight years confinement near Bristol, had acquired a good knowledge of the English language: he spoke with gratitude of his treatment as a prisoner.' In Pau, Marianne saw the rising moon and wrote: 'I could have wished for Lord Byron's muse, or Sir Walter Scott's descriptive pen, to paint the effect of the transition.'

On 19 June they arrived in Bagnères-de-Bigorre where they spent seven weeks at the Spa, which had all the facilities of a modern hotel: steam-baths, restaurant, billiard room, reading room, library, assembly room and concert and card rooms. Their fellow guests were mainly English with some Spanish, French and a few Swiss and Germans: 'a most easy and agreeable society was formed, free from the shackles of etiquette or the parade of ostentation'.

Once they resumed their travels, they visited the cascades of Pont d'Espagne on 10 September, taking the 'celebrated' route along a narrow path with Edward on foot armed with a long spiked wooden pole while Marianne was carried in a 'chaise à porteur' or sedan chair. Her bearers wore sandals of raw calfskin to reduce slipping and they trod on the pointed edges of rocks thereby causing their feet to cling like those of a mountain goat. Beyond the path was an abyss and Marianne clung tightly to her chair on the descent but denied that she felt scared.

On 1 November they left Orleans and travelled once more to Paris where they saw the King travel by open carriage and were introduced to the Duc de Bordeaux. Marianne commented on the subject of regulation, saying that the French love of regulation 'would too much interfere with the independent spirit of our countrymen, who are habituated to exercise the right of thinking, and acting for themselves.' They celebrated the New Year 1821 in Paris before returning to England, taking home a high opinion of their hosts: 'The gaiety, the politeness, and the *savoir vivre*, which are the peculiar attributes of the French nation.'

5

The Colstons at Roundway Park

ON THEIR ARRIVAL at New Park in 1840, Edward and Marianne changed the name to Roundway Park, and began to make improvements to the house, gardens and estate and to entertain on an extensive scale. They now had a family of four children: in addition to Arabella they had three sons, Edward, Samuel and William.

By 1846 they had spent £30,000 (£3.4m today) on the house and estate with most of the expenditure being on improvements to the gardens, parkland and estate. The house itself was in good condition, so spending was relatively limited and focused on reorganising the entrance area and the downstairs rooms.[102] Not everyone thought their changes were for the better. Thomas Finden's designs were censured in the *Civil Engineer and Architect's Journal* in 1841:

> New Park near Devizes, showing the principal front, with alterations and new carriage entrance, does not impress us with any very high idea of the taste or ability of Messrs. Finden and Green. How far they have doctored up the house, we know not: for aught we can tell they may have improved it, but if they have it must have been deplorably bad indeed before, since it is bad enough – we should say, intolerably bad even now.[103]

Portico in the courtyard behind the west front (Historic England).

The main reception rooms were rearranged with the dining room and drawing room located at opposite ends of the west front of the house. The old drawing room now became the dining room with an arch inserted at its south end to delineate a serving area. The fireplace was probably installed at this time. Wyatt's oval dining room was reordered as a small library or writing room with the buffet alcove refitted with bookshelves. The large picture gallery or music or ballroom, which was next to the conservatory, now served as the principal drawing room. Its double entrance doors were faced with mirror glass, and niches were introduced at the north end of the room to hold full-length statues.

This rearrangement of Wyatt's rooms reflected the changes in lifestyle and entertaining in the first part of the 19th century. Dinner was now served at about 7pm compared to at or before 5pm at the time when Roundway was built, although it remained the main meal of the day. Guests gathered in the drawing room before dinner and then processioned through the connecting rooms to the dining room where the meal was served in style with footmen in attendance. The ladies then withdrew to the drawing room at the other end of the house while the men continued to sit in the dining room, drinking, smoking and talking. In this way, the separation of the dining and drawing rooms ensured that the noise and smoking of the men did not disturb the ladies and, as a result, the former came to be seen as a masculine enclave and the latter a feminine room. The procession between the two rooms at either end of the house also provided a sense of theatre and the opportunity to show off the paintings, furniture and other works of art in the connecting rooms.

Drawing room at Roundway c1860s with marble statues.

A key ingredient of the Grand Tour was the acquisition of works of art, although Marianne seldom mentioned such purchases in her journal. It is difficult to know whether this was through discretion or simply because they made few acquisitions. There was certainly a fine collection of Old Master paintings at Roundway although it is not clear when or how these were acquired. A photograph of the drawing room in the mid 19th century shows two marble statues of *Dancer*, reputed to have been by Antonio Canova (the first version of the dancer with both hands on her hips is dated 1810 while the other figure is dated 1809).[104] Marianne mentions visiting artists' studios in her journal, including Canova's in 1820 in Rome:

> Here, indeed, the wonders of 'the marble art' are displayed! I had no idea of the powerful effect of statuary till I came to Rome, and now I confess, that this sublime, majestic art, claims a high pre-eminence above her 'rainbow sister' … Here are an exquisitely beautiful Magdalen; a Hebe; the inimitable Three Graces, the original of which is possessed by the Duke of Bedford …

The Colstons also owned a particularly beautiful oil painting by Dutch painter Caspar van Wittel (also known as Vanvitelli) of the Villa Aldobrandini near Frascati, a place that Marianne and Edward had visited while in Rome: 'We visited the Aldobrandini villa, which is called Belvidere, from its delightful situation. It belongs to the Borghese family. The casino is adorned with fine marbles, and paintings, by Cavaliere d'Arpino; the gardens contain a variety of statues, cascades, fountains etc., by which latter several very pretty water-works are performed.'

Villa Aldobrandini by Caspar van Wittel, also known as Vanvitelli.

A little later on their travels in 1820, in the Palazzo Barni in Lodi, Marianne had revealed her keen eye for pictures and their value when she encountered a striking painting of the Madonna: 'The painter of this extraordinary picture is unknown; but though I do not pretend to any great connoisseurship, I have little doubt that it is by Correggio … The owner of this picture had bought it for the ridiculously trifling sum of five francs; he had been offered for it 1700 francs, and perhaps if it were proved an original of Correggio's, it might, in England, produce the same number of pounds.'

In 1841 a large estate map was drawn up (shown on page 36): *A Map of Roundway Park, formerly called New Park, the Property and Residence of Edward Francis Colston Esquire, 1841.*[105] Roundway's setting clearly fulfilled the Colstons' taste for the picturesque, to which Marianne referred in her journal. She had criticised, for example, a chateau she saw near Alençon, in 1821, for its 'straight avenues of trees' which 'afford no variety and little beauty to the eye'. She and Edward had preferred instead the countryside at Mount Soracte in the Apennines, which they visited in 1820: 'In many parts of this extensive tract, the turf was as fine and soft as in any gentleman's lawn in England; and the beautiful timber with which it was clothed, gave it the air of one continued park. Were this lovely scenery to be found in England, how soon would it be enlivened and adorned with the seats of noblemen and gentry!' The Colstons also had considerable knowledge of trees and plants, as Marianne revealed in her journal, which they put to good effect at Roundway.

Their improvements to the estate aroused considerable local resentment when in 1842 they enclosed 'Sheep Wash Dell' to extend the parkland, thereby depriving usage as common land.[106] They erected the lodge on London Road at this time, its classical style designed to complement the architecture of the Wyatt house. By contrast, they built Quakers Walk Lodge, on the west side of the park by the canal, in a Jacobethan style with their coat-of-arms, at some point between 1841 and 1845. A small red-brick gardener's cottage was also erected close to the walled kitchen garden.[107]

Left: Quakers Walk Lodge and *right:* Marlborough Road Lodge on the London Road.

The Swiss Cottage, which is marked within the woods on the northern edge of the estate on Edward Colston's map of 1841, may have been erected for either the Estcourt or the Colston family at the same time as the nearby waterfall and its rustic bridge were engineered to create a pleasing focus for walks from the house. The cottage stood in a clearing and was used as a shooting lodge. It consisted of three sections, with an upper chamber reached by outside steps to a veranda, which served as a tearoom or gazebo. The walls were clad with logs arranged vertically except for one panel next to the veranda on a side wall where the logs

Left: Postcard of the Swiss Cottage (©Wiltshire Museum, Devizes) and *right*: Swiss Cottage.

were arranged in the pattern of a spider's web. The rest of the cottage was brick built and lived in by the gamekeeper. It is little changed in appearance today.

One gamekeeper who lived there in the mid-19th century was Eli Barrett who came to Wiltshire from Ireland at the time of the potato famine. There is a story of a member of the Barrett family being caught in the deep snow of 1881, taking refuge in a barn on the estate and waking up to find that he had been sleeping next to a travelling bear.[108]

Left and middle: Waterfall and rustic bridge in the Pleasure Gardens.
Right: Watercolour of the rockhead above the waterfall by Agnes Baynes, 1874.

The water gardens consisted of a lake fed by the most easterly source of the Bristol Avon, which flowed into two successive waterfalls. The Colstons liked to walk in the woods and the water gardens after church. In 1956 the remains of another building were found by two boys on the hillside at Roundway Hill who uncovered a tiled floor (and hoped in vain that they had discovered a Roman temple). There is a print of uncertain date showing a building on the hillside there.[109]

Like many country estates, in 1846 Roundway Park was threatened by the second period of railway speculation, dominated by George Hudson the 'Railway King', which increased railway track in Britain from about 2,000 miles in 1843 to 5,000 miles by 1848. Edward Colston was unhappy with the plans for the new London, Newbury and Bath (Direct) Railway to travel across parts of the estate and commissioned expert witness Francis Fuller to outline the case against the route in a document entitled 'Proof of F. Fuller Esq.' which also provides a detailed description of the estate:

Mr Colston has recently erected at considerable cost a Lodge at the end of the Quakers Walk which this Railway would sever. The Line passes thro' the Deer Park and ornamental lands adjoining Roundway House. That from such examination Witness finds that the extreme distance such line will be from Mr Colston's Mansion is about 440 yards and the nearest approach to the Pleasure Grounds is about 200 yards (this is at the point adjoining the Trellis work Gardens, a favourite resort of the Inhabitants of Roundway) ...

Quakers Walk Lodge in Victorian times.

The park in front of the Mansion is also finely timbered and is of an undulating nature. The gardens and ornamental walks etc have been laid out with the most perfect taste and at a large outlay. At the bottom of the Park and close to the London Newbury & Bath Railway are 3 pieces of ornamental water with waterfalls etc. These have been artificially made and the large pieces of Rock forming the bed of the waterfalls as Witness has been informed have been brought at a great expense from Melksham a distance of 10 miles – many of which are several tons weight. This particular part of the Park is extremely beautiful and picturesque and is a favourite resort of the Inhabitants and Visitors at Roundway. The line of the London Newbury and Bath Railway will render this part of the Park totally useless as a place of resort as the line will be close to it and the Banks or rather slopes of the cutting will come down close upon the ornamental pieces of water. Adjoining this part is a thickly wooded Hill with ornamental Walks called the Grotto Retreat. This will be intersected and consequently destroyed by the line ...

Any works or buildings that may be erected on the land pointed out to Witness as the station for such line at Devizes would be visible from Roundway House and would overlook the Park Grounds and Pleasure Gardens. Noise of engines easily heard at Roundway House during day and night. That no plantations which might be formed on Mr Hughes' land would screen such Station from the view of the house …[110]

In the event, no railway was built across the Colstons' land. Indeed, the first train did not arrive in Devizes until 1857, on a single-line broad-gauge track from Holt Junction owned by the Wiltshire, Somerset and Weymouth Railway, and it was not until 1862 that the town acquired a direct line to London. The absence of significant manufacturing activity in the town as well as the protestations of landowners such as the Colstons were key reasons for the relatively late arrival of the railway in Devizes.[111]

Edward's responsibilities for his estates beyond Roundway can be seen in the work that he carried out with his uncle William on the church at West Lydford in the 1840s. The West Lydford estate in Somerset, which mainly lay west of the Fosse Way between Shepton Mallet and Ilchester, had been bought by their ancestor Edward Colston the Philanthropist in 1704 from Sir Edward and Lady Hungerford.[112] The Manor was slightly larger than the parish and totalled 1,802 acres at the end of the 18th century. At some stage in the 19th century, the Colstons also bought Lydford Park but it was not held on a long-term basis.[113]

Between 1797, when William started as Rector, and the major church re-building in the 1840s, he had built the Rectory in 1800 and carried out various improvements to the church including erecting the screen in 1799, repairing the tower and re-hanging the bells in 1805, and installing the pulpit in 1821. The church was prone to flooding, which probably explains why re-building works were required in the 1840s.[114] This theory is supported by the fact that Edward and

St Peters Church in West Lydford.

William restored the bridge at the same time with floodwater arches.[115] The plaque dated 1846 on the wall of the church records that: 'The Body of this Church was rebuilt and the Tower repaired by Edward Francis Colston, Esq. of Roundway Park, Wilts AD Mdcccxlvi. The Chancel was rebuilt in the same year by the Rev. William Hungerford Colston D.D. Rector of this Parish.'[116]

A flavour of Colston family life at Roundway in the 1840s can be found in the diary of Louisa Ruperta (known as Louisa) Murray, written when she stayed at the house aged 19 in August 1845.[117] Three years later she married Edward and Marianne Colston's eldest son, Edward, and it is possible that this visit in August 1845 was the first time she had met her future husband, then a 23-year-old officer (cornet) in the 15th Hussars. Louisa was the grand-daughter of Rt. Rev. Lord George Murray (1761–1803), Bishop of St David's, and the second son of John Murray, the 3rd Duke of Atholl.[118]

Edward Colston the Hussar
by James Godsell Middleton.

Louisa's father, also called George, was vicar of Northolt in Middlesex and Prebendary of St Paul's and her mother, Ruperta Catherine Wright, was the only child of the late Sir George Wright, Bt, HM Minister Resident in Venice.[119] The name Ruperta is a reference to the alleged descendancy of Sir George Wright's mother's family, the Stapletons, from Prince Rupert of the Rhine (1619–82), grandson of James I.[120] It was repeated down the generations in the name of the eldest daughter in the Murray family and then the Colston and Baynes families.

Louisa recorded in her diary for August 1845 how she and her brother Charles left London 'by the 11 o'clock train on the Great Western to Chippenham', from where they were 'collected in a Phaeton', arriving at Roundway before six. Her eldest brother, Augustus, a naval officer, 'came down from Town by a Coach having missed the train'. The four-day visit coincided with the Devizes Assizes, and the Roundway party was involved daily, visiting the Court House or entertaining the High Sheriff, his wife, his Chaplain, and various connected officials. Twenty-six people dined in the house on 11 August 'with singing in the evening and a Polka afterwards', while on 13 August, 'There were 28 people at dinner and we danced all sorts of dances ending with a Cotillon and Sir Roger de Coverley which I played.'

After all the investment and work in improving the house and estate at Roundway, Edward and Marianne must have taken great pleasure and satisfaction in seeing Roundway full of activity and being enjoyed by their children and friends.

6

Lives Cut Short

TRAGEDY STRUCK ROUNDWAY in 1847, when Edward Colston's drowned body was discovered in the park's fishponds by a passing labourer on 16 February, the day after Edward's 52nd birthday. The death was reported in the *London Illustrated News* on 24 April 1847:

EDWARD FRANCIS COLSTON, ESQ.,
OF ROUNDWAY PARK, WILTS.

The melancholy death of this gentleman has occasioned deep regret throughout the neighbourhood of Devizes. On Friday, the 16th instant, as a labourer was passing near the newly formed fish-ponds in Roundway Park, he discovered the body of Mr Colston floating in the water.

From the evidence adduced at the Coroner's Inquest it appeared that the deceased was taking the shortest way across a steep bank, upwards of twenty feet high, when, either from apoplexy, to which he was predisposed, or from some accidental stumbling, he fell into the water.

The lamentable event is much deplored. Of a cheerful and amiable disposition – courteous, affable and kind-hearted – Mr Colston enjoyed universal esteem. His chief delight seemed to be in 'living at home', in improving his estate, in employing the poor, and in dispensing hospitalities to his friends and neighbours. He held the Commission of the Peace for the counties of Somerset, Wilts and Oxford, and possessed large property in each. His father, the late Colonel Colston, of Filkin's Hall, was grandson and heir of Alexander Ready Esq., who took the name of Colston from his third wife's great uncle, EDWARD COLSTON, the philanthropist of Bristol. The gentleman whose decease has given rise to this brief notice had completed his fifty-second year the day before he died.

It is fair to assume that Marianne was much involved in protecting her son Edward the Hussar, now aged 25, and his best interests as a major landowner as well as solving the many problems caused by her husband's sudden death, including substantial debts most probably caused by the high level of investment in Roundway.[121]

Fortunately, Marianne was financially independent due to a substantial inheritance from her father. The will of William Jenkins provided £30,000 (£3.3m) for Marianne in the event of her surviving her husband Edward.[122] She was also left the two portraits of her mother and the portrait of her paternal grandmother. Her son Edward the Hussar was excluded from the will, given that he had the Colston inheritance, but Arabella was left £1,000 (£100,000 today), and her other sons, William and Samuel, received £500 each. Marianne was also left a life interest in all the freehold and leasehold property at Strickland Farm as well as in West Bradley and Barton Saint David, which were to pass to her sons William and Samuel on her death.

Marianne's son Edward the Hussar was promoted in February 1848 to lieutenant from cornet. On 20 June he married Louisa Murray, and about this time sold the Filkins estate in Oxfordshire, most likely to pay off his father's debts.[123] He sold his commission in the Hussars that December and, two months later, was appointed a lieutenant in the Royal Gloucestershire Hussars, a yeomanry regiment with which he served for 12 years until May 1861.

Portrait of Edward the Hussar by James Godsell Middleton.

Louisa's first child, a boy, was born in 1849 and, following the family tradition, was christened Edward. He was soon joined by two sisters, Amy Ruperta in 1850 and Lilian in 1852, and then by a brother Charles in 1854. As well as this growing family, the 1851 census recorded that the Roundway household was served by 11 living-in servants as shown below. Of these, only the butler, Henry Blancourd (known as

From left: Amy, Charles and Lilian Colston as children.

Blenco), was married and all the servants were under the age of 40. There is no mention of a cook, although he or she may have been living elsewhere on the estate and therefore not in the main house.

Susan Higgins	Nurse	Unmarried	Aged 28	Servant
Matilda Green	Nurse	Unmarried	Aged 19	Servant
Henry Blancourd	Butler	Married	Aged 36	Servant
Arthur Gain	Footman	Unmarried	Aged 24	Servant
Robert Jones	Footman	Unmarried	Aged 27	Servant
George Hudson	Coachman	Unmarried	Aged 22	Servant
John Turvey	Groom	Unmarried	Aged 22	Servant
Elizabeth Hughes	Housekeeper	Unmarried	Aged 38	Servant
Esther Cockbell	Lady's Maid	Unmarried	Aged 39	Servant
Elizabeth Aplaud	Lady's Maid	Unmarried	Aged 27	Servant
Mary Garrard	Housemaid	Unmarried	Aged 27	Servant

Edward and Louisa's eldest son suffered from tuberculosis, known then as consumption, and they built a little house and garden on the estate near Quakers Walk and Belvedere Wood called Newlands where little Edward could be treated in the manner then thought best, namely by complete isolation with plenty of fresh air. A wide flight of steps led to a raised ground floor room provided with a fireplace. A hatch door in the ceiling gave access to a roof space used

Edward Colston (1849–59) and Newlands cottage (John Girvan *Devizes Hidden Secrets* and Don King).

for storage. In the basement there was a kitchen with a cast-iron cooking range and outside a large garden.[124] It must have been an extremely lonely life for the little boy.

Edward died at the age of ten in 1859 when staying at his mother's family house near Brecon in Wales. A sense of the aching loss to the family is communicated by the poignant memorial by John Hancock in St James's Church in Devizes. It shows angels reaching down to take the boy up to heaven with his three surviving siblings looking distraught at his bedside with this inscription:

> *Suffer little children to come unto me for such is the Kingdom of Heaven.*
> *Around the throne of God in Heaven,*
> *Thousands of children stand,*
> *Children, whose sins are all forgiven,*
> *A Holy, Happy Band*
> *Singing Glory, Glory, Glory.*

Edward is also commemorated with his mother Louisa in a stained-glass window in the church at the east end of the north wall and the Colston family by the two large wooden prayer chairs. Also at the church is a three-tiered granite grave to the Blenco family for whom memorial stones were later discovered at Newlands. Henry Blenco, butler at Roundway in the 1851

In St James's Church in Devizes (*from left to right*): Colston stained glass window.

Memorial to young Edward Colston.

Colston prayer chairs.

census, later became the innkeeper at the Castle Hotel in New Park Street. It is likely that Henry or members of his family played a key part in looking after Edward and that the Colston family wanted a memorial to their connection with the little boy to be placed at Newlands.

Louisa's Letts No 10 diary for 1861, inscribed on the inside cover: 'Louisa Colston, Glanoysk, Senny Bridge, Brecon, South Wales, 1861', shows that the family spent a significant part of the year away from Roundway, possibly in order to have some independence from the indomitable Marianne. The diary also gives us an insight into life at Roundway at that time.

Situated on the river Usk, the house at Glanoysk (now Glanusk House with the name of the nearby town now known as Sennybridge) may have been bought in 1829 at auction by Louisa's parents, George and Ruperta Catherine, inspired by the Welsh connections of her grandfather the Rt. Rev. Lord George Murray, Bishop of St David's. Louisa, Edward the Hussar and the three children were to spend most of the summer of 1861 there, from June through October, returning to Roundway for November and December.

Glanusk House, Sennybridge, near Brecon, Powys.

Other than an asterisk each month to record her menstrual cycle, there is very little about Louisa's own health, in contrast to that of her husband. There are frequent entries such as this one on 29 April: 'Ed's back still sore and also a bad fit of gout in his great toe' while on 20 September Ed was 'not quite the thing and did not go out shooting'.

The most serious, however, was the entry for 13 April during a visit to Padworth House, the home near Aldermarston in Berkshire of Edward's sister Arabella, 'Araby', and her husband Christopher Darby Griffith: 'Dear Ed taken ill with an epileptic at luncheon …' In view of this, Edward wrote to his commanding officer in the Gloucestershire Hussars, the Duke of Beaufort, to offer his resignation. Letters came from the Duke between 21 and 26 April on three occasions, accepting his resignation, commiserating with him and thanking him for his 12 years' service with the regiment.

Edward's epilepsy was managed at home for the rest of his life without recourse to an institution. There was no known cure for epilepsy at the time; it was much misunderstood as an illness and the cause of much cruelty to some sufferers who were considered deranged and consigned to an asylum.[125] The latter came into existence as a result of the 1845 Lunatics Act with the construction of the Wiltshire County Lunatic Asylum in Devizes being approved in 1848.

Louisa's diary presents a picture of a simple, rather restricted existence at Roundway. She mentions the weather every day, and refers to letters that she has received and written with mention of cheques sent. By 1861 mail was being carried all over Great Britain, still partly by mail-coach in remote parts, but increasingly by rail between major towns. Letters and parcels reached their destinations promptly and families could keep in touch almost on a daily basis. Since the reforms of Rowland Hill in 1840, and his introduction of the one-penny stamp, the postal service was now cheap as well as frequent and efficient.

Sunday entries in the diary almost always told of two visits to church, sometimes walking with Edward and the children. On one occasion at Roundway she notes that Mr Thrupp, the rector, came on a Saturday 'to give the Blessed Sacrament to Mrs Colston and to some of the servants and to me' at the house (Louisa's mother-in-law, Marianne, is always referred to in the diary as Mrs Colston).

The need to give Holy Communion to Mrs Colston at home suggests that Marianne was beginning to fail physically at the age of 69, though she was still as mentally alert as ever. On 2 April, Louisa records that it being a fine day, 'Mrs Colston went out in her chair for the 1st time this year.' She went out regularly in the following months but always in some form of carriage, frequently taking Louisa with her who tacitly gives the impression that these outings were an unavoidable duty.

At other times Louisa went out on foot, taking the children with her whenever possible, and sometimes accompanied by her husband or his brother Willie (now aged 37) who was unmarried and still lived at Roundway. They often walked to the Swiss Cottage, or down Quakers Walk into Devizes. On 1 May there were three outings: 'I walked to the Watermill with Lilie before lunch, and afterwards drove with Mrs Colston to Devizes, and Ed, the children and I then walked to see the new purchases at Newlands.'

A weekend visit to London in early May with Edward and Lilian was also family oriented. Taking the 7.30am train from Devizes they arrived in time for lunch with Louisa's widowed mother, Mrs Murray, at her home in Manchester Square, then went down to stay with Louisa's sister and brother-in-law, Emma and Robert Lawes, at their house in Kingston Hill. The following morning, they went to church and 'heard a very good sermon about "the Tares and the Wheat"'. That afternoon the party made the 12-mile journey to Whitton Park in Middlesex, to spend the rest of the day with Louisa's brother Charles Gostling Murray and his wife Emily, returning to Kingston for the night. From there an early train on 6 May took them up to London, where Edward hired a hansom cab for the day to take them round the shops and to a bazaar. Catching the 4pm train from Paddington they were home at Roundway by 9pm.

There are frequent entries referring to Glanoysk: Mr Jones despatched the first salmon from the river Usk to Roundway in March; in April, Louisa wrote to a Brecon plumber. By the end of May, all the extensive preparations for the family's summer visit were complete. Following a visit to the dentist Mr Ayton in Devizes and a walk 'with the children to say good-bye to some of the poor people and gave away 2 frocks', they left Roundway for Wales. On Saturday 1 June, accompanied by a children's nursemaid named Elizabeth and a groom by the name of Pettitt, they drove to Chippenham and then travelled by rail via Swindon to Llandovery on the South Wales railway. The 14-mile journey to Senny Bridge was made in a 'Bus' with four horses.

The next morning Louisa walked a mile to church in the nearby village of Defynnog with her two daughters. In the afternoon she took all three children to the Kydbree Chapel in Senny Bridge. This became the regular pattern of their Sundays while at Glanoysk, with Edward at times accompanying them, and on occasions some of the servants as well.

The mail service to Senny Bridge was as efficient as elsewhere in Britain, and Louisa continued to write letters almost daily to Mrs Colston and also frequently to her mother and her sister-in-law Araby Darby Griffith at Padworth. Louisa was clearly happy to be living the simple rural life at Glanoysk. To ensure that the children's education did not suffer, they employed a French governess 'Mamselle de Karp' for two months, after which Mr Davies, the local schoolmaster, came to give the children lessons until they returned to Roundway.[126]

Edward the Hussar's epilepsy led to his early death at the age of 42 in 1864. His will had been drawn up in 1856 and seemed to anticipate the premature death of his eldest son, Edward (1849–59), by focusing on his younger son, Charles. It makes reference to the fact that Charles would inherit, at the age of 25, the estate of their cousin John Morris Colston and his wife Isobel of Kensington Gardens Terrace, Hyde Park. Edward's two daughters, Amy and Lilian, each inherited £25,000 (£3.1m today) which accorded them the status of heiresses in their own right.

Colston family tomb by the Crammer pond.

The early death of her eldest son may well have contributed to Marianne's own death a year later in 1865. She had already lost her younger son Samuel ten years earlier in 1854 when he was just 29, a graduate of St John's College, Oxford, and unmarried. Marianne left effects valued at about £40,000 (£4.9m today) and was buried in the graveyard at St James's Church in Devizes in a handsome family tomb which was erected beside the Crammer pond.[127]

In 1866, a year after Marianne's death, her only remaining son, William, died at a similar age to Edward, aged 41, but unmarried. We do not know if either he or Samuel also suffered from epilepsy. This left only Arabella Darby Griffith of the four Colston siblings; she went on to live until the age of 71, dying on 13 March 1891.

Marianne's father, William Jenkins, had stipulated in his will that the land and property at places such as West Pennard and Barton St David were for the use of Marianne during her lifetime and were then to pass to her younger sons, Samuel and William. After the deaths of the two sons, they passed to her grandson, Charles Colston, with the provision that his aunt Arabella had the income from the estates for her lifetime.[128] There was then some reorganisation of these assets: for instance, in 1866 the estate at Barton St David, which by then totalled 223.5 acres, was divided up and sold.[129]

When William Jenkins drew up his will, nobody would have expected his land and property to be inherited by Charles but rather to have been split up between his other grandchildren and their descendants. The twist of fate that benefited Charles financially also greatly favoured Roundway's long-term prospects by providing a substantial financial cushion when economic prospects worsened for the Colston family in the late 19th and early 20th century. Both Charles and his son Edward were to receive other substantial inheritances from relations over the next 70 years.

At the age of 39, Louisa now became the dominant figure in the household at Roundway, with responsibility for guarding her son Charles's inheritance – he was only ten years old at the time of his father's death – and for ensuring that his education and upbringing prepared him well for the day when he would take control of it himself.

$$ 7 $$

Love and Marriage

LOUISA COLSTON was assisted in her role as head of the family by her sister-in-law Arabella's husband, Christopher Darby Griffith (1804–85), who assumed some of the duties of a father to her children. Christopher and Arabella's only child, Christopher, was similar in age to the Colston children, being only four years younger than Charles.

Left: Arabella Darby Griffith with young Christopher.
Right: Christopher Darby Griffith.

Christopher, who lived at Padworth House in Berkshire, was the MP for Devizes at the time, so it suited him from a professional as well as a personal point of view to spend time at Roundway. He was an independent-minded Conservative with a shrewd humour and aptitude for making amusing speeches 'spiced with eccentricity'. Together with many other Conservative colleagues, he

Left: Padworth House entrance front and *right*: the hall (*Country Life*, September 1922).

supported the Liberal Prime Minister Lord Palmerston whom he is said to have enjoyed baiting with perplexing questions, which were parried with ready humour and repartee.[130]

Christopher, however, lost his seat in Devizes in the 1868 election, held after Disraeli's Reform Act of 1867 which had greatly extended the franchise, increasing the number of men eligible to vote by 1,000 in the town, and had made Devizes a one rather than two-member constituency. He failed again to be re-elected for Devizes in 1874 when Disraeli won a handsome majority and, likewise, he was not elected for the county of Berkshire, where Padworth was situated, in a by-election in 1876. It was not until 1892 that another member of the extended Roundway family would become an MP, when Charles Colston was elected the member for Thornbury, near Bristol.

It is likely that Christopher had a significant influence over Charles's education, as his nephew followed him to Eton and Christ Church, Oxford, where he read Modern History. In 1868, the year that Charles went to Eton, the Darby Griffith family held a ball at Padworth for their niece Amy's coming out at the age of 18. For this happy occasion, Christopher wrote a poem entitled 'Impromptu', which can be best described as cheerful doggerel and begins:

> *Oh happy Teen, oh! bright teen!*
> *The very golden age, I ween,*
> *Full of hope and viscus bright*
> *And slumbers calm – except that night*
> *When Padworth saw a sudden light …*
> *And then there came the last*
> *And brightest of the scene*
> *Oh proud Cotillon! Lift thy happy head,*
> *For at that witching time a Murray led*
> *The Lady of the Night, from Roundway flown …*

Another crucial support for Louisa was her numerous and close-knit Murray family with whom she remained close throughout her life. In 1872, Amy married Christopher Baynes (1847–1936) whom it is likely she met through her mother's family, the Murrays, friends of the Baynes family.

Colonel Murray's drag at Roundway, September 1869.

From now on, the Baynes family plays an important role in the history of Roundway Park and the people associated with the estate. Christopher Baynes had been educated at Harrow, which he had left at the age of 16 due to scarlet fever, and he had then gone into the City, joining Gregson's, his father's merchant trading business, in 1869. The third of nine children, he was the eldest son of William (1820–97) and Margaret (1819–1911) Baynes. In a character reference for Christopher provided in 1871 by Frederic Farrar, then Master of Marlborough College and formerly a housemaster at Harrow, Christopher was praised for the 'sterling worth of his character and the steadiness of principle by which he was guided'.

Miniatures of Amy Ruperta and Christopher Baynes c1880.

Margaret and William Baynes c1880.

Sir William and Lady Baynes lived at Coombe Wood in Kingston-upon-Thames after a peripatetic lifestyle in pursuit of peaceful places in the country to soothe William's persistent headaches (probably migraines). In the seven years before moving to Coombe Wood, they lived in Norwood, near Hyde Park, followed by Ashtead, near Epsom, Cannizaro House in Wimbledon and Crabbett Park in Sussex, with frequent visits to Brighton where they rented houses on the sea-front.

Christopher's family originally came from Nidderdale in Yorkshire[131] but William's great-grandfather, also William (1719–98), came to London and made a fortune as a merchant in the City, mainly in the wine trade. In 1772 he bought Harefield Place in Middlesex and, partly through the connections of his wife Mary, whose father was a Director of the East

India Company, he became a Gentleman of the Privy Chamber to George II and III (he is also reputed to have lent money to the Royal Family). His son Christopher (1753–1837) was made a baronet in 1801, having raised the Uxbridge Yeomanry and helped found Atlas Assurance, which included George IV among its Lives Assured.[132] Christopher was then made an offer he could not refuse for the house and part of the estate at Harefield Place, which he sold in 1812 for £33,000 (£2.3m today) but shortly afterwards lost all the money in a speculative investment in either canals or coal in the slump after the end of the Napoleonic Wars.

Harefield Place, Middlesex, from *The Beauties of England & Wales* by John Britton (1825).

Undaunted, Christopher's son William (1789–1866) re-made the family fortune by working for the East India Company, becoming Super Cargo (Manager) of their factory in Canton. His beautiful and spirited wife, Julia, was a celebrated figure in Chinese history as she fraternised with the Chinese, then forbidden, which contributed to her husband's eventual dismissal by the East India Company in 1837, as detailed in the recently published book *Imperial Twilight* by Stephen R Platt. William retired a wealthy man, however, from the commission he earned in China (£79,000 or £8.7m today) which helped his son William to finance his partnership in Gregson's and buy the lease on Coombe Wood near Kingston in 1859 for £16,000.

Coombe Wood, a large house in the Gothic style and now part of Kingston University's campus, lay in then unspoilt countryside (now a stone's throw from the Robin Hood roundabout on the A3). William fell out with author John Galsworthy's father, who lived nearby. This resulted in the Baynes family being portrayed by name in an unflattering light in Galsworthy's *The Forsyte Saga*. William is portrayed in the first book, *The Man of Property*, as the architect Baynes (uncle of Bosinney) who was 'a bit of an old woman' and built a

Coombe Wood, Kingston-upon-Thames in 1860s.

row of 'crimson houses in Kensington which compete with so many others for the title of "the ugliest in London"'. Margaret's feelings are not spared either and she is described as a self-important humbug with a 'bulky frame' and a look of 'hard, ugly directness' in her eye. Both are described as mercenary, and Baynes's knighthood is described as being awarded because 'he built that public Musem of Art which has given so much employment to officials, and so little pleasure to those working classes for whom it was designed'.

William and Margaret were certainly formidable characters, as family stories attest, but also lively and cheerful. The root of Galsworthy's hostility was apparently envy of William's house at Coombe Wood, which commanded the best views in the area and which are described in detail in *The Forsyte Saga* in the portrayal of Robin Hill.

Margaret was the third daughter of the newspaper proprietor Daniel Stuart (1766–1846) who owned *The Morning Post* and, later, *The Daily Courier,* in which he championed not only parliamentary reform[133] but also the work of the Lake Poets, particularly Wordsworth, Southey and Coleridge (the latter in 1816 wrote of Stuart: '... you are superior to any man I ever met with in my life time').[134] The Stuarts lived at Wykham Park in Oxfordshire (now Tudor Hall School) and 9 Upper Harley Street in London.[135] Daniel had a fine collection of paintings, including Sir David Wilkie's *The Blind Fiddler*, which he acquired in 1806 for five guineas (now in the Tate Collection). He refused a peerage in order to maintain his independence as a newspaper proprietor.

The wedding of Christopher and Amy Ruperta in 1872 was reported in great detail in the *Devizes Advertiser* with a special pull-out description of the wedding day on 20 June printed in gold:

The wedding cortege left Roundway Park at about 11 o'clock, and consisted of nine carriages. It proceeded by the carriage way leading into the London road and thence to the Church, the drives for the greater part of the distance being decorated with lines of flags, evergreens, &c., while at the Lodge at the London-road was a graceful archway, covered with flowers and gay flags and streamers, and suspended from which was the inscription, intended to greet the happy couple on their return from Church – 'Welcome to Roundway, Mr. and Mrs. Baynes'.

Arriving at the church, they were greeted with a hearty cheer from hundreds of spectators, who had been unable to obtain admittance; the pathway was carpeted, and overhead was an awning, extending from the gate-way to the church door, intended as a protection from the rain which yesterday it was feared might fall, but happily it was not needed for that purpose, for a more lovely morning for a wedding could not have been desired, and if the saying is true – 'Happy is the bride that the sun shines on' – there will be a life of sunshine indeed for the newly-made wife of this morning.

Amy's brother Charles gave her away and she had six bridesmaids, including Rosalind Murray, who was herself to become a Colston bride when she married Charles seven years later in 1879. The newspaper reported that, after the service, the party returned to Roundway to a wedding breakfast for 55 guests in the conservatory, which was 'supplied in most elegant style by Mr. Michel of Sloane-street'. Later in the day, after the new couple

Conservatory at Roundway in the 1870s.

had left for their honeymoon in Switzerland, a dinner was given for all the inhabitants of Roundway and workers on the estate in celebration.

Among the 132 wedding presents itemised in the newspaper report were those given by the townspeople of Devizes, the staff at Roundway and the clerks at Gregson's:

Handsome waiter, engraved with beautiful pattern of ferns – Presented by Tradesmen of Devizes

Round engraved waiter – Presented by workpeople on the Roundway estate

Walnut and brass inkstand – Presented by clerks in Sir W. Baynes' office

Two pincushions fully trimmed – Lady's maid

Chinese dessert service, bird and flower pattern on green ground – Butler and footman at Roundway

Worked sofa cushion – The Housekeeper

Bible, presented by the Southbroom School Children and their Teachers

Subsequent events confirmed that this marriage was a love match but it was nonetheless accompanied, as was the custom in those days, by an extensive marriage settlement at the time of the couple's engagement and the union displayed a symmetry of benefits: Amy brought money and landed status while Christopher provided a title.

Two years before the couple's engagement, the first Married Women's Property Act of 1870 established that the property and wages earned by a woman in her lifetime would be regarded as her separate property and would not automatically become that of her husband as had previously been the case. It was to be another 12 years before the 1882 Married Women's Property Act established that all property of a married woman was hers and hers alone regardless of its provenance and the time that it was acquired. It also protected her from her husband's creditors.

The Colston–Baynes marriage settlement[136] therefore offered an important safeguard for Amy by ensuring that her interests were protected and that she would be provided for in both life and widowhood. Amy had two 'settled fortunes': she was entitled to £8,000 (£900,000 today) of real estate from her late father's assets and also a share of the estate of John Morris Colston on the death of his widow. She also held £800 of railway stock in her own right. All of these assets were assigned to a trust with four trustees for the benefit of the couple; but the income from Amy's two settled fortunes was for her use alone.

The trust also contained Christopher's Life Assurance policy which had a substantial annual premium of £500 (£55,500 today), which he guaranteed to pay and of which his father, Sir William, promised to pay £100 pa. The settlement also stated that the couple's daughters required their parents' approval for marriage up to the age of 21 and provided for potential financial difficulties on Christopher's part by saying that the trustees could be lenient to him if he had problems paying his Life Assurance premiums.[137] Amy's mother Louisa took into account her daughter's financial situation when drawing up her own will in 1878, which prompted this touching letter from Roundway on 24 January:

My dearest Amy,

Though I know there is little danger of your misunderstanding me, I think it right for others, just to leave a Memorandum of my reason for making dear Lilie take rather a larger share of the small sum I leave by Will, than I give to you. Your portion having been already as one may say partly forestalled by £1500 [£167,000 today] having been laid out in Trousseau, Furniture, Linen, Breakfast and £200 in advance and also the little sum of £4 yearly. Another reason for leaving the larger sum to Lilie is her being unmarried, so that she has to make a home for herself.

I know my Darling you will understand this and believe that as long as I lived I loved you both equally. In the fervent hope of meeting you and all my loved ones before the Throne of God where I trust our merciful Saviour will present us all washed from our Sins.

I am yr ever loving Mother

LR Colston

The happiness of Amy and Christopher is captured in a letter from the young bride to her mother in the summer of 1872 on their return from honeymoon to their marital home at 62 Upper Berkeley Street in Mayfair. It is full of reports about hiring servants, unpacking boxes, looking at wedding presents, thank you letters to be written, plans to visit family members and this comment relayed from Christopher: 'My husband says I am to tell you with his love and best thanks that if you had wished to "win his affections" you could not have thought of a better plan than presenting him with a barrel of XX (Wadworth mild beer from Devizes), as it is a beverage he much appreciates!!' The letter ends: 'I wish I could write twice as fast and tell you a few more of the many things I want to; we feel as though we ought to be thanking you perpetually for all you have done. I don't think there ever was such a dear kind Mother as the one I possess!'

8

Family Life

AMY followed her mother Louisa in keeping a regular diary, and the one for 1873 describes a busy social life in London with visits to and from friends and family members. Both the Colston and Baynes families were tight knit with many family members living nearby. These visits were interspersed with attendance at church, shopping (including buying furniture from Maple & Co for their house), trips to the theatre and the Horticultural Gardens, dinner parties, dances, summer events such as Ascot, cricket at Lord's and other such activities. Christopher's work in the City is frequently referred to and clearly kept him busy, including on Saturday mornings.

Amy's lifestyle was still old-fashioned with the practice, in the days before the telephone, of making calls upon people (without prior communication) and leaving a visiting card if they were out. Her references to people in the privacy of her diary are still formal; she always uses titles, for example describing Christopher's grandmother Julia as 'the Dowager Lady Baynes'. This entry from Amy's diary for Saturday 1 February is typical:

> Very cold and it snowed a little. A box containing pheasants, a sponge cake, apple jelly etc came up from Roundway (for Monday evening). I wrote to my Mother, Aunt Emma and Cousin Rosalind. After lunch I drove in a brougham to Charing Cross to meet Christie and we drove to call on Lady Lee, Mrs Selwyn, Mrs A Chapman and the Ravenshaws, all of whom were out. We also drove to Kensington to enquire for Mr Reeves; and went to two or three shops. Col. & Mrs E. Neville called late this evening but did not come in as we were dressing for dinner.

As this diary entry shows, Roundway continued to play an important role in Amy's life. It was the provider to 62 Upper Berkeley Street of fresh food (another entry for 25 April records the arrival of a suckling pig and the first strawberries), flowers (snowdrops and hothouse flowers arrived on 4 February), staff (the lady's maid Francesca came to stay for a few days from Roundway on 21 January to alter some of Amy's dresses due to her pregnancy) and Devizes tradesmen such as Mr Price, who came to tune the piano on 11 February.

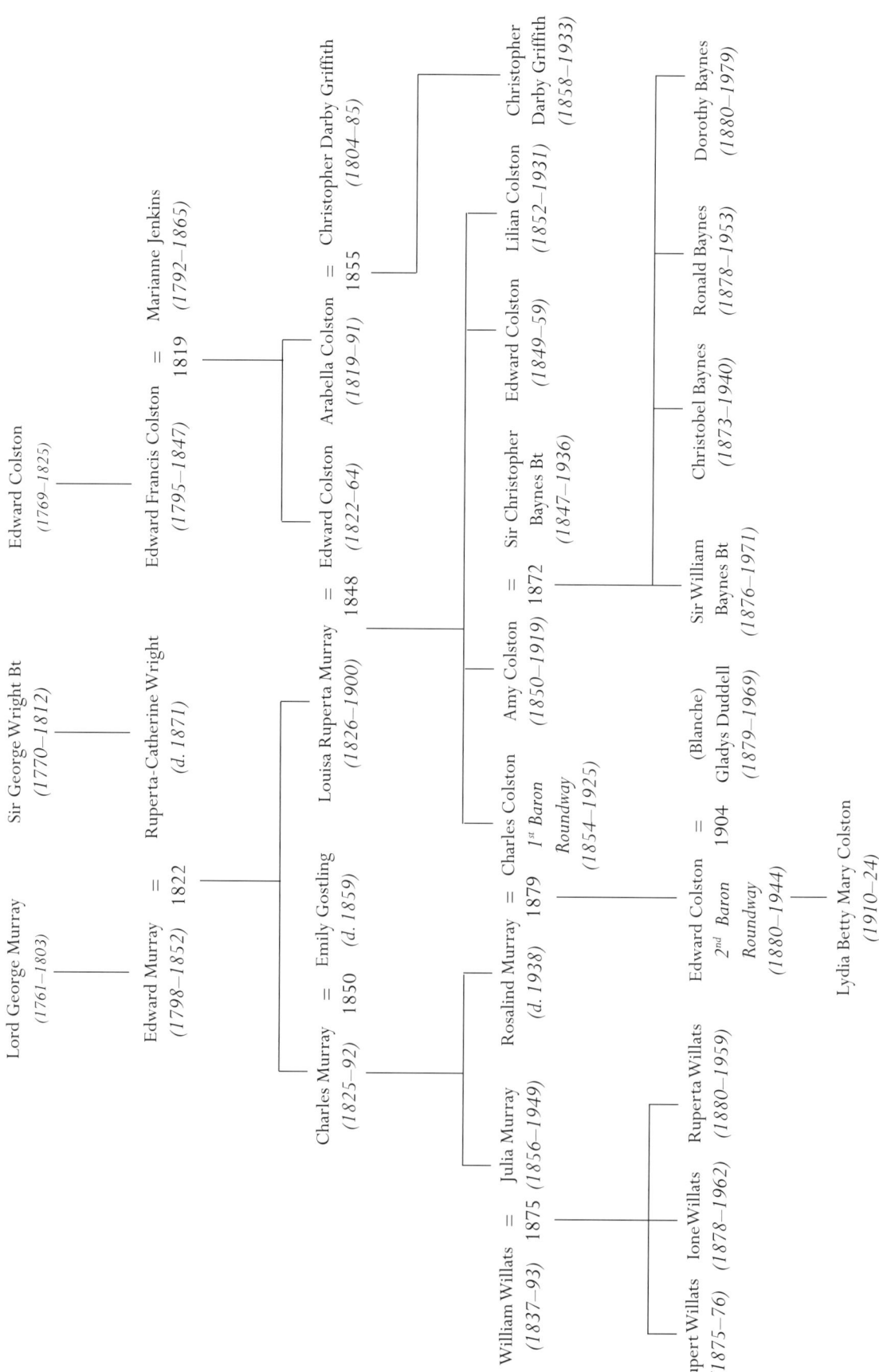

The Colston–Murray–Baynes Family Tree

Amy's diary entries also provide news of life at Roundway, showing that Louisa Colston was very active socially ('My Mother gave a dance at Roundway this evening' Amy wrote on 10 January), not least because she was promoting the marital prospects of both Charles and Lilian ('My Mother and Lily have gone to stay with the Knyftons for a Ball' on 21 January).

The daily life at Roundway is described in Amy's diary entries for 10–16 April 1873 when they went to stay there for a few days for Easter. At this time, she was pregnant with her first child. She celebrated her 23rd birthday on 10 April and travelled after dinner by train from Paddington, arriving at 10.30pm. They were met in the estate omnibus at Devizes by Charles and there were several relations staying.

On Good Friday, after church (or reading the service at home for Louisa who had a cough), they picked flowers in the woods with which to decorate the church on Easter Day. On Saturday, Charles and Christopher went hunting after breakfast until 4pm. The ladies made the flowers into wreaths and bunches in the study in the morning and, after lunch, walked through the park to the Newlands Woods where they found some 'Star of Bethlehem' just coming out and then went to visit Mrs Barby, whose husband was the coachman.

Circular room and west facade from the parkland c1870s.

On Easter Monday, Lily and Amy drove round the village of Roundway in the morning in a little cart drawn by a blind pony ('Wiltshire walking' as Amy described it) and they made visits to a dozen cottages. Charles and Christopher went hunting again with the Roundway harriers and were out all day long. In the afternoon, Amy and the others went to the Swiss Cottage for tea, walked back through the woods and then there were 18 for dinner.

On Tuesday they all climbed Roundway Hill in the morning and then Christopher went trout fishing. The following day Amy picked primroses to take back to London and then drove to the Cottage Hospital in Devizes to thank the matron, Mrs Wiltshire, for a beautifully worked robe (presumably for the baby). In the evening Charlie took them to Devizes station and they arrived back at Upper Berkeley Street at 11pm.

For the Season in 1873, Louisa took the house next door to Amy and Christopher in Upper Berkeley Street. Decamping to London from Roundway was a major logistical exercise. On

30 April, Amy wrote: 'Some of the servants came up from Roundway this morning and went to the next house, no. 63. Barby also came up with the horses and carriage … I went with Christie before dinner to 63, saw the servants and went over the house to see that all was ready and nice for Mother and Lily.' The following day the party arrived from Roundway, including more servants, ready to stay for three months.

The Baynes and Colston families were in and out of each other's houses every day and fully participated in the busy Season: for instance, Lily attended the Goldsmiths Ball in the City on 9 May with the Darby Griffiths, Lady Sidmouth's party (At Home) in Mansfield Street on 15 May and a family outing to hear Adelina Pattie sing at the Floral Hall on 19 May. Lady Langton's 'At Home' on 23 May had included 'speeches by ladies on "Women's Rights"'. The staff also enjoyed themselves; Amy recorded on 3 June: 'Our three servants went this evening to see a conjurer.'

Amy and Christopher were pleased to have the use of the Roundway carriage in London rather than having to hire such transport as they usually did. On 10 May they drove with the carriage top down in bright sunshine with Louisa and Lilian to have lunch with Christopher's parents. Four days later they drove up and down Hyde Park till nearly 7pm and saw the Princess of Wales, just as Amy had, as a small child, encountered Queen Victoria riding in her carriage in the park.[138] On 23 May, the large number of carriages in Hyde Park led to a traffic jam: 'Mother and I stayed in the carriage and were in such a "block" that we hardly moved for two hours.'

Amy Baynes with baby Christobel in 1874.

At this time, Amy was collecting in a blue notebook all sorts of advice about bringing up children, which included articles by Hon. Mrs Norton advising that: 'Grown persons are apt to put a lower estimate than is just on the understanding of children. They rate them by what they know, and children know very little, but their capacity of comprehension is great.' Mrs Craik in 'Sermons out of Church' contended that: 'Everyone's natural genius should be carried as far as it could, but to attempt the putting another upon him, will be but labour in vain …'

The birth of Christobel on Tuesday 17 June seems to have been straightforward and Amy wrote that she was 'confined of a dear little girl' at about 11.30pm. She began to 'nurse

Baby a little' the following day, family members visited and then friends called after the birth was announced in the papers on 19 June. Not surprisingly there is a hiatus in the diary after this but the entries resume in July and record how 'Baby' (as Christobel was invariably called, even after her christening on 21 July) is taken, often with her doting Colston grandmother, on walks as well as outings in the carriage to call on people. On 28 July she was photographed with her mother at photographers Fry & Eliot in Baker Street.

The last section of the diary is missing from 7 August, just when they decamped to a rented house, Howard Villa, in Putney. This period was overshadowed by the demise of Sir William Baynes's business Gregson & Co., which could no longer compete with the better capitalised Joint Stock Banks in its activities as an East India Agent and merchant trader. Sir William, however, paid off all his creditors, a process that had necessitated the sale of the lease in 1872 on Coombe Wood to Lord Kenry for £20,000 (£2.2m today), and resulted in his move to Forest Lodge in Putney, close to Christopher and Amy's rented house.

Watercolours by Christopher's sister, Agnes Baynes (*left*): Forest Lodge, 1874 and *right*: Roundway Park, 1873.

The demise of Gregson's also meant that Christopher, in his own words written later in life, was now 'thrown out of employment'. He did not work again until January 1877 when he was appointed Sub-Agent of the Portsmouth Branch of the Bank of England (in those days all appointments of Agents were from outside of the Bank staff). The job involved traditional retail and private banking and came with an annual salary of £500 (£58,000 today) as well as a residence, 25 High Street, next to the Branch. His father stood surety for £2,000 (£230,000 today) on this appointment and Christopher stayed with the bank for the rest of his career. It is difficult to know the effect that this period of unemployment of almost four years had on the young couple but it is probable that it played a major part in Christopher's irascibility, which was much remarked upon by later generations. Amy's substantial dowry would have kept them afloat financially and they both had supportive and close families but the uncertainty, particularly when comparisons were drawn with the wealth of the Colstons, must have been difficult.

This uncertain period probably explains the gap in the births of their children given that the second, William, was not born until 1876, three years after Christobel. As there was no male heir to Roundway at the time, he was christened William Edward Colston Baynes in case the estate might one day come to him. Ronald ('Ronnie') was born in Portsmouth on 12 November 1878 and then, finally, Dorothy in 1880 in Edgbaston in Birmingham where the family was then living during Christopher's posting there for the Bank of England between 1879 and 1881.[139]

Christobel, Ronald, Dorothy and William as children.

In her autobiographical book, *Enter A Child*, Dorothy describes in detail her upbringing in the following way which she contrasts unfavourably with the more liberal regime at Roundway: 'My parents had not the slightest intention of making my life miserable; no parents could have been better-intentioned, but they were obsessed by the idea of doing their duty by me, and seeing that I did mine by them. The question: "Is this child happy or unhappy?" would never have occurred to them. Neither would they ever have thought of applying such a question to themselves. Their minds simply did not work that way. They saw life in terms of necessity, duty and convention, and if I had been capable of summing up in words the unsatisfactoriness of my days, they would merely have been genuinely shocked at such a reaction to their parental goodness.' They were conditioned by their own upbringing which, in the case of her mother Amy, had been 'so old-fashioned that I may say I was, practically, brought up according to the ideas of two generations before my own'.

Apart from the birth of her son, William, Amy's 1876 diary also records the celebrations of her brother Charles's Coming of Age.[140] Although Charles turned 21 in 1875 the celebrations were delayed until the following year so he could complete his studies at Oxford. The party took place at the Colston's estate at West Lydford, a pretty Somerset village which is little changed to this day. A flavour of the event is given by these extracts from the account in the local paper, which also show a more general sense of the relationship between a landowner and his tenants at the time:

The weather was propitious, and the village was profusely decorated with arches and ornamental fir trees from West Lydford; while almost every cottage showed its bunting. At the Cross Keys-inn an elaborate arch displayed the Colston arms, and a banner with 'Welcome to the Colston family'. At the Fosse-road, the entrance to the village, the Bridge farm, the Rectory-gate, and at the keeper's lodge were arches with appropriate mottoes, such as 'Long live our noble squire', 'Many happy returns of the day', 'Success to the house of Colston' and 'Blessings follow thee'. At night these decorations were prettily and effectively illuminated with variegated lamps, coloured lanterns, etc. Mr Colston, who was staying at the Rectory as the guest of Rev. W. Homes Orr, drove his drag and four handsome bays to the Cross Keys where he was met at noon by his mother and sisters, and Mr and Mrs Knyfton [the latter Charles's cousin], of Uphill Castle, Weston-super-Mare. The horses were removed from the carriage, which was drawn by 100 men to the Rectory, where an excellent dinner was provided by the Misses Barratt, of Castle Cary, to which the tenants on the estate, 18 in number, sat down. The health of 'the Queen' was proposed by Mr Colston and duly honoured, after which the following address was read by the Rev. W. H. Orr:-

To C. Edward Colston, Esq.

It is with very great pleasure that we, the tenants of your West Lydford estate, this day offer you our best and most cordial congratulations upon the recent attainment of your majority and we pray that every blessing, both spiritual and temporal, may attend you through life.

We have noticed with extreme pleasure your brilliant career through the University, and while we hope that your course through life may more fully call forth the talents you undoubtedly possess, we also hope that with such powers and knowledge, and as an extensive landowner, you may be enabled largely to contribute to the welfare and happiness of those with whom you may be connected; and that the same good feeling which has so long existed between the Colston family and their tenantry may still continue. We would also respectfully offer every kind and good wish to your esteemed mother and sisters. May you and they long be spared and blest to each other.

Signed on behalf of the tenants of the West Lydford Estate,

ROBERT WELCHMAN, W. BENJAMIN, W. CREES, Sept. 19th, 1876.

Charles responded to a toast proposed by a Mr C Wainwright of Shepton Mallett by saying:

> Succeeding as I have after a long minority, I have to buy my own experience, and
> if I fail in any of my duties and responsibilities as a landlord be assured it will be
> unintentional on my part, for my greatest wish and ambition is to act in a fair and
> straightforward way, as between 'man and man', and to recognise that the interests
> of landlord and tenant are not opposed to each other, but on the contrary are bound
> up as it were together. Englishmen have always been conspicuous for their love of
> anything that is old – what has been handed down from generation to generation
> acquires a certain feeling of love and veneration in our minds, and in nothing is this
> more felt than as regards landed property, and no one can share in those feelings more
> deeply than I do myself …

> The health of Mrs Knyfton was proposed by Mr Chard, and that of Mrs Colston by Mr
> Orr. The party then proceeded to a large tent in the Rectory grounds, where about
> 130 workmen were entertained to a substantial repast, after which tea was provided
> for about 180 women and children. The band of the Somerton Rifle Volunteers was in
> attendance throughout the day and various amusements were provided, including pony
> and donkey racing, dancing, running in sacks, women's and other races. At nightfall
> there was a dance in Mr Robert Welchman's barn, which was kept up till midnight.
> Supper terminated a day that will long be remembered in the annals of Lydford.

Georgie Knyfton, née Colston, had married Thomas Tutton Knyfton in 1855 and they lived
at Uphill Castle, decorated in the High Gothic style with furniture made to Augustus Pugin
designs, near Weston-super-Mare in Somerset.[141] It is probable that she kept an eye on matters
for Charles and his mother in West Lydford, where her father, William, had been Rector.

Left: Georgie Knyfton and *right*: Uphill Castle, Weston-super-Mare in Somerset.

Charles's inheritance was very considerable, as was shown in the government's 1873 *Return of Owners of Land,* dubbed the New Domesday Book. He inherited 8,364 acres with an income of £13,726 (£1.5m today):

Wiltshire:	*1,955 acres and income of £2,526*
Somerset:	*2,409 acres and income of £3,700*
Gloucestershire:	*4,000 acres and income of £7,500*

The New Domesday Book was used as the basis for John Bateman's *The Great Landowners of Great Britain and Ireland,* the fourth edition of which in 1883 recorded that there were 1,363 large landowners in England of whom 331 owned over 10,000 acres (which was Bateman's definition of a 'great landowner') and 1,032 over 3,000 acres. By this measure, Charles, only 1,636 acres short of 10,000, was nudging the category of 'great landowner'.

Rosalind and Charles Colston.

In 1879 Charles married his first cousin Rosalind, the daughter of Louisa's brother Charles Murray (1825–92), now Col Charles Gostling Murray, having assumed his wife Emily's surname Gostling when she inherited Whitton Park,[142] a Palladian villa in Middlesex, from her father. Charles was a barrister and honorary colonel in the service

Whitton Park, Twickenham, in Middlesex.

of the 2ⁿᵈ Volunteer Battalion, Middlesex Regiment. On New Year's Eve 1880 Rosalind gave birth to her first and only child, a son named Edward, as might be expected, but always known as Ted. He was the same age as his cousin Dorothy Baynes, a bond that underpinned their close relationship throughout their lives.

Amy's and Charles's sister Lilian never married and there is a vivid pen portrait of her in *Enter A Child*:

> Aunt Lilian had a tall agile figure, and a face sculptured on lines at once plain and aristocratic. But this plainness was lost in the effervescence of her personality. From her tiny green eyes poured rays of kindness – and, on occasion, when she was religiously shocked, darts of flint – and from her good-humoured, too large mouth a spate of conversation. But for two hostile chances, two slight swerves of fate, Aunt Lilian would have been Vicereine of India. But fate defaulted, and instead of her lot being red carpets, bowing Maharajas, and a personal association with the National Anthem, it was self-immolation to my grandmother in a small house in Curzon Street: a lifelong conversation with her maid on the slings and arrows of daily existence and her being,

Lilian Colston in a studio portrait and on horseback.

> in appearance, chained to her writing-table for hours at a time, composing letters of extraordinary complexity to tradesmen and charitable organisations, or else making up her accounts. When these proved satisfactory, she hurried off to Christie's and bought another writing-table; for to collect old furniture was her delight. She possessed a stick-at-nothing quality which made her the beloved family butt.

Lilian Colston's bureau.

Elsewhere, Dorothy related how when Lilian was 12, she was staying with her cousins the Astleys at their house Chequers Court (now the Prime Minister's official country residence), and Disraeli and his wife came to stay:

> She remembered seeing him walk down the stairs backwards holding out his arms to catch his wife in case she fell – she coming down just above. For some reason at that time the stairs had been built up at the side with planks, this making the staircase dark. And, too, she told me that the house party posed out of doors to be photographed and that Disraeli called out to her: 'Come here, little girl, and see if the curl on my forehead is straight.'

Throughout their lives, the three Colston siblings remained close to each other and to their numerous cousins, many of whom derived from the large and well-connected Murray family. These relations provided companionship and friendship throughout their lives in good times and bad.

A Murray family photograph of Chequers Court in Buckinghamshire c1870.

PART 2

HEYDAY

Left: The Quakers Walk drive c1880.

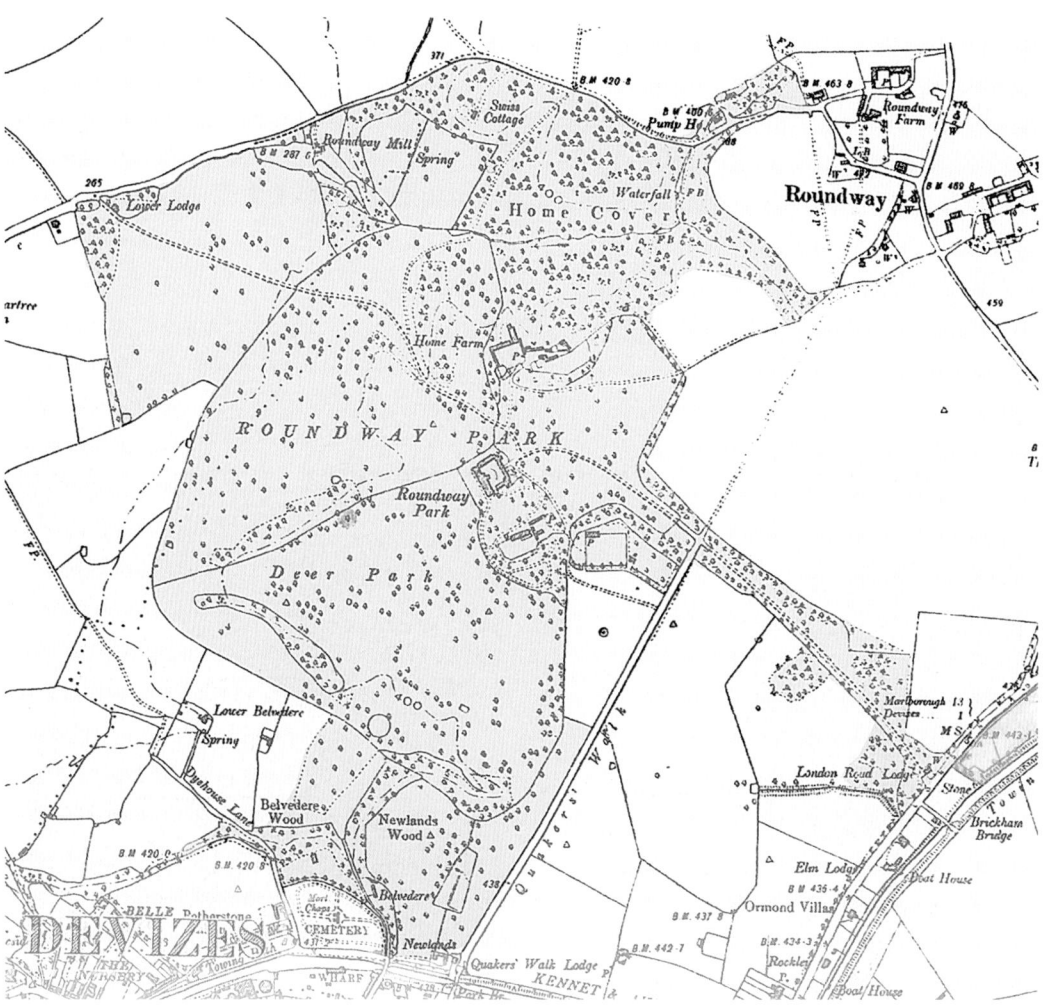

Map of Roundway Park c1895 with the estate in green.

9

Roundway Park's Victorian Heyday

WHEN CHARLES came into his inheritance in 1875, Britain was at the height of its economic power. In 1870 the volume of Britain's external trade was greater than that of Germany, France and Italy combined and was almost four times that of the US. Britain was enjoying an unparalleled period of peace and its industrial and commercial might combined with its mastery of the seas and burgeoning empire gave it the status of a 'superpower'.

Charles Colston's stewardship of Roundway bears out John Martin Robinson's observation in *Felling the Ancient Oaks* that this period saw the highpoint of the English landed estate: 'In retrospect, the Victorian estate seems to capture the best of both worlds, combining the mature visual results of Georgian Augustan improvement with the philanthropic and humanitarian achievements and technical progress of the nineteenth century.'

The Colstons were always very closely involved in the activities of Devizes. As a result of their donation of land, the Devizes Cottage Hospital – later becoming the Devizes Hospital – was opened in 1872 in New Park Road. They also held events on the parkland for local organisations and made it

Charles Colston at his desk in 1880s.

available for festivities such as the Grand Fete organised by the Devizes charitable organisation the Independent Order of Oddfellows in 1876. Apart from foot-racing, athletic sports and archery, there was a 'bizarre line-up' featuring London Star Artistes, Montgomery's New York Minstrels with Wonderful Performing Elephants, canine wonders and a child wire walker.

Three years later, the August Bank Holiday of 1879 brought the Jubilee celebrations of the Oddfellows and the procession through the town was 'Decidedly, the handsomest thing of a

Horses harrowing in the parkland.

kind ever seen in Devizes'. Members of kindred societies taking part included The Providential Dolphin Lodge of Oddfellows, The Ancient Order of Foresters, Court Dolphin, United Patriots, The Rationals and The Hearts of Oak. After parading the town, the whole entourage proceeded up Quakers Walk for the day's festivities. The field had been marked out for the races and various sporting events and, alongside, numerous marquees offered alternative entertainments. Imported from London, the star-studded acts included performances on the trapeze by the Brothers de Castro and the dancing sisters Rosina and Lucy.[143]

The Wiltshire Volunteers in mid-19th century.

Charles became a Justice of the Peace for Wiltshire in 1877 and was High Sheriff of the county in 1885. He was chairman of the 2nd Court of Quarter Sessions for many years and would become chairman of the 1st Court towards the end of his life in 1923. In 1882, he became Hon. Colonel of the Wiltshire Volunteer Battalion until it was transformed into the Territorial force. This, as the 4th Battalion Wilts Regiment, he continued to command until 1909. His involvement with the Volunteers had started at Eton as a cadet (where he had been in the rifle corps and also in the school's shooting eleven) and continued with his becoming a captain in the 5th Wiltshire Volunteer Corps in 1873 when he

Charles Colston on his polo pony c1880s.

was at Oxford. In later life, he was vice-chairman of the Territorial Force County Association and was instrumental in raising the National Reserve Force in East Wiltshire. He was also a keen polo player.

The benign presence of Charles and Rosalind created a childhood paradise at Roundway. They are described in glowing terms by Dorothy in *Enter A Child*:

They were not only my uncle and aunt, not only my host and hostess, but in my mind two beings set apart. They were both of pale gold fairness, and this golden quality seemed to run into all their words and actions, giving a gracious sweetness to their whole atmosphere. I could remember clearly how once, at the age of three, as I lay in bed gently whimpering over some child misery, my uncle had strolled into the room. 'What is the matter, my little dear?' he asked. The sudden vision of that glimmering shirt-front, the gentleness of the voice coming from that dimly seen face, kindness when according to nursery rule I deserved a scolding, so surprised me that from that moment my heart was his. As for my aunt: 'L'or! What a picture!' my nurse would exclaim in admiration as, on party occasions, we peered at her from over top-stair banister or from nursery window. And my nurse was right.

Roundway

Dear Christobel

Thank you so very much for the Shop I do like it so very much. I opened some of the little bottles & Mother ties them up again for me. I am so glad to have Willie as I like him as he is so amusing!

Give my love to Aunt Amy & I am

Ever Your affec^te Edward

A thank-you letter from Ted Colston to his cousin Christobel Baynes c1885.

The central theme of *Enter A Child* is that Dorothy's upbringing was overshadowed by her difficult relationship with her father and the dreariness of their life in London which contrasted starkly with her idyllic holidays at Roundway in the relaxed household of her Colston relatives (see Appendix IV for more detail on this and the rest of Dorothy's life as a very successful writer but eccentric character).

Amy's diary for 1885 records her family's annual Easter visit to Roundway, when Dorothy was aged five, and a second visit in the autumn. The second visit involved sending the children (minus William, who was now boarding at prep school) on ahead to spend a month there with

Left: Autumn view of the west facade and *right*: conservatory facade c1880.

their nurse, after which Amy and Christopher joined them on 1 November. This month-long stay for the children may well have been a form of respite from London for health reasons as Christobel had contracted scarlet fever earlier in the year.[144]

The November visit to Roundway was dominated by politics in the run-up to the 1885 General Election in which Charles was standing for parliament for the first time, for the Conservatives in Bristol.[145] There was a meeting at the Town Hall in Devizes on 3 November of the 'Church Defence Institution' at which the local MP Walter Long and others spoke. Charles and Rosalind were often in Bristol campaigning and, on 9 November, Lilian was in Roundway village helping the Primrose League, an organisation founded in 1883 for spreading Conservative principles, which took Disraeli's favourite flower as its emblem: 'Lilian gave away a number of political and Primrose League Pamphlets to the villagers.' On 19 November: 'Mrs Simpson came up to talk over the Elections and the votes of the working men here,' a priority given the extension of the franchise, and on Sunday 22 November Christopher went to church at the 'Independent Chapel (!) in Devizes, expecting a Political Sermon'.

Charles's election result in Bristol was among the first to be announced and led to this diary entry by Amy for 26 November: 'Heard this morning that Charlie has been beaten in the Election at Bristol by Fry who got 4,000 votes and Charlie 3,000.' The final results from the general election did not come in until 18 December from far-flung corners of the kingdom and resulted in Gladstone being returned as Prime Minister.

Amy's 1886 diary recorded her annual Easter and late summer visits to Roundway in which the routine is similar to previous accounts. Amy and Lilian were exemplary in their visits to

Left: Circular room from the parkland and *right*: thatched cottage c1880.

people locally, particularly on the estate, and they often took gifts with them, sometimes of the Baynes children's clothes, which they had grown out of. There was also much music-making in these pre-gramophone days, with Lilian playing the harp and both Rosalind and Amy playing the piano. Charles and Lilian joined the Volunteers at their Review in April and the children rode Ted's pony. There were many walks around the estate and tea was taken at the Swiss Cottage. The summer visit also included shooting for Christopher and William. Amy and Christopher made another visit to Roundway in November 1886, which involved Christopher shooting at the West Lydford estate with Charles and a 'Petticoat Party' made up of the abandoned wives and female relatives at Roundway.

Amy Baynes c1890s.

Amy's diary for 1887 has similar entries for the annual visits to Roundway but also mentions a stag hunt during the Easter visit on 12 April 'near the Barracks; we and the 5 children [including Ted] all drove first to the Market Place in Devizes where the meet was to be, then we drove on to Coate where the stag was un-carted and a great many people riding or driving were there. We had a good view and drove about until 1.30pm.' There was also a concert in the Town Hall, which the adults attended, the annual Sham Fight at Spye Park, which involved, among others, the Volunteers and the Yeomanry, and a circus on the Green in Devizes to which Ted

Wiltshire Yeomanry in Devizes c1890.

and William went with Ted's nurse. On Saturday 16 April, Rosalind drove Amy in the dog-cart to the meet at Derry Hill while Charles and Lilian rode there and they saw the hounds and many friends either out hunting or driving.

In the August visit to Roundway in 1887, Christopher started to teach William to shoot and the older children had riding lessons in Devizes. Amy gave all the children academic lessons in the absence of their governess, Miss Goodworth, who was on holiday and they went to the Tennis Club in Devizes to watch a tournament after which Rosie gave out the six prizes to the winners.

In November Amy and other members of the Colston family attended the annual Colston Day in Bristol which, out of respect for the

Charles Colston in his hunting clothes c1880s.

Sabbath, was held a day late on Monday 14 November: 'We arrived at the Cathedral in time for the sermon by Mr Burnaby; Julia Colston met us there and then we all went to lunch with the Colston Boys, and then drove to Clifton to lunch with Mrs Parr; then saw Colston's monument in All Saints Church, then the lovely Church of St Mary Redcliffe, then drove to the station and we all returned back to Weston and drove to Uphill Castle (except Charlie who stayed for the Dolphin Dinner and Speeches).'

Amy's diary for 1888 is not among her papers and it is probable that she did not keep one for that year as she caught scarlet fever, which very nearly proved fatal. The profound relief of Christopher (who had contracted scarlet fever as a teenager) during Amy's recovery from the illness is movingly expressed in this letter of 10 September 1888 to his mother-in-law Louisa, written from London after a visit to Amy who was recuperating in a rented holiday home:

My dear Mother,

Yesterday was one of the most happy days I have ever spent, as I found dear Amy in tremendous spirits and quite as strong as I could possibly expect. The journey and excitement had naturally tired her, and I should think today she will feel even more tired, but she promised to keep very quiet and we arranged she is to do no housekeeping but sit and get strong.

> We had a short walk before lunch, and afterwards packed Dorothy off with Rickwell,
> and Amy had two hours in a chair; though the wind was rather cold, the air was
> delicious, and we enjoyed ourselves immensely and agreed that until this illness we
> did not know how much we cared for each other!!

In January 1889 Charles was elected to Wiltshire County Council when it was first created, a position he held until his death in 1925.[146] The Local Government Act of 1888 had established elected county councils in rural areas thereby replacing the administrative work of the Justices of the Peace, such as Charles, although they continued in their judicial capacity as magistrates. Analysis of the 1889 County Council elections in the local Wiltshire newspapers shows how the landed classes were now jostling for position with those from commercial and professional classes. The report in the *Wiltshire Gazette* started by observing that: 'The number of candidates before the electors proves that the apathy that has caused so much comment in the Metropolis and elsewhere is not experienced generally in Wiltshire, although even here there are cases of very little interest being taken in the elections.'

There were 101 candidates for 60 seats and the newspaper listed them by profession, which showed how the advent of local democracy was being used by the non-landed classes to increase their power and influence:

Professional or commercial pursuits	35	*Labour candidates*	5
County Magistrates	29	*MPs*	4
Farmers	18	*Ministers of Religion*	2
Brewers	8		

County magistrates mainly consisted of aristocrats, such as the Marquess of Bath and the Earl of Pembroke, who were returned unopposed for Warminster and Wilton respectively, and the landed gentry, such as Charles, who was unsuccessfully opposed for the Cannings ward by the brewer T.A. Berry. The newspaper report carried a biographical sketch of each candidate, which mentioned Charles's positions as magistrate and Deputy Lieutenant of Wiltshire, and also that he was the lord of the manors of estates beyond Wiltshire, such as West Lydford, Westerleigh and Henbury.

Amy and her family were back at Roundway in 1889 as usual in April and again in August. On 27 August they enjoyed lovely weather by driving 'in the break up to the hill where we got out and played "tip and run" for an hour with the 5 children; then walked home through the woods, stopping to have tea at Swiss Cottage on the way'. There were visits to the Horse Show in Bath and to Mrs St George's Garden Party in Rowdeford, riding for the boys with their father, reading and sketching in the garden for the girls with their mother, cricket at Hillworth for Christopher and William and a trip to the toy-shop in Devizes for Ronnie and Dorothy.

They drove across the Downs for tea and croquet with the Heneages at Compton and 'Charles and Rosie gave a large Garden Party and Fete to all the Volunteers and their wives (over 500); a great many neighbours also came; there was tennis and other games, and a large tent for refreshments.'

Above: Family sketch of Roundway Park.

Below: The Colston coach outside the west front of Roundway in the 1890s.

The next major event was the annual school feast, which the family gave at Roundway: preparations involved shopping in Devizes for toys and 'Christobel and I sat on the Terrace making dolls frocks for the school feast'. The great day dawned on 13 September: 'Very fine. All the school children (over 500) from Southbroom came from 2 till 7 and they had tea sitting on the grass in the park and we all helped; and then there were games and races and Rosie gave each child a toy. The band played as they went away.'

Fortune favoured Charles's next attempt to enter the House of Commons in 1892 when, aged 38, he won Thornbury, a constituency ten miles north of Bristol (he was a substantial landowner in Somerset and Gloucestershire), although the national majority in the election went to the Liberals, returning Gladstone as Prime Minister. It was probably at this time that the light-hearted observation on political life below was written, quite possibly by Charles. The Julia to whom it refers was most likely Charles's first cousin and sister-in-law Julia Ruperta Murray (1856–1949) who had married William Willats in 1875 and lived at Denton Court in Kent. Their two daughters, Ruperta and Ione, remained close to their Colston and Baynes cousins throughout their lives.

Left: Ione and Julia Willats in 1896 and *right*: Ruperta Willats as a bridesmaid.

To calculate with due precision
The moment of the next Division
The Art in proper time to cough
The Mysteries of pairing off.
When to be silent, when to cheer,
A modest Member with a leer
The doubt in Debates begin
Of Whipping out and Whipping in
From Bellamys with checked digestion
Just as the Speaker pops the question –
These Julia are the hard conditions
Imposed on Lucking Politicians.

HRH The Prince of Wales inspecting the Royal Wiltshire Yeomanry on the Roundway Downs with Charles Colston in 1893 (reproduced by kind permission of the Royal Wiltshire Yeomanry Historic Property Collection, Swindon).

In 1892, the same year that he became an MP, Charles made the first of two enlargements to the house at Roundway. We can assume that Charles's inheritance, reputed to be £188,000 (£23.5m today), from his cousin Georgie Knyfton on her death in November 1891 made these alterations possible financially.[147] This money came to Charles just before death duties were introduced by the Liberal Chancellor Sir William Harcourt in 1894 at a rate

The Prince of Wales in the centre of Devizes in 1893.

of 8 per cent on estates of £2m. Also, in 1891, with the death of his aunt Arabella Darby Griffith, he started to receive the income from his Jenkins grandfather's fortune, which had been enjoyed by Arabella since her mother's death (Charles had already inherited the capital). The timing of Charles's alterations was also probably affected by the impending visit to Devizes of Edward, Prince of Wales, in 1893, when Charles took the prince in the Roundway drag to inspect the Wiltshire Yeomanry drawn up on Roundway Down and accompanied him on a visit to the town.

The west front of Roundway after the alterations of 1892.

Left: The main front from the courtyard, showing the infill to the left of the portico and *right*: view from south-west after the 1892 additions.

The alterations consisted of an enlargement to the southern end of the main west front.[148] On the ground floor a billiard room was built on the courtyard side of the principal drawing room and a first-floor bedroom storey was added above it. The west front was then altered and given an upper storey, with two bow windows continuous through both floors, topped with balustrading, the whole in a neo-Jacobean style, reminiscent of the 17th-century alterations to Kirby Hall in Northamptonshire. It looked out over the deer park which, by 1892, comprised about 120 acres, enclosed by continuous iron fencing and containing about 200 fallow deer.[149]

It was probably at this time that the lodge at the Conscience Lane gates was modified by re-facing the lower section in stone and putting up two stone plaques with the Colston arms carved on them.

Conscience Lane Lodge and the Colston crest on the lodge.

Charles was also a railway enthusiast; he had a miniature steam model railway which he used to set up on the lawn as well as in the house as described by Dorothy in *Enter A Child*:

All the male members of the family were pressed into the service of laying down the rails – which were heavy. In this Wyatt house the billiard-room, drawing-rooms, hall, library, and dining-room all opened out of each other: when all the double mahogany doors were thrown back there was revealed a charming landscape of room beyond room, the whole suffused with streams of light from the windows at one side. But when the rails were down, crossing every room, running through every doorway, it gave a most desolate look. But still that was not the point; the point was to make the engine go …

And then suddenly there would be a cry, 'She's off!' There would be a fizzing and a puffing, and actually, yes, actually, there was the little creature moving along the rails of its own accord … beginning to go quite quickly … quicker … now really fast; and my uncle, flushed with success, brandishing a walking stick (which he used for poking into the engine's tender when he wanted it to stop) would run along by its side, occasionally, for some strategic purpose, vaulting over the rails.

The indoor railway at Roundway (John Girvan Collection and Mike Thomas).

Uncle Charlie, by his leaps over the rails, invariably got left behind by the engine which, now at the height of its form, would rush from room to room, a terrifying demon that no one of us dared interfere with for fear – as was constantly impressed on us – that it would either explode, burn one's fingers, or set the house on fire.[150]

Charles also had a horse-drawn railway in the grounds from which visitors could view the estate. It is referred to in Amy's diary entry of Saturday 27 August 1887: 'I went in the small railroad Charlie has just made in the Park, down the steep slope where it goes at a tremendous pace and is pulled up by a horse.' It is believed that the railway ran along the top of Belvedere Wood, over the bridge in Dyehouse Lane (where there were until recently iron hooks in the footpath and there are still the remains of two brick piers that may have supported the track) and then on up to the house itself. The last port of call was a summerhouse where there were very good views of Chippenham, Bromham and Rowde. There was also reputed to be a track to the Swiss Cottage. In later years, after the railway track had been removed, Rosalind would often drive along the path in her pony and trap.[151]

Charles may have acquired the track from the old horse-drawn railway at the Caen Hill flight of locks on the Kennet and Avon Canal. This was a temporary 1.5-mile-long line, constructed when the locks were first being built in 1794. It was used by horse-drawn wagons carrying building materials and coal until the canal opened in 1810. The line is marked on the Ordnance Survey map of 1884 and could have been acquired by Charles a couple of years later. It is thought to have followed the boundaries of the present-day cemetery and to have passed close to an old grotto. Devizes resident Clive Leach's uncle, born in 1880, remembered the estate hanging game and deer in the grotto where it was cold and safe from foxes. The grotto has since been pulled to pieces by children playing and the passage of time.[152]

Rosalind and Ted on their bicycles at Roundway in 1896.

In the 1890s bicycling became popular and the family participated with enthusiasm as can be seen from photograph albums which include one of Christopher falling off his bicycle, much to the amusement of his children. Previously he used to ride a tricycle: Amy recorded in her diary for 12 June 1886 that Christopher 'started at 12 to go on a tricycling tour of a few days with Mr Barham' and for 12 August 1886, when on holiday with their children in Norfolk, she wrote that Christopher 'took the little ones by turns on a small tricycle'.

Charles was also keen on coaching as is captured in the description by Dorothy in *Enter A Child* of a picnic on the Downs in the Roundway coach. The roads of Wiltshire and elsewhere in Britain's countryside were relatively quiet at this time in the early 1890s with much of the traffic drawn away by the railways and before the appearance of the motor car. Dorothy described how the family gathered in the courtyard to mount the coach, 'from the door of the coach-house the stablemen were watching us: at an upper window two of the housemaids gazed as from a box in the theatre at this equine display'.

Roundway coach in the courtyard preparing to leave.

The coach then made its way up the drive and 'the big white gate in the park, which a groom jumped down to open, was left behind us, lazily click-clicketing. Now we were in the avenue that led to the high road. Joe was standing up with the horn, about to warn Mrs Harris at the lodge of the splendour that was bearing down upon her.'

As they reached the Downs, 'the sense of airy void was growing upon us; we seemed to be shrinking smaller and smaller; we seemed now a little fussy thing clattering its way into a vast silence. The clouds like huge galleons were adrift above us.' They stopped after a while for a picnic tea: 'Far below lay the great valley: hedgerow and field, field and hedgerow, lapping away and away to the diaphanous horizon. I tried to discover which clump of trees enclosed Roundway. Roundway, in whose rooms of sunlit emptiness my great-grandmother was sitting even at this moment with her crochet, faintly disapproving.'[153]

Colston coach on the Roundway Downs in the late 19th century.

Darkness was falling on their return and, as they were just about to turn into the archway leading to the back quadrangle, 'the long horn was upraised: in the dark its leaping ribbon was of a clearer gold. Then we were home again. We crowded into the brightly lit hall. There was

Louisa Colston with her crochet c1890.

my grandmother, there was the butler, there were the hall tables, the great china jars, the staircase, and the pictures on its walls, but in some indefinable way the downs had come in with us.'

As in this excerpt, elsewhere in *Enter A Child*, Dorothy makes frequent reference to her 'great-grandmother' in a distinctly unflattering light, depicting her as gloomy and of a sour disposition. Given that none of Dorothy's great-grandmothers was alive in 1890, we can assume that this is in fact a portrayal of her grandmother (who certainly looks fairly miserable in family photographs) which lies at odds with the affection shown to Louisa Colston in letters and comments by her three children.

Left: Louisa Colston in 1890s (centre) with Lilian and Charles (back row, left and middle) and Rosalind (front row, left) and two unknown sitters) and *right*: Louisa Colston with her grandchildren at Roundway in the 1890s.

The order and rhythm of rural England, typified by the exchanges at Charles's Coming of Age celebrations back in 1876, seemed very much intact as the Colstons continued to live a life apparently little touched by the economic and social changes of the last quarter of the 19th century.

In 1895 Charles was returned as MP for Thornbury with a much-increased majority. He was content with remaining a backbencher and spoke infrequently. In that same year the statue to Edward Colston the Philanthropist was unveiled in Bristol, with very large crowds attending.

Charles was also still in a position to expand his landholdings: in 1896, he bought the neighbouring Rowdeford estate (excluding the main house) on the death of Wadham Locke and in June 1899 he purchased West End Farm at Rowde from the same estate for £900 (£114,000 today) at auction.[154] Rowdeford House itself had been sold by auction in December 1889, before Wadham Locke's death. The auction took place over five days in December 1889, with items for sale ranging from Chippendale furniture to mahogany bidettes and night commodes.[155]

There were, however, underlying financial concerns for Charles at this time. The high point of the income from his estates coincided with his 21st birthday, after which there was a decline in British agriculture which was to last his lifetime and mirror the relative decline of Britain's economic strength. From 1875 onwards, agricultural prices started to fall due to cheap imports from abroad, particularly of wheat from Russia and the prairies of the

US, which were facilitated by improved internal transport and competitive international steamships. There were also poor harvests in the UK due to wet summers from 1878 to 1882 and, a decade later, due to severe droughts between 1892 and 1895. The invention of refrigerated ships at this time made the import of meat possible, particularly from the Empire.

Rents declined for landowners by between 50 and 75 per cent between 1872 and the 1890s, which forced landowners to reduce investment in their estates. The decline also led to diversification, particularly investment in industry and finance, so that by 1896 over a quarter of the peerage held directorships, often in companies in which they had an economic interest, whereas in the 1880s this had been relatively unusual. Lord Randolph Churchill remarked in 1884 that land as an investment was 'no longer safe, and the bloom had been altogether rubbed off the peach'.[156]

In the short-term, Charles was insulated from these problems, not only by the scale of his wealth but also by inheritance and diversification, such as the coal mines he owned in the West Country. This explains why he was able to take advantage of the economic situation by buying the Rowdeford estate. Longer-term, however, he was no more immune to these factors than any other landowner in England.

View of the north front with the circular room in the early 1900s (©Wiltshire Museum, Devizes).

10

A Day in the Life of Roundway Park

IN THE LAST THREE CHAPTERS of *Enter A Child*, Dorothy's description of a typical morning, afternoon and evening, from the point of view of a ten-year-old girl in 1890, brings Roundway vividly to life:[157]

I would be wakened by the ringing of the house bell which announced to everyone at Roundway, both within the house and without, that it was eight o'clock. When I escaped from the hands of my mother's maid, I started to run down the stairs. A question was in my mind as I ran; would I be in time for prayers? For, my grandmother's spirit imprinting itself on the household, family prayers were still kept up at a time when in nearly every other house they had been dropped. If I now met the head housemaid giving the final flick of her feather-brush to the pot pourri bowls on the landing ('Good-morning, Bertha', 'Good-morning, Miss Dolly'), then I was certainly in time. If there was no Bertha on the stairs, then there was a doubt.

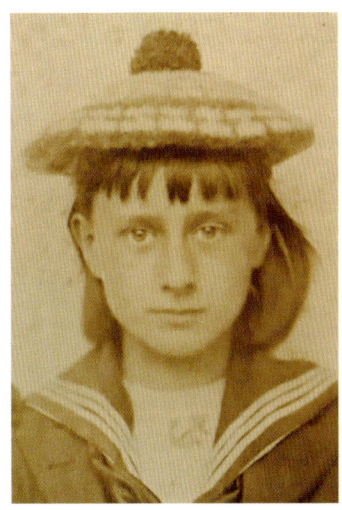

Dorothy aged about ten.

Now I was at the dining-room door, putting my head sideways against its glossy mahogany panels to discover whether I was in time or not. If the sound was low, continuous droning, I thought 'late again', and turned back to the library. Here I was kept company by a stuffed eagle in a glass case. I would wander over to the writing-table in the window and examine a big red-leather book marked on the cover in gold letters, *Visitors' Book*. It was odd how many ways there were of writing a signature. I would pore over them, greatly impressed by those which used up most ink: violent, powerful signatures that rushed convulsively from one side of the page to the other.

But now there came from the other side of the door the low scraping of chairs that meant that the long row of servants were getting up from their knees, and that prayers were over. I turned the door-handle, and there the whole breakfast-scene lay before me: the big green-walled dining-room; the big table frothed over with orchids, pink china, and silver; the pictures in their gold frames crowding the walls; my tall uncle standing up unfolding and refolding the sheets of his morning paper; Savage the butler stooping down to the wick of the spirit-lamp; figures of relations here and there sitting down shaking out their napkin, or standing peering into hot dishes on the side-table; while through the open windows could be seen the water-wagtails running up and down the dew-whitened lawn quirking their tails. The day, the gorgeous Roundway day, had begun.

The upper lawn had always played the part of outdoor nursery, chiefly, I imagine, because there was a summer-house at one side of it dear to the nurses. When I was smaller, my old nurse and the old Roundway nurse, Mrs Turner, would sit side by side casketed in this summer-house like two ancient female images in a shrine.

Ted Colston as a young boy.

Surrounding the upper lawn was a dense shrubbery of laurel but if there had ever been paths in the Roundway shrubberies they had become overgrown, and when my cousin Ted and I decided that morning to build a hut among the laurels it meant cutting a path as well. All the time I was pottering I was aware in a vague subconscious way of the cradling softness of the garden atmosphere around me: of the sunlight that soundlessly shifted and changed with the moving hours: of the flowers' starred faces bared unflinchingly to the sky as they stood tranced in their own secret, self-sufficing world: all this was the accustomed silent accompaniment to our garden life …

There was a sense at once of freedom and yet of people all the time moving about in the house and garden that to me was so satisfactory. Was I happy? Was I content? The words are too pale. I was a child Eve in a Wiltshire garden of Eden.

At five minutes to one the first, the warning, luncheon bell came ringing from the house across the lawns. To wait till we heard this was cutting it fine; it meant only four

Laurels in the gardens to the south of the house c1890, just as Dorothy remembered them.

minutes to wash and tidy up, and when that plangent sound fell on our ears, without exchanging a word we would start hurling things into the wheelbarrow … a brief: 'Got everything?' from Ted and we were off at a rush.

This frantic rush across the garden in answer to the bell was one of the things I liked best in the day … I have only to shut my eyes, and I am back there now … the lawn, broadly banded with lighter and darker green from the morning's mowing, stretches before me as I run … run … Behind me come sounds of a wildly shoved-along wheelbarrow, and of Ted shouting … the air is nectar-pure upon my face, the sky clear midday blue; all around are suspended glittering banners of green. The outspread beds of begonias and geraniums are all ablaze as I tear by.

Each time of the day at Roundway had its own special feel and texture, and none more so than the quarter of an hour after luncheon when the grown-ups dawdled about before returning to their day-long and, to my mind, unspeakably dreary occupations.

But for this short time we all idled in company. The dining-room doors open, we straggled into the library, and through library to hall. Here, in the centre of the stone floor, was a great square rug, and this rug had given rise to the game of Goats. To play Goats you crossed your arms on your chest to make your body compact, and then, hopping on one leg, tried to butt, push, hustle your opponent, also on one leg, off the square of carpet. Ted and I adored it. We charged, we shoved, we squealed. The laughter and cheers of the grown-ups were spurs to our excitement.

Amy Baynes c1890.

But within a short time the grown-ups were sauntering away, returning to their writing-tables, their newspapers, their embroidery-frames. 'Now, dears!' my mother would say to Ted and me, and lead the way to the drawing-room. Arrived there, Ted and I flung ourselves flat on our backs on the floor, and my mother began to read aloud. The idea was rest and instruction combined. Most soothing and pleasant it was to lie there in the dimmed light vaguely listening to my mother's beautiful reading voice, idly tracing with my eyes the pattern of mediaeval birds and flowers on the chintz valance within a few inches of my face.

In the afternoon Ted had to do an hour's work with his tutor Mr Ridford: and while this was in progress I hung about waiting for him to come out. Hence my presence alone in the quadrangle: hence my loitering. As I stood there I became aware of the lovely afternoon silence, not the silence of isolation but the suspended silence that enwrapped Roundway between the comings and goings of the morning and the reawakening about tea-time. And if one listened right into this silence, then one could hear gentle, far-off sounds … a voice singing somewhere in the kitchen part of the servants' wing … wheels of a cart going across a field … and, now, somewhere in the very heart of the house, a gush of water from a tap plashing into a

Painting by Dorothy of the portico and quadrangle at Roundway.

pail … and then suddenly, cutting stridently across these muted sounds, the clattering clogs of a stableman as he crossed the cobbles on the further side of the quadrangle.

The stables in the quadrangle held for me an almost mystical charm: that subtle, uplifting smell which met one the moment one pushed open the door, that special horse-and-straw atmosphere, that quick pull on the halter and swung-round enquiring face, those stirrings in further stalls, that rustling of straw, that occasional deep, patient sigh. Eager to be drawn into still closer communion with the stable-world, I would open the bin against the wall and eat the oats.

Several weeks before the Roundway school-treat which took place every August, parcels of small naked dolls

A scene in the quadrangle by the stables from the time of the childhood of Dorothy and Ted.

would arrive from the toy shop in Devizes. The aunts and grown-up cousins would then set to work to dress them with scraps of stuff. Very soon after luncheon on the day itself Ted and I would scuttle upstairs to the Red dressing-room that looked over the drive, for from here could be seen the first sign of the children. Before us lay the drive, the great white gate at the end, now fixed expectantly open, then more drive, and trees.

'There they are!' Mrs Turner would cry suddenly, 'Look there's one of their banners!' Yes, flecks of bright colours of banner and, now, flecks of light colours of children's dresses were clearly there where before there had been nothing but road and trees. An endless serpent of children was coming towards us, barred every few yards by a banner.

The park was to be the afternoon's playroom. As each block of children arrived their conversation rose to fever pitch. Now the children were running everywhere, hurling themselves down on the long dank grass, screaming, jumping in the air, or rolling down the park slope.

At four o'clock the cry went up: 'Tea! Tea!' Now the figures of the butler Savage and the footmen mingling with figures of housemaids and kitchen-maids were seen moving about within the shade made by the great beech-trees near the servants' wing. To and fro they ran from house to park, from park to house, bearing heaped-up trays and all the hot-water cans, large and small, that Roundway possessed. When the long trestles under the trees had had alternate plates of cake and bread-and-butter placed all down their centre, and the children were scrambling on to the wooden benches, then was the moment for Ted and myself.

Each snatching up a small hot-water can from the collection put ready under a tree, we held them out open to Savage and his enormous can. Smiling with benevolence, like a god pouring out gifts from a cornucopia, Savage poured forth the boiling tea. From big can to little can, from little can to thick white mug, from white mug to draining mouth, such was the route of these gallons and gallons of tea. Even when one would have thought each child must be full of tea from head to foot the cry of 'More tea please, Miss!' still rose in the air.

On the children's departure along the drive, it was just the same as their arrival, only the other way round, and now, instead of talking they were singing. These departing children seemed to be bearing away the summer day with them, the summer day and all the school-treat fun … it was all over now … all over for a whole year … but there was no time to feel melancholy about it, for Ted and I had already turned back to the house for a last run through the whole length of rooms before the double doors were shut. For on the school-treat day, as on engine day, every door was flung wide, and one could see room after room, from billiard room at one end to Circular room at the other.

On ordinary Roundway days the time between tea and dinner, with the low light slanting through the tree branches in the park, was as delectable as any other part of the day. The Cabinet room was so called because the walls were lined with glass cupboards. These cupboards were filled with china, and among the Lowestoft and Rockingham tea-sets, the Bow and Bristol figures, stood a Sevres mug said to have been used by Napoleon on his campaigns. In the evening when the blinds were pulled up, the park, the deer, and the setting sun would be reflected in these glass doors, and there within this confused mirror one would see a fallow deer moving across the tea-cups, and, enmeshed within the branches of an elm, Napoleon bearing his part in this tranquil English scene.

The only occasions when I didn't like the early evening were when, towards the end of our visit, and the days drawing in, Aunt Lilian would act as show-man to the sunset. Crossing the hall, I would see her peering through the glass of the terrace-door while at the same time keeping a sharp look-out for anyone passing by within the house, so as to urge them to come and reinforce her enthusiasm.

The cabinet room (Historic England).

Now everything was growing darker. The solemn hush of the sky was absorbing the valley, the lawn, ourselves where we stood, the whole of Roundway. If only Frederick would come pushing through the swing door with his stool to light the gas and ... oh, relief! There he was, carrying his stool in one hand and a lighted taper in the other, placing his stool beneath the gas chandelier, climbing on to his stool, gingerly applying his taper beneath gas globe ... pop of gas ... five more globes, five more pops, and Frederick's work of salvation was complete. Light, reassuring, insistent light, flooded the hall. One disciplined taper had defeated Aunt Lilian and her sunset.

I could see him as he went through the open door into the dark drawing-room, placing the lamps about, one on each small table. Then I heard him drawing the window curtains, the clicketing of the curtain-rings sounding fainter as he gradually moved further down the big room.

Eight o'clock in the evening. Escaped from the hands of my mother's maid, newly washed and dressed, I was in the drawing-room standing in my party-frock and silk stockings watching the grown-ups gradually collect. At dinner Ted and I always sat next to each other, and no sooner had we sat down than we started the water-bottle game. The object of the game was to collect round us and drain to the dregs as many of the glass water-bottles as possible, and, the table being long, there were any number of these bottles of a unique and a particularly lovely design. The supreme moments of the game were when Aunt Lilian, for instance, needing some more water, would look up and down the table in a puzzled way and exclaim, 'Where *have* all the water-bottles got to?' And another voice would chime in, 'Yes … very odd … I can't see *one!*'

Rosalind Colston.

When, after dinner, we were all collected in the drawing-room among the orchids that fantastically displayed themselves on every table beneath the rays of the little lamps, then my dearest wish was that Aunt Rosie would sing. Usually, before this happened, some other members of the family sang or played. Aunt Lilian would sit down to her harp and … thrip … thrip … would go her long white fingers on the tautened strings. I found this thrip-thripping a thin bloodless affair, and for me the only charm in the performance was when, with a louder but deadened thrip, one of her harp strings snapped. Then Aunt Rosie got up from the sofa and sat down at the piano, her wild-rose fairness lit by the candles on either side. Her voice was afloat in the air … winging about the room like a bird. The gentle melancholy, the sweet nostalgic sentiment of her songs was honey to my crude being. But on Sunday evenings Aunt Rosie did not sing. On Sunday evenings my grandmother demanded hymns. I enjoyed these evenings. It was fun to see who chose which hymn; for the rule was that each member of the family should choose in succession.

As I stood in my usual place by the piano, the beautiful Wyatt room lay spread out before me. The silk-shaded lamps threw a subdued light on to the ceiling where drifted white-limbed goddesses reclining on clouds, clouds brought into being by Angelica Kauffmann, different from those that floated above the downs, but, in their way, even more emotional and spectacular. In the centre of the ceiling hung a crystal chandelier whose thousand facets had once glittered in a boudoir of Marie Antoinette; while at the further end of the room, within curved alcoves on each side of the mahogany doors, two nude marble figures held their eternal poses of grace.

Then there was the evening, the supreme evening when Miss Witherington played the piano. Miss Witherington had been music teacher to Aunt Rosie and Aunt Lilian. Dinner was over, and Miss Witherington, with Aunt Lilian acting as aide-de-camp, was preparing to play. Standing imposingly in her dress of purple lace by the side of the keyboard, Miss Witherington began to direct and rearrange the positions of her listeners. 'My dear Rosie, I advise you not to sit quite so close … and you, dear Charlie, on the contrary, are really a leetle far off, are you not?'

The drawing room in the late 19th century with the piano at the back on the right.

Ted sidled up to me. He was biting his underlip. 'We'd better get out of this,' he muttered, 'or I shall explode.' We slipped through the open doors into the Cabinet room. Here we could hear without being seen. We flung ourselves, one on the floor and one on the sofa, and each seizing a cushion we smothered our laughter in their depths. There was a moment's silence in the next room, and then, 'May I ask for complete – but complete silence!' I rammed my face further into the pleated silk. Miss Witherington began to play …

Later, in bed, I smiled to myself in the darkness because I was thinking that though this day was over, I was still at Roundway; safely there for weeks to come. A long vista of garlanded hours lay before me. Roundway! The very name spelt all the sweetness of living.

The hounds at Roundway c1900 (John Girvan Collection and Mike Thomas).

11

Henry Robinson: Butler Extraordinaire

IN 1892, during the preparations for the visit of the Prince of Wales, a seemingly minor appointment was made at Roundway in the form of Henry Robinson (1874–1959), who joined the staff as second footman at the age of 18. He went on to play a central role in the life of Roundway particularly with the Roundway harriers, remaining on the staff until his retirement in 1945 and on the estate in the Quakers Walk Lodge until his death in 1959. For much of this time, he was close to Ted Colston, being only six years older, and went on to be his footman and then butler. His letters provide some of the most engaging and at times poignant commentary on the fortunes of the family and estate during his half century of devoted service to the Colston family.

'He was destined', wrote Daphne Moore, the well-known author of many books and articles on hunting, in 1979, 'to become, by his own efforts, an outstanding character whose like will never be seen again. He was born in a spacious age and lived all his working days in great houses, where his quick perception and exceptional intelligence enabled him to become an authority on such diverse subjects as heraldry, hunting, forestry, old silver, paintings, genealogy and architecture.'[158]

Henry Robinson was born in 1874 in Berkshire where his father was the butler at Kingston House. His mother had been a lady's maid. He was educated at the village school in Kingston Bagpuize, where he learnt to write with a fluent hand and laid the foundations of a lifetime search for knowledge. Living close to the kennels of the Old Berkshire hounds, young Henry spent much of his available free

Henry Robinson c1900.

Dog leads with rosettes in glass cases at Roundway.

Young Ted Colston with the hounds in the late 1890s.

time there, and it was here that he first developed what was to become his life-long interest in hound breeding, and his love of hunting. Whenever possible he followed the pack on foot, at times playing truant from school to run after the hounds all day.

Having left school at 14 he spent four happy years as hall-boy at Woolley Park, near Farnborough, the home of the Wroughton family (Mr William Wroughton was the late Master of the Pytchley Hunt from 1894 to 1902 and of the Woodland Pytchley for a further six seasons). This was his only other employment apart from his time at Roundway. In his early days as a footman, his hair was powdered and knee breeches were worn with his livery, as was still the custom in many great houses before 1914.

Among his first duties at Roundway, Henry acted as valet to Ted Colston during his school holidays from Eton. This not only led to a strong bond between them but also, in 1897, to Henry becoming whipper-in of Ted's own private pack of 16in foot harriers, the Roundway Harriers. In 1896 the Eton College Beagles spent a restorative summer at Roundway and between that year and 1911 the 'Roundway' built up a classic foot pack and hunted the strong hares around Devizes.[159] By 1911, the Roundway had extended its area to include more open downland above Devizes, which led to it becoming a mounted pack in order to keep up with the hounds in the open countryside. Reports of the Harriers' meets were well covered in the local press.

In 1898 Ted, now 18 and having completed his education at Eton, where he rowed for the school, decided on a military career, and hoped to be granted a commission in the Grenadier Guards. Instead of attempting to do this via a cadetship at the Royal Military College, Sandhurst, he chose the other method then available, which was through a commission in a militia regiment. This route entailed a period of recruit training at a regimental depot; two attendances at month-long camps with the militia battalion; an attachment with a regular battalion; and finally passing a competitive examination. To many young men it had more appeal than two years at the RMC Sandhurst under conditions much like school. Militia commanding officers were mostly peers and large landowners and they selected officers from their own families and friends.

When Ted joined the North Staffordshire Militia in 1900 Henry accompanied him as his footman. In the extract below from one of Henry's letters, written to Dorothy in a mood of reminiscence in January 1944,[160] Henry described his arrival with Ted in 1900 at Woolwich for militia training:

The Infantry Barracks were full up so we had quarters in the Artillery Barracks; the cab horse jibbed at the station, ran back and turned the cab over, but we both just scrabbled out in time. As the Barracks were not far and we were rather late he said he would leave me to come on or he would be late for Mess.

Of course, it was a long time before I could find his room in the Artillery Barracks and when I did, Oh, you should have seen the panes of glass out of the window, ashes in the grate up to the mantelpiece; never shall I forget it and wondered whatever his father and mother would have said had they seen it.

Ted Colston in the uniform of the North Staffordshire Militia.

Well, I blocked the broken windows up. No blinds but some old curtains, which when I went to draw the poles fell down. Then went foraging for some sticks and coal after cleaning a barrow load of ashes away; fortunately, I had his own bed and bedding. After about 2 hours I got things a little ship-shape and in he comes with the head of a small loaf, some cheese and a bottle of Bass. Then he said 'sit down and have that for I'm sure you can do with it'.

Fortunately, I had got a room with a widow just outside the barracks for myself, such a nice old lady. So, when I left him and said good night after shutting his door, I noticed there was a crack in the door nearly an inch wide. So, went back and hung his topcoat over it to keep out the draft and when I turned in to my snug little room there was no question who had the best bedroom. Of course, about the next day he had a cold which was not an ordinary one and the following one it took a much more serious turn and we went back to Green Street [the Colstons' London house in Mayfair] though he was very loath to go and Mrs Oliver came up to Green St. to look after him and he spent his birthday in bed …

Ted's illness was 'immortalised' in a poem written at Roundway by his cousins Christobel, Dorothy, Ione and Ruperta to console him on his birthday, which fell on New Year's Eve; it was accompanied by a drawing of the invalid in bed and the first two and the last of its eight verses are quoted here:

A Birthday Ditty

Now Greetings to our Cheshire Cat
From we his Cousins Four,
And hearing of his fate so sad
We all that fate deplore.
Alas! that on his Natal Day
(The 31ˢᵗ we think?)
He should be stretched upon his bed
And given nasty drink.

The elements since ere you left
Have shrieked and wailed your loss,
With rain, with snow, with mist, and hail,
And we have wept of course.
At last to cheer our woeful hearts
We sallied for a walk,
And all the way our Cousin's health
The subject of our talk …

Today the sunshine greets our eyes
Farewell to storm and rain,
We trust our Cousin soon will rise
Restored to health again.
Now Greetings to our Cheshire Cat
From us his Cousins Four.
We hope he'll kick the 'flu' away
And wish him joys galore.

"*Alas! that on his Natal Day He should be stretched upon his bed*
(The 31st we think?) And given nasty drink!"

The sketch accompanying the Birthday Ditty.

Returning to Henry's letter, he then reported on Ted's recovery:

Well after he recovered we went back to Woolwich, this time in the Infantry Barracks, and his room was quite chic after I had scrubbed the floors and cleaned the windows etc, which I had only finished by 3pm when I expected him, as I had left London early to have his room ready.

There was a bang at the door and a sergeant with 'Get ready for the sweep'. Oh, I replied, 'I have only just cleaned the room' – 'Doesn't matter about that,' he replied and in came the sweep. I said to the sweep: 'Look here, I don't want a mess about here; I have just cleaned this room and expecting my master; here's a 1/- for you, just put the brush up about a foot.'

Says he: 'Do you see that Sergt. out there on the barrack square?' Yes, says I. Well, he said, 'He's waiting to see the brush go up through the top of the chimney.' Just then someone called the Sergt. away and he took the 1/- and my advice and as he walked out his Lordship walked in and had a good laugh at my strategy.

There had been a very hard frost and a rapid thaw set in. The next morning when I called his Lordship he was curled up at the foot of the bed. A tank had burst and flooded his bed; he was fast asleep when it happened and thought he was in a leaking tent. You never saw such a state his bed and bedding was in, and this after just recovering from influenza. However, he luckily took no harm and with a big fire I got going and managed to dry everything.

That day the whole militia regiment volunteered on parade for active service and the next we had orders for Newry, Ireland. I had just packed already when a wire came saying he was gazetted to the Grenadier Guards. So off he went to Windsor after a day or two at Green St. to get his kit together as the only barrack furniture found in those days was a small table, coal box, a chair and a poker. Bed, bedding, chest of drawers etc all found by the officer himself.

Your grandfather's chests – XV Hussars – were used long after I came here to Roundway for taking the harness to London for the season by Barby and one of these was used at Curzon St. by your grandmother to keep potatoes in the area cellar. And a very unique table of his was the carving table in the dining room at Roundway long after I came here. It folded up very cleverly and was always of great interest to the London waiters that used to come here in the old days to our big shooting parties.

I always remember our first night at Windsor. Lord Henry Seymour, son of the Marquis of Hertford, had the next room (my father was 1st footman to the Marquis of Hertford) and on the other side was a Lieut. Vivian (my mother was lady's maid to Lady Vivian) so I felt rather at home.

Just before dinner young Vivian and Fisher Rowe, two old schoolfellows of his Lordship at Eton, came into his room to take him in the mess and as his mess kit had not arrived he went in ordinary dinner dress. Just before going, he said to them: 'Now, am I alright?' They had a look at him and as was usual there was braid down the side of his evening trousers. One said – 'Well, Ted, I should take that braid off your trousers.'

'Get the scissors, Henry,' he said 'and take it off.' So the first night to dinner in the Guards Mess I took the braid off his trousers, why for I never knew.

About the 3rd night Lord Douro's servant (son of the then Duke of Wellington) came to me and said just come and look at my room. You never saw such a mess, he had been 'ragged'. They had taken his bed to pieces and piled it in the middle of the room, broken all his pictures, thrown his cigars etc on the fire, cut his uniform trousers etc and he had slept on the floor in a corner, so I expected the same to happen to us. So for the next two or three nights I sat in his Lordship's room with a big stick waiting for an attack which never came and said nothing; however, about the 4th night I said to his Lordship: 'They served Lord Douro very badly the other night' – 'Serve him right' he said but gave no reason and I never asked, but often wondered why it was; at the same time I felt very relieved.

Then I had all his Lordship's belts, sword slings etc arrive, all natural yellow colour, and the soldier servants wondered what I was going to do to put them right; by night I had finished them and all the other servants came to look at them. Of course, any servant that can clean leather hunting breeches can manage that kind of work and the older soldier servants there were soon unlocking doors to show me their breeches and top boots of the officers there who were hunting and I had quite an interesting time.

One Sunday when he was on guard at Windsor Castle his father and mother had tea with him and I had tea also before I packed the things up and they went to the evening service in St George's Chapel. I went early to have a look round and then when people began to come in I took a seat; there were not many people and I was so intent on the ceiling and everything that I did not notice that with only a few people there, some 1/4 of an hour before the service commenced, I had taken my seat next to the late Lord and Lady Roundway but did not notice this for some minutes when of course I moved away.

When his Lordship saw me afterwards he said in his nice way: 'Why did you move away from us Henry?'

'Well,' I said, 'why did I sit there for it looked just as if I had done so intentionally as there was so much other room.'

Ted Colston
in Grenadier Guards uniform.

Ted continued to serve with his regiment and, in 1908, was promoted to Captain and awarded the MVO, Member of the Royal Victorian Order. He and Henry Robinson continued to build up the Roundway Harriers as is described in this newspaper article by Keith Gardner:

> In 1911 the Roundway extended their country to include more of the open downland above Devizes and thus became a mounted pack, as the new country gave hounds 'every chance of shooting away from those who are not mounted'. A pack of larger harriers could now be used and as Mr. Herbert Connop was giving up the N. Montgomeryshire Harriers to take the United Foxhounds, Mr. Colston purchased them. (The field staff were supplemented by the addition of Jack Bond the first coachman, as second whip to Henry Robinson – who by now was first footman / first whip!) …
>
> Mr. Colston's eye for quality both in his own and other's breeding must have been superb for within a year he had won both the dog and bitch 19in Harrier classes at Peterborough – with Warrior and Wallflower by Tanatside Warrior out of their Roguish.

The hounds outside the south front at Roundway with (from left to right) Henry Robinson, Ted Colston and William Baynes.

A key part of this success was Henry's encyclopaedic knowledge of hound pedigrees. When he became whipper-in, he began to study their blood-lines in depth, and to start writing out their pedigrees, described by Daphne Moore as 'tracing back to the 18th and 19th centuries, exquisitely written with a fine pen in microscopic lettering of amazing clarity'. She also wrote that he became one of the great authorities of all time on this absorbing subject:

> His 'double life' began at 6am on non-hunting days, when he would go hound-exercising on his bicycle, prior to starting work in the house in the capacity of footman, and, years later, as butler. When hounds came to be shown at Peterborough (where they achieved no small success) he would always accompany them as official whipper-in and great must have been the rejoicing when they won … The late Earl Bathurst regarded him highly as a student in this field and acknowledges his help in the Preface of one of his erudite books; whilst the Duke of Beaufort described him as one of the three great experts of his day on this subject.

The Peterborough Harrier Show proved successful where, according to *The Times* of 11 July 1913, Ted 'swept the board'. He was helped by his purchase of the residue of Mr Barclay's pack known as the Epping Forest (Mr Pelly's) Harriers, which were added to the Roundway pack.[161]

Henry Robinson with the victorious hounds and rosettes at the Peterborough Harrier Show in 1913.

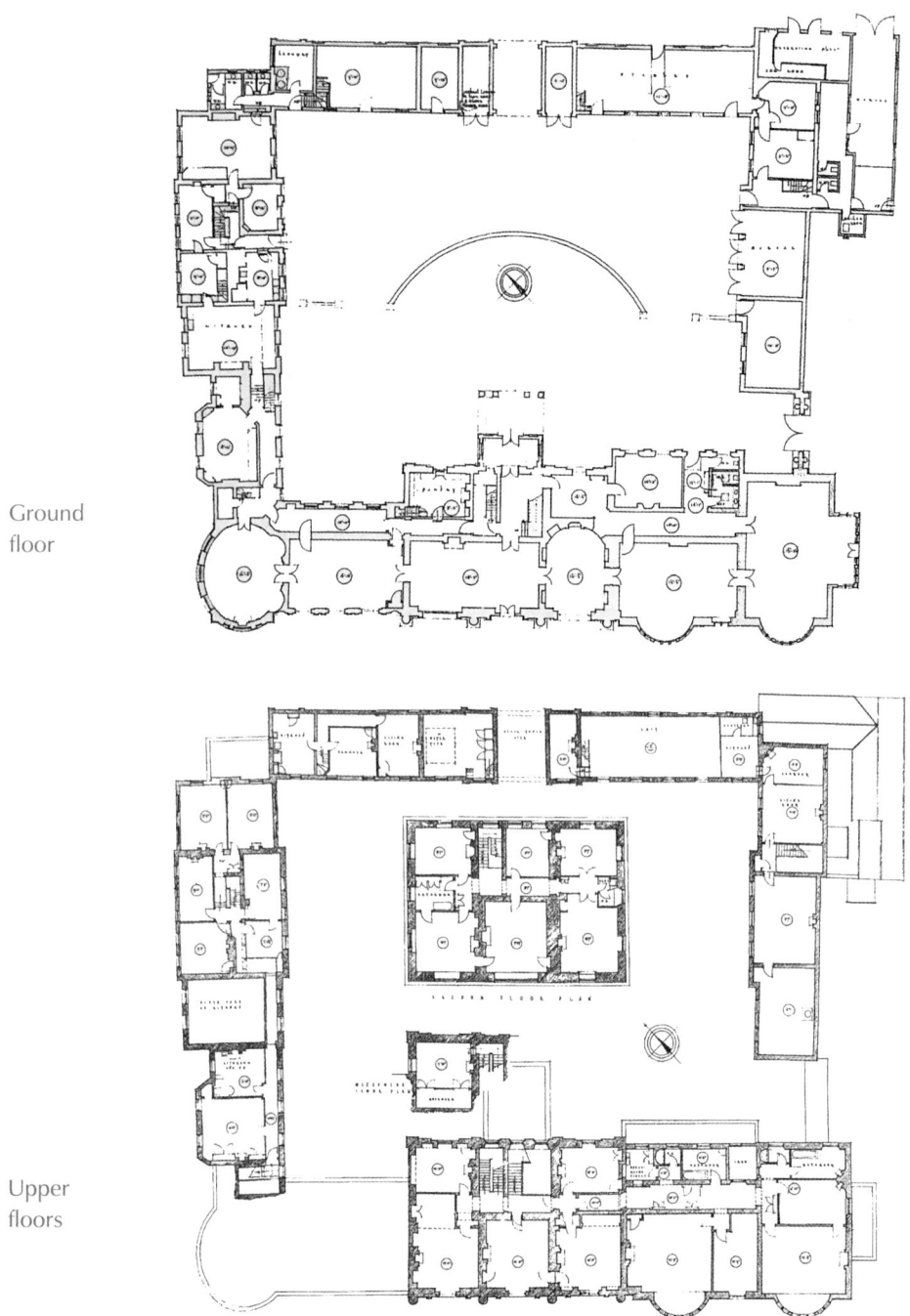

Ground
floor

Upper
floors

Floorplans of the mansion house showing the layout of the rooms on the ground and upper floors after
Charles Colston's alterations of 1901 which remained unchanged until these plans were drawn by
Frank S. Bowden, Wiltshire County Architect, in 1952 prior to partial demolition of the house.

$\text{\small ❧}$ **12** $\text{\small ❧}$

The New Century

THE EXPERIENCES of the Colston family during the Edwardian era reflected many of the changes and paradoxes of this time. Britain was still in the ascendant internationally in terms of its wealth and power but its position was being increasingly challenged by the US and Germany. The Empire was near its zenith but the Boer War proved an acute reminder of the difficulties of maintaining Britain's influence overseas and its effects were felt by families like the Colstons across the country as their sons were wounded or killed in the conflict.

In general, however, the landed classes in Britain started the new century in an optimistic mood, as shown by Charles's unopposed re-election as MP for Thornbury in 1900 and his improvements at Roundway. In June of the same year Roundway was featured in *The Pictorial Record* with photographs of the mansion house, the Shooting Box (the Swiss Cottage) and the waterfall in the grounds. It was described as 'one of the finest country seats in Wiltshire'. Shortly after this, Charles doubled the previous addition to the west front, thereby filling

View of the west front of Roundway after early 20th century changes.

Newly installed oak panelling in the library in 1900 in Edwardian times (John Girvan Collection and Mike Thomas).

View from the library after 1900 (John Girvan Collection and Mike Thomas).

Edwardian gardens at Roundway.

in the gap between the southern end and Wyatt's original central block. This created three extra bedrooms and three additional bathrooms on the first floor. It replicated the neo-Jacobean style of the previous addition thereby further compromising not only the symmetry of Wyatt's design but also the original Palladian style.

Internally, Wyatt's original entrance vestibule and the adjoining sitting-room were thrown together to create a new much larger entrance hall with a marble fireplace ornamented with birds, fruit, flowers and figures. This enlarged room was lined with 89ft of panelling of white-painted deal taken from Whitton Park, described as being 'fine 13ft-high panelling … with fern ornamentation on fluted pilasters with heavy cornice with broken rose and foliage decoration'.[162] The conservatory was refenestrated and completely redesigned as a library with oak panelling above a strapwork decorated dado and a heraldic stone fireplace with a carved overmantle incorporating the Colston-Murray family crests. Outside the library, a yew walk with borders was planted leading to the walled garden.

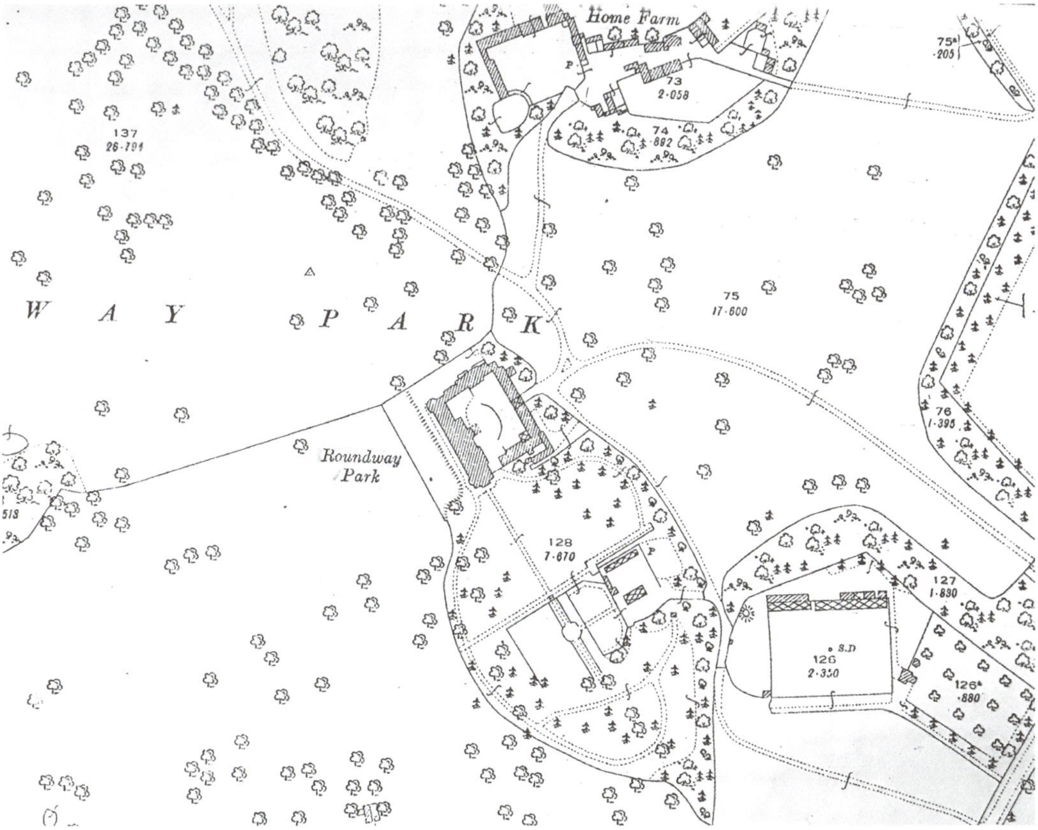

Roundway estate map in 1924.

View of the west front after 1900 addition (©Wiltshire Museum, Devizes).

The death of Louisa Colston, who had been ill for some time, at the age of 76 on 20 November 1900 marked the passing of the old century. Her funeral was at St James's Church in Devizes where she was buried in the family tomb. A glowing tribute was paid to her in the *Devizes Gazette* as a kind-hearted and charitable person with a sweet-natured disposition.

Two months after Louisa's death, on 22 January 1901, Queen Victoria died and a letter from Lilian to Amy, written from Roundway on black-edged paper, shows the interweaving of the two events in the concerns of the Colston family. She referred to Charles's efforts to obtain tickets for viewing the Royal funeral procession and then responded to concerns about her grief and loneliness due to their mother's death by saying that she was keeping herself occupied and enjoying the break at Roundway but 'it is mostly at night or early morning that sad thoughts will come, but I try to shake off depressing thoughts by trying to realise how perfect our Darling's happiness must be now; we firmly trust. I do not grieve for Her, only for my shortcomings to her. Yes – she would have taken such intense interest in all these accounts in the Papers as you say, and would have felt the dear Queen's death very acutely.'

Louisa's death coincided with that of her cousin and friend Rosalind Astley of Chequers Court, now the Prime Minister's country house,[163]

Ted Colston in uniform before the Boer War.

and the latter's son Bertie Astley wrote Lilian a touching letter of sympathy of which this is an extract: 'How singular it is that those two devoted friends and cousins – our two Mothers – should have passed almost hand in hand to the grave, leaving <u>such</u> records in this world. There was much that was alike in them – the charm of manner, the singular sympathy and power of attraction – the love of fun and, above all, the devoted unselfishness of their lives. I somehow feel we shall <u>never</u> see their like again.'

After being gazetted to the Grenadiers as a 2nd lieutenant, Ted was sent to South Africa to fight in the Boer War from 1901 to 1902. This letter, from Charles to Amy dated 29 November 1901 from Roundway, captures the worry felt by parents as their sons went off to war:

It was so good of you to write us such a dear sweet letter. The whole thing is like a horrid nightmare and the strain is such an effort to sustain, but we try and not show it more than we can help. You will be glad to hear that we got a wire this afternoon saying that he had arrived at Cape Town, had been inoculated, and was quite well – for which we were very thankful as the innoc makes some people awfully ill, and the fact that they had scarlet fever on board was not pleasant.

He was going on to Durban and so to Fouriesberg[164] which according to the map is 60–80 miles from Harrismith. I suppose he will rail from Durban to H, and then have to march along the chain of mountains for several days. I do wish he had some other officer with him, as the District seems very disturbed and I see some of their men (2nd Grenadiers) were badly wounded near Fouriesberg a few days ago, but I daresay some one will meet him at Harrismith. The Battalion appears to have left H and moved to F during the last week or so. I don't think R has found out about the above casualties which is a good thing.

Rosalind, writing on 28 November 1901, also thanked Amy for the same letter:

I cannot tell you how much we appreciated your dear letter. Indeed, we did not think you did not sympathize; we knew what you felt for us, it was really kinder not to say much as it was very difficult to get through everything without utterly breaking down. I think one realizes it more now one is alone, and I must say at times I do feel it dreadfully. One can only pray that he may come back to us again.

Rosalind Colston.

A letter written from Ted to Dorothy from South Africa on 26 May 1902, refers to their childhood gardening at Roundway and also to the building works being carried out there. It starts with Dorothy's nickname 'Tabby', which is repeated in various formulations in family correspondence quoted in this book. It is a reference to her paternal great-great-great-grandmother, Tabitha Baynes (née Prickett).[165]

Dear Tabby,

Many thanks for your last letter. I am afraid I do not often honour you with one but I expect you hear all my news, and I have not a great deal of spare time. You see my Company No. 4 is spread out over nearly 5 miles so it takes some little while visiting all our Battalions of which we have 11 and we have to go round every day.

We got up a Gymkhana this afternoon. I rode Prances in the polo pony flat race and ought to have been near the front, only my whip broke (it was only a thin switch) and so I finished only fifth which was rather bad luck. It was quite a good race, a field of 12 runners. I took some photos of the various events which I am sending home so I hope you will see some of them.

The seeds I have sown all seem coming up well. I have not done any gardening since my youth – do you remember the fun we used to have? I believe the plants I had in my garden are still in existence. Roundway must be in a most awful mess; I expect the result will be splendid when <u>really</u> finished. I hear there are any amount of Beagle puppies …

Much love to all.
Yr very affectionate cousin Ted (ie) The C. C. [Colston Cat]

PS Please thank W[illiam] for his letter and congratulate him on the success of his book.

In another letter to Dorothy of 19 August 1902 Ted wrote how 'Life is very dull here, polo and driving are really the only amusements …' In September, however, events changed radically and he was wounded during operations in the Orange River Colony and was awarded the Queen's South Africa Medal three clasps. This resulted in his return to England and his postponed 21st birthday Coming of Age party in October 1902 at Roundway, which was vividly described in letters from Dorothy and Lilian to Amy, who was not able to attend. Dorothy described Ted's arrival at the station in Devizes, which 'was announced by cheers and then the Mayor speechified and gave him a pipe. Then he mounted the box with Uncle Charlie and Aunt Rosie and Barbie [Barby, the head groom] <u>inside</u>! … I thought they would never have done cheering and singing "He's a jolly good Fellow" when they once got him home.' Lilian then takes up the story:

Edward jumped off the box seat of the Break at the front door and kissed the girls and me in a <u>blaze</u> of coloured lights and torches (the men holding them having formed up all round the quadrangle as they drove in). The Band played 'Home, Sweet Home' and everyone cheered again and again! Many of the people in the crowd 'hoped he be as <u>good</u> a man as his Father' and said the reception was as much to show their appreciation of Charlie's 'invariable courtesy and kindness' as to welcome the 'young squire' that they came up that night. I think all the Tenants were here, and nearly <u>all</u> the Tradespeople (they were all carrying lighted torches).

Beer and ginger beer was given from the Brew House to all who cared to have it; Savage said the crowd were so orderly and all waited to be invited to take something which was very nice. Barby, Harrison, the Stablemen and Harding all handed it out. Savage remarked gravely to Charlie afterwards that he was so glad that C had kindly offered refreshments 'as it gives a house such a good name'!

The Presentation of the <u>Servants</u> beautiful Bowl, and Hall, Hanley and Margaret's Tortoiseshell and silver Paper Knife, was on Friday (as the girls have probably told you). All the Servants and Workpeople were present in the Billiard Room and Barby acted as spokesman and made such a nice little speech. Edward thanked them all in a very hearty and capital speech. He was <u>immensely</u> pleased with their presents, and almost overcome with it all dear Boy.

Port wine and biscuits were handed round to the company before they departed and lusty cheers were given – Charlie made an excellent short speech too. Please forgive the incoherent epistle and all mistakes, I am writing in fits and starts, between strolls in the sun in the garden, and tea, and now winding it up nearly in the dark.

Ted seized the opportunity created by the late arrival of the entertainers, who had missed their train at Paddington, to show slides of his time in South Africa on a magic lantern to the assembled guests. And there was this touching postscript described by Dorothy to Amy: 'One man took the glass he had his beer in home with him and wrote a letter to Uncle Charlie asking if he might keep it in memory of the occasion.'

New Year at Roundway is neatly summarised in this letter from Rosalind to Amy, dated 1 December 1902: 'A line to say that we propose having our festivities as follows: Dinner for Tenants, Tradespeople etc on Wednesday Dec. 31st, then County Ball on Thursday Jan. 1st and Village Tea or Dinner on Friday 2nd. We hope you will <u>all</u> be able to come for them.'

Another theme of the correspondence at this time was technological progress: Charles bought a motor car in 1903 and this, combined with Ted's shortage of leave from the army, led him to write in February 1903 to Amy that the horses at Roundway 'do nothing. I hope to sell some soon but am too screwy myself to try them and settle what to keep and what to sell.' For many years afterwards motorised and horse-drawn transport co-existed and ownership of a car continued to be a rarity: in 1924 only five per cent of households nationally owned a car and it took until 1938 for this figure to rise to 20 per cent.[166] In a letter to Amy of 17 May 1904, Charles wrote about the Darby Griffiths' home: 'The electric light at Padworth is charming and the whole place is really in beautiful order.'

In the same year, 1904, two years after his return from active service, Ted married Blanche Gladys du Bois Duddell (the 'u' pronounced as in 'dew'). Charles had written to Amy about the young couple's engagement in November 1903 from his house at 54 Green Street in Mayfair:

> We are here for the night en route tomorrow for the Wyndham Murrays[167] and Edward has just left us for Aldershot. He seems as devoted as ever to Miss Duddell, so we have consented to an engagement, and I know Dear you will be interested to hear about it. We do not know much of the young lady but Ruperta [Willats] who knows her well, is very fond of her, and we have great confidence in her judgement, so we have every reason to hope the young people will be very happy together.

Blanche, preferring to use her middle name, Gladys, was described as beautiful by the *Wiltshire Gazette* and an expert skater, winning a waltzing competition before the King. She was also, in the words of the *Daily Express,* a 'splendid tennis player'. She regularly partnered the German Crown Prince at Bad Homburg and her skill won her many prizes. In 1901, Gladys had been the finalist in the German Ladies Tennis Championship but was beaten by the extraordinary Toupie Lowther who was not only a fine tennis player but also an exceptional fencer, a highly accomplished pianist and composer and a boxer.[168]

Gladys was the daughter of George Duddell (1821–87) who had made a fortune in Hong Kong (having also traded in Canada, Australia and Burma) as a pioneering property owner and auctioneer. There is a street named after Duddell in Hong Kong[169] and, despite a question mark over his business practices, he was appointed the Government Auctioneer. After his return to England in 1857, George moved to Brighton in 1863 where he bought Attree's Villa and land at Queens Park.[170] He was a Liberal Town Councillor and published a local newspaper.

Duddell had a complicated private life and he sired several children by different partners.[171] Gladys was born out of wedlock in 1879 although her father and mother, Kate

Dubois (who was also George's great niece), married shortly afterwards in 1881, aged 60 and 28 respectively. He died in 1887 after which the Brighton property was sold, in 1890, by Kate Duddell and later opened to the public as Queens Park, which it remains to this day.

The wedding of Ted and Gladys was held on 28 April 1904 at the Guards' Chapel, Wellington Barracks, in London and was reported in the following day's edition of the *Daily Graphic*, which stated that the bride was accompanied by her uncle, General Sir Ronald Thynne,[172] and given away by her mother. Viscount Mahon (eldest son of Earl Stanhope) acted as best man.[173] There were seven bridesmaids, including their cousins Ruperta Willats, Dorothy Baynes and Angela Thynne, and Gladys was dressed in a 'gown of old Brussels point appliqué lace, caught up with a fringe of orange flowers, and tulle veil over a coronet of orange blossoms. Her only ornament was a single row of pearls, the gift of her mother …' The reception was held by Gladys's mother, now Mrs Smithers, at 47 Hans Place and the couple received over 300 wedding presents.

Duddell's Villa sale particulars.

Newspaper report of the wedding of Ted and Gladys Colston.

After their marriage, Ted and Gladys lived in London at 1 Queensbury Place in Kensington while Charles and Rosalind were chiefly resident at Roundway. There is an amusing letter from Ted's old nanny Mrs Oliver to Dorothy in which she complains that he has been 'taken away' from her by Gladys (to whom she refers as Mrs Edward):

I am glad to hear that Mrs Edward (how queer it sounds) is really better. Mrs Smithers has given a <u>very nice</u> Photo of her to me. I was afraid I was not going to have one, or that Mrs Edward thought I did not deserve one. You know, she said I would not look at her at Roundway. I hope I was not really rude to her, but somehow I could not help feeling that <u>she had stolen my last nursling away</u>, therefore I was jealous of her. I have quite given him up now, and hope they are very happy. I do not expect I shall hear <u>from</u> him, but shall be very pleased to hear of him in your own, as well as Miss Ruperta's letters.

Six years later Gladys gave birth to Elizabeth Lydia, always known as Betty, who came to love Roundway as much as the rest of her family.

Betty Colston as a young girl at Roundway (John Girvan Collection and Mike Thomas).

13

The World at their Feet

IN JUNE 1907 Charles became world champion in coaching at Olympia, against stiff competition from the Vanderbilt family of the US, about which the *Wiltshire Telegraph* said: 'The first prize Park team at Olympia, Mr Colston beats the world.'[174] His victory was also reported in *The Times*, which described how the Gold Cup was presented by the Prince of Wales. Ted also won second prize in the class for pairs in victorias or sociables at the same contest. In 1909 Charles repeated his success in winning first prize for single horse and Brougham.

The above-mentioned report in the *Wiltshire Telegraph* of 15 June 1907 paid tribute to the role that the firms and townspeople of Devizes played in the Colstons' success:

> That Mr Colston's coach and team took the first prize in a competition open to the world, shows that Wiltshire can do something when it puts its mind to it. Mr Colston, it is well-known, makes the selection and training of his horses a personal matter, and he is well backed up by his staff at Roundway Park stables, who have all the keen personal interest in them we should expect. But in this event the horses did not secure all the points; they counted for 50 per cent., but the drags were to be good for 25 per cent., the harness 15 per cent., and the liveries 10 per cent. In all these details Devizes tradesmen were engaged by Mr Colston, and it says much for his confidence in them, as well as for his loyalty to Devizes, that he trusted them instead of going to 'town' for details on which much depended.

The repairing and re-painting of the coach was entrusted to the firm of Messrs. Willis and Son, of the Market Place, Devizes, and excellent as their work has been in the past, special praise is due to them for the high standard of proficiency reached on this occasion, especially so when it is considered that stipulated colours – the Colston colours: blue picked out with white – had to be adopted throughout. The harness, supplied by Messrs. W. S. Banbury and Son, of Wine Street, Devizes, was made in black with silver mountings (the latter having the crest engraved upon it); it was greatly admired – the workmanship being of the highest standard. The making of the liveries was in the capable hands of Mr W. H. Farley, also of Devizes Market Place; they were made of dark blue cloth, with velvet collars and silver buttons, the latter bearing the Colston family crest (the dolphin). The top boots of the attendants were supplied by Mr Tanner, of No. 22, 23, the Brittox, and this well-known establishment may also take credit for assisting in securing for Mr Colston pride of place. And everyone who knows Barby, the former stud groom at Roundway Park for so many years, will be pleased to know that he was not 'out of it', though he is on the retired list, for he made the whip …

Black and white photograph of the painting of Charles Colston's coach-and-four (John Girvan Collection and Mike Thomas).

As this newspaper article demonstrates, Devizes was a self-sufficient market town which supplied many of the needs of its people and the surrounding villages for food and clothing (there were dressmakers in abundance), transport and other attendant trades.[175] At this time the town had a population, including the outlying hamlet of Roundway, of about 7,000 people (it had doubled in the 19th century) although the town centre was relatively small and compact. The biggest employer was Brown & May's foundry in Estcourt Street, the second largest was E&W Anstie's snuff works and there were few people unemployed.

There was the thriving market, a wide range of shops, Wadworth and other breweries and 32 pubs. A significant professional and managerial class ran institutions such as the schools, the station, three banks, the cottage hospital, the asylum and the three newspapers. The Colstons made land available for local businesses such as Townsend's Nursery and for the allotments by the Quakers Walk gates; many families grew their own vegetables on allotments rather than buying produce in local shops so there was an extensive acreage of allotments in the town of which the largest was at Forty Acres. There was plenty of local entertainment with sport, theatre, music and events such as those hosted by the Colstons on the parkland at Roundway. Cinema reached Devizes in 1912 with the opening of The New Electric Theatre in the Market Place.

Charles's victory at Olympia in 1907 had come as a welcome antidote to his defeat in the 1906 General Election, which saw a landslide for the Liberals. He expressed his feelings in this letter to Amy in a letter from Roundway dated 28 January:

> Thank you so much for your dear letter – it is a great wrench to get such a slap in the face, but it can't be helped, and it has always been a wonder to me that the Constituency ever returned a Conservative – seeing the crowds of bootmakers and Miners in it. At some of my meetings their faces were white with passion and I could not get a hearing at all so had little chance to reply to the wholesale lies of our opponents and at Kingswood they stormed our platform and sent us all flying.
>
> I put in as many as 8 meetings one day, so you can imagine how worn out I feel and dear R is rather seedy with a chill. I fear she overdid it – the campaign – 3–4 weeks – has been a time of tremendous strain and labour but I kept pretty well all the time I'm thankful to say. Arrears of work – letters – bills – terrible. I must get on with them. These Rads will warm us up presently. We got home last night, most comfortably, in the Motor.

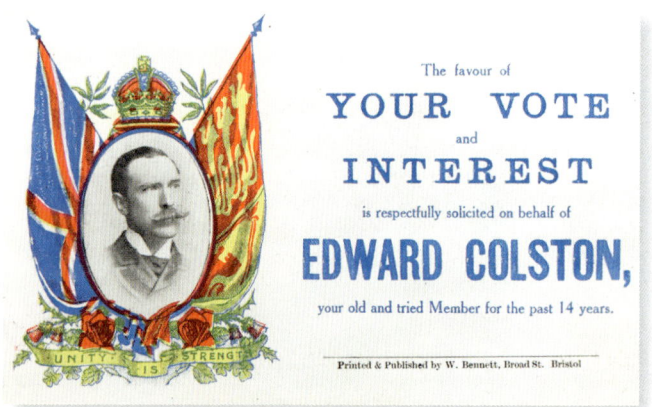

Charles's election literature in the 1906 General Election.

Charles's electoral defeat was a reflection of the seismic political changes which, under the new Liberal government, led to Lloyd George's People's Budget of 1909, the battle to curb the powers of the House of Lords, labour unrest and the Suffragettes' campaign for votes for women. For landowners such as Charles, Lloyd George's budget of 1909 introduced four new land taxes, albeit not on agricultural land.[176] Anxiety on the part of the owners of estates about the future contributed to an estimated 800,000 acres of land (equivalent to 200 estates) being sold in the years before the First World War.[177]

Despite these political concerns, day-to-day life continued as usual at Roundway, as is shown in Amy's diary for 1908. The annual summer visit by the Baynes family to Roundway took place between 18 and 29 August. It followed the usual traditions and also included playing 'Fives' in the Billiard Room, a visit from Rosie's Swedish masseuse Miss Widdigrin and Christobel helping Lilian to give her annual tea at the Devizes Union Workhouse. The family returned to Roundway for Christmas where they joined the Boxing Day meet for Charles's harriers at the Lower Lodge and, due to heavy snow that night, held their Sunday observance in the dining room with the servants the following day with Charles reading the service. They also visited the Kings in the Lower Lodge and Barby at the Quakers Walk Lodge who were ill.

An Edwardian summer afternoon in the garden at Roundway.

Amy and Christopher Baynes by Hugh Riviere (1905).

Charles's victory at Olympia also shows an increasingly international dimension to the Colstons' lives in the Edwardian era, which was in marked contrast to the more domestic existence of previous generations. The Empire provided opportunities for travel and also employment for many young men, including William, who was employed in the Egyptian Legal Service, and his cousin Rory Baynes who, as a young soldier, was posted from India to South Africa in December 1909.

A vivid picture of life in the Empire is provided in the letters that William wrote to his mother from Egypt, many of which remain from the period between October 1911 and the end of 1914.[178] After Harrow and Trinity College, Cambridge, William was called to the Bar in 1900 and then qualified in Paris as Licencié en Droit Francais in order to practise law in Egypt where he went to live in 1905.

In November 1911 William wrote to his mother: 'I should be very pleased to see my cousins Geoffrey and Marion [Lord and Lady Saye and Sele][179] out here … are they really going to attend the Durbar [the King and Queen's state entrance into Delhi took place on 7 December], or are

William in Egypt in 1907.

they merely going to Ceylon?' He enjoyed riding on his pony: 'I had a delightful ride this morning among palms sprinkled over downy sands with view of the sea all the time.' He also wrote about Lord Kitchener, at this time the British Agent and Consul-General in Egypt, saying that a judge named Vaux described Kitchener as 'a mastiff lying on the hearthrug, with no particular plans, but just growling whenever anyone in the room dared to move, which promptly made them all sit quiet again'.

In 1913 Christopher, recently retired from the Bank of England, and Christobel came out to Egypt to stay with William. The Baynes and Colston families had rarely holidayed abroad before this time. Father and daughter set sail in the New Year of 1913 for Egypt and Christopher wrote this letter to Amy on 7 February 1913 on board R.M.S. *Osterley* (Orient Line of Royal Mail Steamers):

> We are just through the strait between Sardinia and Corsica, perfectly lovely view, air pretty clear; both islands wild and rugged, Corsica the most, and we saw snow on the top of the mountains. We are so pleased we went into Toulon, the approach of the sea was magnificent, the entrance to the harbour very intricate but a splendid anchorage. The harbour is very large and is surrounded by high rocky hills some little way off, a very strong place – I am bad at description (want of poetry in my nature I suppose) but the hills, with the town along the water and the side bays and colour altogether was very impressive.

He went on to describe the 'fine lot of Battleships' in the harbour at Toulon and '4 other Battleships steaming towards the harbour for firing practice', a reminder of the rearming taking place between the Great Powers at that time. In a postscript, he said that 'Elgar the composer is on board – he was self-taught.' When they reached Cairo, Christopher wrote from Shepheard's Hotel to Amy, whom he addressed as 'My darling Wifey':

> We have just been in Cairo 10 minutes, all our baggage has been handed over to Willie's boy Hassan, and we have come here to tea and then go on to Maadi. Bill seems very well and in great spirits: no news yet. Xobel is in bounding spirits, all the squabbling, confusion and excitement keeps her in continual laughter ... The country was most interesting, it looked so rich and thickly populated, the colouring altogether beautiful – camels, goats, sheep and oxen in plenty.

On 23 February, William's birthday, Christopher wrote from Maadi and this letter in particular glows with happiness and a sense of discovery.

We get such early starts in the day as we breakfast at 8 (5 o'clock with you) as Willie goes into Cairo by the 8.49 train. It is a real pleasure to see him so well and happy, always 'merry and bright', talking away to everyone he meets and full of 'rag': the constant sun is certainly very charming and the dry atmosphere; this spot is very fresh and much better for Willie than Cairo, except for the question of promotion. I am sorry he cannot remain here, but he is very keen about Assiut and we must visit him there next! Mr Barnet (who W is to succeed) is dining here tomorrow so we may hear more about the place. W's description of the house sounds very nice and W will get plenty of society …

I am much looking forward to our walks and talks in the Park again my darling, as I feel all my letters do not convey to you half what I want to, it is so much easier to express in talking. W's and Xobel's rooms open out of one another. W told me had given me his room so that he could be close to X in case she wanted anything in the night; but of course the real object was that they could have some gossips together.

The letter is a reminder of Christopher's great affection for his children and love for Amy and does much to counterbalance the harsh portrayal of him in Dorothy's *Enter A Child*. The portrait of William as outgoing and cheerful also stands at odds with descriptions of his shyness and shows how the Empire not only brought career opportunities but also a welcome escape from the rigid social customs of Britain.

It is curious, however, that so many of Christopher and Amy's children did not marry. Perhaps their strict and class-conscious upbringing was a factor, making them unsure of themselves and reducing their circle of potential suitors. Dorothy and Christobel lived with their parents in Lowndes Square while it seems that class difference was a factor in Amy and Christopher's reluctance to sanction Ronnie's engagement to a woman called Ruby, as painfully charted in several letters that he wrote to his parents at this time, between December 1912 and October 1913. He wrote to his father on 14 December 1912:

Dearest Father,

I can quite understand your wanting time to think things over; and I am quite sure you will decide what you think is best for us both. You can have no idea how very much Ruby means to me, and if you saw her last two letters, you would realise how very, <u>very</u> fond she is of me, and how absolutely essential we are to one another's happiness. Father, I couldn't live without her now.

She <u>knows</u> it will be years before we can ever dream of getting married, and she is more than ready to wait for me as long as necessary. And when we <u>do</u> marry, if we ever do, we should do so in quite a small way; she would make an ideal wife for me (as I shall never be really well off) as she is so used to doing everything as cheaply as possible; as I shall always be a comparatively poor man, it is far better that I should have a wife who has been brought up on so very little, and so simply; rather than one who has been used to all sorts of little luxuries that I could never give her …

Hoping so very, very much that you will give your sanction very soon, if possible before Christmas (as of course my Christmas will be absolutely spoilt) if you don't wish us to become engaged.

Ever yr. very affectionate son

Ronnie

P.S. You know that I am no longer a child, and have a good deal of experience of the world, and I feel absolutely and perfectly convinced that I have at last met the one person destined for me by Providence. R.C.B

Later, in correspondence with his mother, he referred to fits of depression and the worry caused by his chartered surveyor exams and the continuing withholding of consent from his father: 'I do <u>so</u> wish Father would sanction it; of course, we should not <u>dream</u> of getting married on too little, or doing anything silly like that; nor should we put it in the papers etc. but just tell relations, and very intimate friends.' By the spring of 1913, however, parental consent had been given as shown in a letter of 12 April from William to his mother: 'I am so glad to hear R's wishes have been gratified and look forward to hearing (or how) you like his fiancée.'

The correspondence casts a revealing light on the social dynamics of the Edwardian era where social barriers were beginning to break down for the younger generation (even though Ronnie's engagement did not lead to marriage in the end) but a web of social standing and financial considerations still weighed heavily, particularly with the older generations.

14

The Great War

AFTER THE DECLARATION of war by Britain against Germany on 4 August 1914, Ted and the Grenadier Guards were part of the British Expeditionary Force (BEF) of about 100,000 soldiers that was sent to France. The despatch of the BEF led to a vast number of volunteers coming forward (750,000 men enlisted in August and September alone), which led to chaotic scenes as recalled by Rory Baynes, in his memoirs, who was serving with the Cameronians in Scotland at the time:

Ted Colston.

Rory Baynes.

Their tents were pitched in a sort of playing field in the middle of the barracks, and every available space was taken up by men sleeping. There was not enough preparation in the way of food and rations, and we had to send out into Hamilton and collect everything possible in the way of food. The first night things got so bad and the depot was so full, that we had to close the gates and at intervals open them and then charge the people outside thus keeping them from breaking in.

William was on leave in England in August but had to hurry back to Egypt as he described in this letter of 21 August to his mother: 'I am sorry to have to rush off and leave you all in such an unceremonious way, and yesterday I hadn't the least intention of going for good; but on getting to Webb's offices this morning I found that all India as well as Egypt is returning post haste, and it will be more difficult to get back with every week, as all the boats are packed …'
In a letter two days later, he described sailing out of the Thames: 'It was interesting coming round yesterday afternoon, as all the way from the mouth of the Thames down to the Channel

the sea was full of cruisers, torpedo boats and submarines and search lights going down the Channel …'

The sense of disbelief about the war in its very early stages is captured in the final words of his letter of 21 August about his holiday entitlement: '… anyhow I shall have nearly an extra month to play with next year, and in the meantime I look forward to seeing F[ather] and Cbel at Assiut if the war falls through'. His weekly letters home in the preceding months in 1914 betrayed no forebodings about the war and were full of his usual news, plans for the future and amusing comments about his family, including reference (in a letter of 26 June) to his parents taking their 'new motor' over to France in the summer on holiday.

William provided a snapshot of wartime life in Egypt in a letter to his father dated 2 September. He had become a Judge of the Native Courts in the First Instance earlier in 1914 and was preoccupied with the imminent announcement of martial law. He also mentioned that 'about 10,000 English and 30,000 native troops are expected from India any day, but the papers are not allowed to publish any information at all about the troops in the country and their movements'.

In August, the BEF fought the Germans at Mons in Belgium: although they were heavily outnumbered, the BEF repulsed the first German attack but, later, the withdrawal of the French Fifth Army to the east forced the British to conduct retreat from Mons of which Ted was part. The retreat from Belgium continued into France and lasted until 5 September when the British and the French launched a counterattack against the Germans at the Battle of the Marne between Paris and Verdun. Ted was part of the BEF which advanced into the gap between the German First and Second Armies. The fighting resulted in the withdrawal of the German armies and the failure of the Schlieffen Plan, which had envisaged a single victory over the French during the opening weeks of the war. Ted fought a few days later at the Battle of the Aisne, which involved the British and French troops attacking the withdrawing German armies. The attack, however, was strongly resisted by the Germans and the allies' offensive was abandoned. Ted was wounded in the battle and invalided home. He could justifiably be proud of his service on the front line as he was mentioned in despatches six times. His recovery was reported in the *Wiltshire Gazette* on 8 October:

> Captain Colston is now much better than when he reached England. It appears that a lyddite shell burst close to him, and though he mercifully was not hit by any of the pieces, he was knocked over with great violence and was badly strained and bruised. He also had a sharp attack of appendicitis, which is now quiescent; the medical orders are that he must be allowed time to recover from the effects of his fall and shock before any operation takes place.

William referred to Ted's wounding in a letter to his mother dated 14 October and his tone is completely different to that of his letters a few weeks earlier, demonstrating that he now understood the sheer horror of this conflict: 'I am so glad to hear Ted has returned safely, ill as he is: it must be a great relief to Uncle Charlie and Aunt Rosie to see him again; the accounts of the fighting are really terrible. I do hope he is not seriously ill, though I am afraid on the other hand that, if he gets well too soon, he will have to go out again.'

Although older than Ted, William and Ronnie were keen to volunteer and this extract from a letter from Ronnie to his father on 15 September 1914 captures the manoeuvring that took place to secure a commission: 'Thanks for Du Cane's letter; I shall most certainly go to 130 Bunhill Row when I come up, as he suggests. I heard from Lord Clifden [a family friend] yesterday, sending me a form to be filled up and sent to Lt. Colonel Tebbutt, commanding the Cambridgeshire regiment. Lord Clifden is also going to write to Lt. Colonel Tebbutt, but of course there may not be a vacancy. I had to be vetted and then get the form signed by my doctor. I should hear whether or not there is a vacancy by the end of this week.' There was no vacancy for him and he eventually served with the 8th City of London Regiment, gaining the rank of Lieutenant. Viscount Clifden's influence in Cambridgeshire stemmed from his ownership of Wimpole Hall (alongside Lanhydrock in Cornwall).

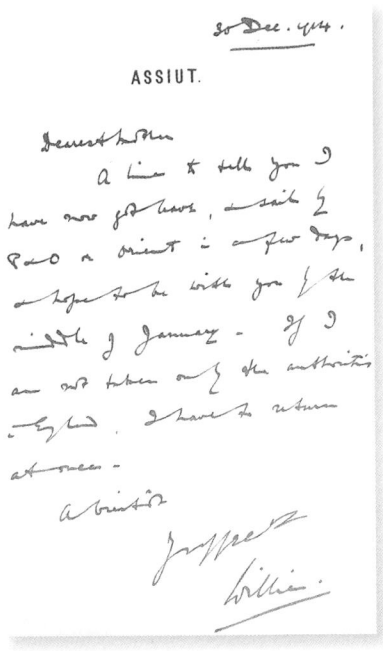

A letter from William in Egypt to Amy at the end of 1914.

Ronnie Baynes in the Great War.

William returned to Britain towards the end of the year, joined the Officers Training Corps in Lincoln's Inn and applied to join the Coldstream Guards Supplementary Reserve. His father knew General Lorne Campbell, late the Scots Guards, who was in charge of Officer Appointments, which, given that William was in his late thirties, facilitated his application.

William was commissioned as an Ensign on 16 February 1915, just before his 39th birthday, and prepared to fight on the Western Front. In March, Rory embarked from Folkestone for Calais on his way to the Front for the first time. His memoirs describe the journey from Calais

William Baynes in 1915.

to Meteren and then to the Front where his regiment, the Cameronians, were fighting as part of the BEF in the battle of Neuve-Chapelle in Artois, north-eastern France.

William arrived in France on 1 May to join the 2nd Battalion of the Coldstream Guards, which was part of the 4th Guards Brigade along with the 2nd Grenadiers, 3rd Coldstream and 1st Irish Guards. This was the same Brigade in which Ted had served as an officer in the 2nd Grenadiers, now preparing for the opening phase of the Battle of Festubert. In a letter[180] of 3 May to his mother, William described his first experience of life on the front line. From his position he could see the church of La Bassée beyond the German trenches, which were about 70 yards away. Censoring some of the soldiers' letters, he found mention of the heavy German shells known as Jack Johnsons flying around, while in reality conditions were relatively peaceful, with little shelling for several days. As a general rule, in a division of 20,000 men, only ten per cent would be at the front at any one time. The others would be in support in the second line of trenches or in reserve further back but still close enough in the case of an emergency.

In the event, the 2nd Coldstream was in reserve throughout this operation and did not go into action. Rory, however, did fight at Festubert and was wounded in the final stages. He was in a dugout when a shell landed beside him and smashed the lower part of one leg as well

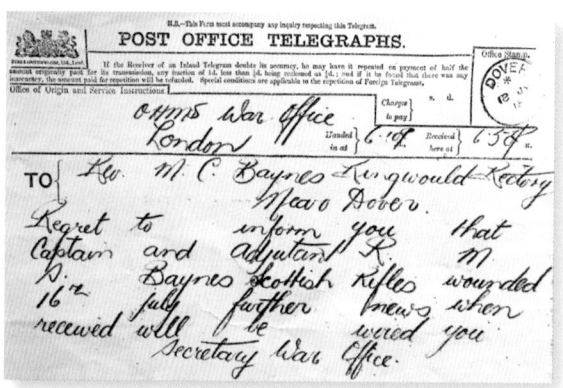

Telegram about Rory Baynes's wounding.

as severely lacerating the other. Back in England his leg was skilfully put together again and mended completely but there was a long period of convalescence and it was many months before he could walk comfortably.

After Festubert, William and the Guards Brigade were employed in various sectors on the front and in a letter of 13 June he wrote about the affliction which was to be mentioned so often in his letters and in so many other accounts of life in the trenches – mud: 'It is quite wonderful how well the men turn out after a tiring, muddy, rainy night: I do not know how they manage to clean themselves, and their rifles are always spotlessly clean.'

At this time, Ronnie was based in the Post Office Rifles in Ipswich and his name had gone forward for promotion to Lieutenant of the London Regiment. In a letter to his father, he wrote that: 'There are about 25,000 troops in Ipswich, including a lot of naval flying men; there is a large wireless station here too, I believe the Germans object to it. I hope you have all got respirators in case of gas attacks; I have and I gave mine to Ruby for her household.' He also referred to his father serving as a Special Constable: 'I hope your patriotic duties don't tire you out too much; it is rather disturbing to be roused in the middle of the night, isn't it?' Later in the war, Ronnie's professional background as a Chartered Surveyor was put to good use when he became a Danger Building Officer for the Ministry of Munitions.

On 17 August 1915, William was in the care of the 6th Field Ambulance for a few days due to dysentery. A letter told how unimpressed he was by a visiting General, offering odds of 50 to one on the war being over by November. He commented: 'Personally I think these over optimistic views are expressed as a matter of policy by all the high command, and I put little faith in them.'

Ted's recovery from his wounds saw him posted to Egypt in 1915 as head of the Imperial School of Instruction at Zeitoun in Cairo. The School was for the technical training of officers of the Colonial Forces, which Ted built up to a significant size from small beginnings with little assistance, leading to his promotion to Major in 1915 and being awarded the DSO, Distinguished Service Order, in 1916. Egypt's strategic importance had led to it being declared a protectorate in December 1914 by Britain and the deployment of troops to defend the Suez Canal, which connected Britain with the oil-producing countries of the Persian Gulf as well as with India.

Silhouette of Christopher Baynes as a Special Constable (1915–19) in London.

William wrote home on 13 December saying they were back in billets 'after a sopping time in the trenches'. He described a patrol two nights before with a corporal and a few privates to see if the enemy wire had been cut by the British artillery. On the way back, having found the wire uncut, he went up to his waist in water and 'foolishly lost my revolver'. Back in the battalion area he found that '… special arrangements have now luckily been made, so that all patrollers can get back to a safe place to get dry and a change of clothes, but so far Hemmings [his soldier servant] has been quite unable to get my things clean'. The letter ends with an urgent request for a 'Savage's automatic pistol 380 with three spare magazines loaded, and khaki or leather case to go on the belt', which indicates how ill-equipped the army was on the Western Front.

Four days later, William was back in billets and wrote on 21 December of the Grenadier Regimental Band giving a concert the night before at one of the Soldiers' Clubs: 'The Band is apparently being kept out here now they have come, much against their will, as they are all professional musicians and not soldiers at all, and out here they merely get their pay of one shilling a day or whatever it is, instead of their pay as players at music halls, and such like.'

Six weeks later, on 8 February 1916, the Grenadier Band had gone home and William could write 'to the strains of "Our Band" which has lately arrived'. His long letter ended with an account of a new sport: 'We have spent quite a lot of time ratting in the trenches this last time, as Ferguson brought back a ferret from home with him, and we adopted someone's terrier that was wandering about on its own, and killed about 40 rats in the two days: at night the great moment is to shoot them by the light of an electric torch with a revolver, but the results are not quite so good.'

In April 1916 William's field address was No. 12 Casualty Clearing Station BEF. He explained that during a heavy enemy bombardment a shell 'knocked me down and partially buried me, but I was pleased to find I had one hand free and could clear my face, and I was quickly released, escaping with a slight bruise on my forehead and a few stiff muscles. I have no business to be in hospital at all really, but I do not think I shall be here long.' His wounding was reported in the *Morning Post* List on 10 April, the reading of which on a daily basis must have been harrowing for the soldiers' families back in Britain.

Back at Roundway, there was good news on 30 June in the 1916 King's Birthday Honours list when Charles was raised to the peerage. On 3 June he had written this letter to King George V on hearing that this honour was to be announced at the end of the month (signed in his second name):[181]

> To His Majesty The King
> Sir,
>
> May I be allowed, with my humble duty, to offer to your Majesty my grateful thanks
> for the honour you have been graciously pleased to bestow upon me. I can assure
> your Majesty that I deeply appreciate and value this signal mark of your favour and I
> remain Your Majesty's most obedient humble servant,
>
> Edward Colston

There was some speculation as to whether he would take the title of Baron Colston but his choice fell on the family seat and he became Baron Roundway of Roundway Park, Devizes. He was presented with an album containing over 2,000 signatures from the townspeople of Devizes.

Charles and Rosalind Colston in 1915 by Hugh Riviere (Devizes Town Council).

Charles's peerage was described in this way by Professor Sir David Cannadine in his book *The Decline and Fall of the British Aristocracy*: 'There were also country gentlemen, who had not held ministerial office, but whose claims to a peerage lay in the traditional combination of landownership, good works at the county level, and unostentatious service on the backbenches. They may already have been a dwindling band in the Commons, but those who survived were still able to go into the Lords … such creations continued throughout the First World War … Mr Charles Edward Colston of Roundway Park was created Lord Roundway …[182]

Charles was also Remount Officer for the district and Colonel of the Wiltshire Volunteer Battalion with which he had been involved throughout his adult life. He bought his own horses, worth perhaps thousands of pounds at £60 apiece, for his work as Remount Officer.

Charles Colston (front row centre) with the Wiltshire Yeomanry c1916.

Due to his lifelong deafness, Henry Robinson was not able to serve in the war. Instead he turned his attention to farming and could be found working on the Home Farm at all hours. In particular, he became an expert on Red Poll cattle of which there was a herd at Roundway.[183] The little house and garden Newlands, that had been built near Belvedere Wood in the 1850s for Charles's brother Edward, who suffered from TB, were used during the War, appropriately enough, by injured soldiers during their recovery at nearby Braeside House.[184] Nowhere else on the Roundway estate was used in this way during the war, unlike the experience of many other country houses at this time, which were requisitioned for use as auxiliary hospitals and convalescent homes.

In France, on 1 July 1916, the Battle of the Somme started after a week of bombardment of the German trenches by the British. Not surprisingly, William was at pains in a letter of 17 July to reassure his family about his safety by claiming that '… you need not be worried about me as I never fight myself. We spend most of our time digging ditches by night'. This proved to be unfounded optimism as only a week later a short note from William dated 24 July from No. 14 General Hospital announced a return to England in a few days: 'I have merely a flesh wound in my arm below the shoulder. A pellet, quite harmless, but will take some weeks to heal. I am not supposed to write, so will wait till we meet.' Fortunately, the bone was not hit. The Battles of Verdun and the Somme continued into the autumn and in September 1916 the Germans started building the Hindenburg Line behind the existing front line. William was back in France on 11 October at the Guards Division Base Depot at Harfleur, near Le Havre. After a spell there, he rejoined the 2nd Battalion of the Coldstream Guards at Carnoy in the Somme sector, where the Division was resting, retraining and receiving reinforcements following heavy fighting: 'I have reached here once more but, as of course I knew, there is hardly an officer here that I know.' His distress at finding that so many of his friends were either dead or wounded was acute; he never really got over their loss throughout the rest of his life.

William's letter of 20 November reported that he had been attached to No. 2 Company because of the inexperience of the officers left there, though only 'as adviser, with strict injunctions not to run the show myself'. These orders proved impracticable and he was forced to assume control due to the 'uselessness of the official Company Commander'. The Somme mud was now so bad that a 'week ago three or four men got stuck and were only released four days later'. He went on to say: 'We remained for three days in these trenches, the most uncomfortable I think I have ever spent.' On the last day, the officers' rations were three sardines and a handful of biscuits each and the relieving battalion eventually arrived six hours late. The letter ended: 'I am perfectly fit and at the same time I cannot understand how anyone survives it.'

After the end of the battle of the Somme, William wrote to his mother on 14 December 1916 that he was back from 'the wettest and muddiest trenches I have yet seen', adding that 'it is astounding that war can be carried on under present conditions'. On a more positive note, he reported that 'I am now commanding No. 2 Company in my own right,' and that his third star has been applied for. He mentioned his platoon commanders: 'One of my officers, Porritt, was very slightly hit the last time in, and I now have Fielding and St Leger with me, both very competent and agreeable.'

With Christmas coming he asked for 17 plum puddings to be sent out, and for any number of balaclavas and socks for the men of the Company. The day after William wrote this letter, the French launched the final attack of the Battle of Verdun and it was not until 6 January 1917 that William and his whole Battalion could have their Christmas dinner which he described in detail in a letter written the following day from 'a comfortable mess room for these parts with a table and two benches, and a fireplace'.

In February, the Germans began their staged withdrawal to the Hindenburg Line. On 13 March it was the turn of the German forces opposite the Guards Division to begin their retreat and, on 18 March, William's letter made a cynical comment on the official British communiqués which were 'taking advantage of the Hun withdrawal to make everyone think that we are doing an enormous push, but I don't suppose any intelligent person pays much attention to them nowadays'. He described some of the booby traps left behind by the withdrawing enemy, including 'jars of beer which explode on touch'. As his Battalion moved forward he wryly observed that: 'There are some cavalry dancing about again, which is always a source of much amusement here.'

In April 1917, the Germans completed their withdrawal to the Hindenburg Line and President Woodrow Wilson of the United States declared war on Germany. At the end of May, William's Division travelled north by train to Belgium to take up a position at Boeringhe, near Ypres, ready for the Battle of Passchendaele. The diary of William St Leger, who was serving with William Baynes, mentions William whom he calls 'Judge' and describes the battle and the horrific sights and dilemmas that the young men had to endure:

> Zero was at 3.50am. There had been firing all the night but at that moment every gun began to speak. The whole horizon to the north-east, east and south-east was lit by one continuous dancing flame composed of jagged flashes of bursting shells. The guns made a deafening row. The solitary broken walls of a ruined village with its shattered spectre of trees showed up grimly against the blazing horizon. Sergeant Harris gave a short laugh: 'A fine picture of civilisation, sir!' he said. 'Fritz's Reveille', said another.

St Leger then led his men forward behind a creeping barrage until digging in on the first objective at 9am under heavy shelling by the enemy. The boundary with the Battalion on the flank had to be decided:

Went across to Grenadiers on right. I found half a dozen who asked permission to shoot a Hun inside a dug-out, who was terribly injured and had, they said, been asking them to shoot him. I did not like the idea, but while I hesitated Judge [William Baynes] came along. I asked the German in my best Dutch whether he would like us to shoot him but he said he could not understand and waved his arms from east to west. I thought he meant his pals would come and eat us. 'He wants to be taken down,' said Judge, 'don't shoot him.'

Shortly afterwards St Leger was wounded and was evacuated from the Front for treatment. William survived unscathed and was awarded the Military Cross for his gallantry, later reported in the *London Gazette*:[185] 'For conspicuous gallantry and devotion to duty during an attack upon an hostile position. He showed the greatest personal courage and contempt of danger, setting such an example to his men that they changed front and formed up on the line marked out for them, as if on parade. He led them through a very heavy barrage, and afterwards during consolidation walked up and down in the open urging his men to dig, exposed all the time to hostile machine-gun fire. It was entirely due to his magnificent example that the difficult manoeuvre of changing front under fire was successfully accomplished.'

This entry in the *London Gazette* was transcribed by his father in the latter's note book of family history and demonstrates the mirror image of the casualty lists in the newspapers, namely the public testimony to soldiers' gallantry of which William's family and friends must have been very proud. Christopher kept a photograph taken in the first part of September 1917 of William's No. 2 Company on the back of which he wrote: 'Captain W.E.C. Baynes in Command in centre of officers. Officer on W.E.C. B's right is Fielding, afterwards killed.'

William Baynes (third row up seated in centre) with No. 2 Company of 2nd Battalion Coldstream Guards.

A month later, on 20 September, the focus of the British offensive at Ypres changed and in the battle of Menin Road William was wounded. Among his letters there is a short note written on 23 September to one of his subalterns, F. W. Butler-Thwing. On the back there is a brief sentence in another hand: 'Last message from dear old Judge. Wounded 24 Sept. 1917. Please keep.' There is also the official telegram to his father, dated 27 September, recording 'multiple gunshot wounds, severe', which included breaking one of the bones of his right wrist.

Mrs Neil Baynes, wife of William's uncle, was working with a women's charity based at Boulogne and visited him in hospital at Le Touquet.[186] She wrote in a letter to his family that: 'Willy was hit by a shell which apparently burst within two feet of him and killed 12 men.' She said that he was suffering badly from shock and was very weak; also 'he has what he saw very much on his mind – the death of 12 of his men'. He wanted, however, for his parents to be told that he was 'perfectly well'. Although he made a good recovery, William did not return to the Battalion but had a spell on the staff at London District Headquarters in Carlton House Terrace, where he was a staff captain.

In 1918, the tide of the War was finally turning in the allies' favour. In the Middle East, the British made a major breakthrough at the Battle of Megiddo against the Turkish forces in Palestine, and there was little opposition to General Sir Edmund Allenby's advance towards Damascus and beyond. In the autumn William was posted to GHQ Egypt, where he became legal adviser to Allenby who, by 1 November, had completed the capture of Baghdad, Beirut and the oil fields of Mosul. It is likely that William made contact with Ted Colston, who was by then commanding 233

Ted Colston (from second left) in Egypt in his uniform as a brigadier.

Infantry Brigade (Egyptian Expeditionary Force) as a temporary Brigadier-General and for which he was awarded the CMG, Companion of the Order of St Michael and St George, in 1918.

With the allies' corresponding advance on the Western Front, a German delegation came to discuss terms for an armistice on 7 November. Kaiser Wilhelm II abdicated on 9 November and the armistice came into force on 11 November at 11am.

PART 3

DECLINE

Left: Details of the Wyatt ceiling in the circular room at Roundway prior to demolition in 1954 (Historic England).

Charles outside Roundway in World War I.

Devizes and Roundway War Memorial (©Wiltshire Museum, Devizes).

15

'Never Glad Confident Morning Again!'

THE GREAT WAR has been memorably described as dividing the period before 1914 and after 1918 'like a band of scorched earth'.[187] On the face of it, this was not the case with Roundway since the Colston and Baynes cousins escaped mortal injury[188] and the day-to-day activities on the estate continued after the war in much the same way as they had been conducted in pre-war times.

Despite the apparent normality at Roundway, the acute strains exerted by the war quickly became apparent in three main ways: illness brought on by stress, financial difficulties and problems of adjustment after four years of conflict. The strain of William serving on the front line most likely contributed to Amy's death at the age of 68 in January 1919. In Lilian's papers there is an envelope with these words written on it: 'Christmas card, letters etc from Darling Amy, Christmas 1918 and Jan. 1919'. There are three letters in the envelope from Amy in London to Lilian at Roundway which are cheerful but the third one hints at Amy's illness in her last days:

Edwardian photographs of Amy in formal attire and writing at her desk in London.

3rd January 1919

Dearest Sister

Thank you so much for your <u>2</u> dear letters, and will you please thank Hall [Lilian's maid] for kindly seeing about the chickens coming up every Saturday; no.1 arrived yesterday and looks a <u>very</u> nice and big one and so fresh that we are keeping it till tomorrow, the weather being good for keeping.

Thank you dear for all you so v. kindly say about my staying with you, but I think I must however look after my own family and household as long as I can. It is a <u>great</u> rest however and pleasant change to have lunch or tea with you now and then, and we have time for a quiet chat.

Thank you for the pretty Xmas roses and bits of green, and for doing them and the lovely orchids up so nicely. I do hope your poor throat is better – we are so glad to hear you will be back on Monday.

In haste – Yr ever loving

Amy

Shortly after this, Amy went to Roundway where she died on 28 January. The nature of her illness is not clear but she had long suffered bouts of ill health, exacerbated by her concern for William during the war. This was the time (January 1918–December 1920) of the Spanish flu pandemic (which infected 500 million people around the world and resulted in 50–100 million deaths) but there is no indication that Amy suffered in this way.

Amy's funeral service at St James's Church was conducted by her brother-in-law Rev. Malcolm Baynes and by Rev. A.S. Bryant. Her coffin, in the words of the *Wiltshire Gazette*, was covered with 'a handsome pall of purple velvet and cream satin, used for the first time at the funeral of Lady Baynes's mother nineteen years ago' and was brought from Roundway on a hand bier with Sir Christopher and Ronnie walking immediately behind (William was unable to attend as he was still in Palestine, about which he must have been devastated given their very close relationship). Amy was buried in the family tomb in the church graveyard by the Crammer pond in Devizes, the entrance to which was lined with ivy by the gardeners at Roundway.

Although Amy was not as vivid and forthright a character as her sister, she was cultured, intelligent, long-suffering and much loved by her husband and her children. Above all, she was a gentle character whom Dorothy described in this way in *Enter A Child*: 'What she really enjoyed was reading her "dear *Times*" over the drawing-room fire, going to concerts, collecting Chelsea figures, and eating buns when they were hot.'

The second post-war problem at Roundway was financial strain. In September 1919 Charles sold 535 acres of land in Rowde, which were bought by Wiltshire County Council by private agreement and sub-divided into smallholdings for men returning from the war. It is possible that Charles made this disposal to help ex-servicemen, to whom he had very close links, and who were returning to a very difficult peace-time environment. During the war, the cost of living increased significantly and there had been strikes and much labour unrest. The first national Remembrance Day ceremony held in 1921 where poppies were on display was also marked by a protest by ex-servicemen about high unemployment, poor housing and delays in the payment of their war pensions.

It is likely, however, that Charles's Rowde disposal was primarily driven by financial necessity. In April 1920 he also sold the family's estate at West Lydford by private contract to a variety of new landowners, mainly tenants of the farms. He retained, however, the gift of the living for the Rector of the Church, which was valued at £350 a year in 1923 (£20,800 today).[189] Charles's land disposals at this time were typical of many landowners who sold peripheral parts of their land holdings rather than the core estate.

The causes of Charles's financial problems pre-dated the war, going back to the agricultural depression of the late 19th century, but the war and its immediate aftermath undoubtedly made things worse, particularly increases in taxation and the Corn Production Act of 1917. In September 1918, income tax doubled as did super-tax from eight per cent to 16 per cent. The 1917 Corn Production Act prevented landowners from increasing agricultural rents and gave the government the power to regulate and enforce cultivation of land in order to maximise food production. It left tenant farmers in a relatively strong position as corn prices were high and rents were frozen, which enabled a significant number to buy their own farms after the war. Landowners such as Charles were now opting to sell as the net yield on their estates had fallen by about 50 per cent on average during the war while the price of land, driven by the demand from tenants benefiting from their favourable farming conditions, had doubled over the same period.

The timing of Charles's disposals proved either very shrewd or extremely fortunate given that, in 1921, after he had sold, land prices started to fall due to declining world food prices and the removal of guaranteed government support. This became known by arable farmers as the 'Great Betrayal' when the government, without warning, stopped guaranteeing corn prices in 1921 and returned to the free market due to the spiralling cost of state subsidy after the sharp fall in world corn prices. Yet, despite his timely sale of land, Charles was still under financial pressure in 1922 with lower cereal prices affecting his remaining land on the Roundway estate as glimpsed in a letter that he wrote to Lilian on 9 August 1922 offering financial advice to his sister, '… you already have great difficulty in keeping your home going, as we have here'.

Charles's disposals were part of an extraordinary break-up of estates between 1918 and 1927 which saw one quarter of all the rural land in England and Wales change hands, with both tenant farmers and new money providing the demand. As a result, owner-occupied land rose from 11 per cent in 1914 to 37 per cent in 1927. A continuation of higher taxation and the resumption of the agricultural depression led to this unprecedented volume of land disposals. The historical context was described by the historian Professor F.M.L. Thompson in these terms: 'Such an enormous and rapid transfer of land had not been seen since the confiscations and sequestrations of the Civil War, such a permanent transfer not since the dissolution of the monasteries in the 16th century. Indeed, a transfer on this scale and in such a short space of time had probably not been equalled since the Norman Conquest.'

Another consequence of the war was its emotional strain and the difficult process of returning to civilian life. By 1929 there were 65,000 ex-servicemen in mental hospitals. Alec Agar-Robartes, son of Viscount Clifden, who maintained a touching correspondence with Dorothy during the war, saw his mental health deteriorate throughout the 1920s and he eventually committed suicide by jumping from an upstairs window at his family's house in Great Stanhope Street in London in 1930.[190] William's anxiety is captured in this excerpt from an article written by his young cousin John Baynes, son of Rory, many years later in the *Guards Magazine*:

> The full significance of that close companionship formed by shared hardships in the trenches was brought home to me in the late 1960s, when I talked to Sir William about the war not long before he died at the age of 95. He started to tell me about the time he returned to the 2nd Coldstream on 2 November 1916 to find so few people left whom he knew. The memory was too much for him and he broke down completely, quite unable to continue the conversation. After a time, we went on to talk of other more mundane matters.

William was demobilised in March 1920, returning for a time to the Egyptian Legal Service where he eventually became the Chief Inspector of Native Courts in the Ministry of Justice. Despite the difficulties of adjustment, it was always a matter of great pride to William that he was one of the few Supplementary Reserve officers to serve with the 2nd Battalion of the Coldstream Guards during the war and that he was among the small number of wartime officers who were invited to become members of the Nulli Secundus Club, the elective dining club for past and present Coldstream Guards officers, after the war. He was also allowed to

A watercolour portrait of William in 1920 and his farm in Somerset.

retain his rank of captain. He later bought and ran a small farm in Somerset, a good place to escape the bitter memories of war.

Despite everything, the Colston family's day-to-day life in the years after the war seemed to continue in much the same way as it had done before. Charles was admitted as an Honorary Freeman of the Society of Merchant Venturers in Bristol and was a Governor of Colston's School from 1916 to 1925. Ted continued with his military career, commanding the 2nd Battalion of the Grenadier Guards in the early 1920s, and he, Gladys and Betty were regular visitors to Roundway and a pony was kept for Betty for her visits in the summer.

Lieut.-Colonel the Hon. E. M. Colston commands the 2nd Battalion Grenadier Guards just ordered to leave Aldershot on Saturday for Chanak, the strategic key of the Dardanelles.

Photograph of Ted in *Daily Sketch* 21st September 1922
(©Wiltshire Museum, Devizes).

Clockwise from top left: Gladys Colston in early 1920s.

Ted and Betty Colston with hounds and horses at Roundway c1920.

Photograph in *The Times* 25th September 1922 of Ted (right) as the Commanding Officer, 2nd Battalion Grenadier Guards.

When in 1920 two West Country packs of harriers – the Stanton Drew and the Wells Subscription – amalgamated as the Stanton Drew and Wells Harriers under the mastership of Capt. Rouse-Boughton, Ted decided to dispose of his hounds to the new hunt. Henry Robinson continued to study hound pedigrees and became one of the leading authorities in the country. That the Roundway pack were so highly valued for the contribution they made to the new improved beagle was as much a credit to him as to Ted.

Henry Robinson was also enjoying his enthusiasm for music. In a letter to Sir Christopher Baynes in 1922 from Roundway, Henry wrote '... the Bandmaster at the Barracks sent over to know if I would play in the Regt String Band for a large Dance in aid of St Dunstans so I had to go through some of the music in spare time. It was a great success with a Whist Drive & Dance and afterwards they cleared about £100.'

At this time Lilian was living in Lowndes Street (just around the corner from the Baynes family in Lowndes Square) and the pattern of her life in the summer months of 1921 and 1922 is recorded on a slip of paper which shows how it revolved around her maid Hall going on holiday and Lilian's visits to her various friends and relations: she was invited in the summer of 1922 to stay at Torry Hill in Kent with the Leigh Pembertons, Seckford Hall in Suffolk with the Woodleys, Much Marcle in Herefordshire with the Whiteheads and Radipole Hall near Weymouth with Mrs Ewart.

Just after the General Election in November 1922, Charles wrote to Christobel to say that she could not use Rosalind's ticket for observing the State Opening of Parliament: 'Alas only the Peeress whose name is inserted on your aunt's ticket can make use of it – it is expressly so stated in the Lord Great Chamberlain's instructions which we have just carefully read. I am more than sorry but I fear I am helpless ... This epistle is wet with my tears. Yr affectionate Uncle.' Rosalind had a rose named after her, 'Lady Roundway', which was raised by B.R. Cant & Sons, Colchester, and awarded the Gold Medal at the Summer Show in 1923.

Normality in the family's life, however, suddenly came to an end. On the morning of 8 August 1924, a crashing of glass awakened Ted and Gladys at one o'clock at their London home,

The Lady Roundway rose.

Hamilton House in Ashburn Place in South Kensington, as was reported in the press. They went up to Betty's bedroom and, to their horror, discovered that the bed was empty and the window open at the bottom sash. Her body was found 50–60ft below, having fallen through the glass-roofed scullery. Her death was instantaneous and her face escaped injury, and when carried back to bed she looked as though she was sleeping peacefully.

That evening Betty, aged 14, had been to the Haymarket Theatre to see the 'Great Adventure' with a Mr Hunter. Before she went to sleep, she checked her caterpillars in a glass box on the windowsill. She had been looking forward to playing in the handicap singles at the Hurlingham tennis tournament later that week and then going for her usual summer holidays at Roundway, where her little pony had been shod in anticipation of her visit.

Ted and Gladys's anguish is glimpsed in two letters from Ted to Dorothy. In the first, written in a poignant postscript to the text that he must have

Betty Colston.

written beforehand, he wrote: 'Betty is dead: it's just too awful. She fell out of her bedroom window and must have been killed instantly, no pain poor darling. The bottom seems to have dropped out of our world.'

The second letter is addressed to Dorothy at 8 York Terrace in Sidmouth where she was on holiday with her sister Christobel:

Tabbie Darling

Thank you so much, I can't say more. The Funeral is on Wed at 2.30 at Devizes, only expecting flowers, please. Ronnie brought round a lovely bunch of lilies.

Please thank Pru for the letter. Gladys can't write at present and I can scarcely see out of my eyes. WDG [William Darby Griffith] has had an operation.

Love to you both, Ted.

PS: The little one goes down by motor Tues. Nothing matters now. Father does not know yet. A wonderful message of sympathy from Queen & King also the Duke, I know them all personally.

The first of these letters was kept by Dorothy in an envelope on which she had written in pencil 'Darling Betty', and also included three photographs of Betty, two of them with Ted which clearly shows their strong bond.

Roundway Park
Devizes.

Dec 24th

Dear Aunt Lily
    Thank you for money and the book and the Calendar, you gave me 2/6 with the book and After you sent me 3/- by Post.

With Love
Betty.

There is also a thank-you letter written by Betty from Roundway to her great Aunt Lilian and a photograph of a cross made of lilies and other flowers, which was probably put on Betty's grave in the Devizes cemetery. Her parents placed a stone angel on her grave and cut an opening in the woods so that the family could watch over her from Roundway Park. The Colston family never fully recovered from Betty's death.

There was much speculation about the cause of Betty's fall from her bedroom window. Jill Hepple, a cousin of Gladys's, was told by her mother, Beatrix Pratt, that Betty had committed suicide on discovering that Ted was not her father. According to Beatrix, Mr Hunter, with whom Betty went to the theatre on her last evening, was indiscreet enough to tell her the truth about her parentage and that he himself was her biological father.[191] It is thought that the conception was one of the earliest cases of artificial insemination by donor (AID) with the donor, Mr Hunter, being a friend who was an admirer of Gladys.[192] It was allegedly necessary because Ted had been rendered infertile by having contracted mumps as a teenager. Another factor may have been reduced fertility in both parents due to inter-marriage in their respective families.

Irene Cooper, who was lady's maid to Rosalind at Roundway between 1934 and 1938, understood that Betty had been sleepwalking to which she was prone and had done so when staying at Roundway.[193] Major John Bartholomew, a family friend and later chairman of Wadworth's Brewery in Devizes, had heard that Betty was leaning out of her bedroom window to see an aeroplane that was flying over, lost her balance and fell on to the conservatory roof below.[194] This seems the most likely explanation, but we do not know for certain.

Betty's grave in the Devizes cemetery in front of the Colston family tomb, surmounted by a cross.

Later, in the early 1930s, Jill Hepple was given Betty's riding clothes and dolls' house while her brothers were given lead soldiers that had been Ted's as a child.[195] It had taken many years before Gladys could bear to part with Betty's possessions.

Ted and Betty Colston standing in the archway at Roundway.

16

The Inter-war Years

CHARLES died a year after Betty on 17 June 1925 at the age of 71. Lilian kept an envelope of keepsakes on which she wrote 'My Darling Brother' in pencil. It includes a copy of the order of service from his funeral; a lock of his son Ted's hair and some photographs, including a picture of him at Eton, in uniform outside the front of Roundway, and at a shooting party in Scotland.

There are also numerous press cuttings about Charles's funeral on Saturday 20 June from both national and local newspapers. The article in the *Morning Post* refers to his health having been 'bad for the past few years' and *The Times* said that 'he had been in failing health for a long time'. There is a magnificent photograph of the funeral cortege in the *Bath and Wilts Chronicle and Herald* dated 22 June. The report in the *Wiltshire Advertiser* provides a vivid account of the funeral and the widespread affection and respect felt for Charles in Devizes and beyond:

> The scene in the Devizes Cemetery on Saturday afternoon last when the body of Lord Roundway was committed to the ground near the grave of the only daughter of his only son, the present Lord Roundway, was a striking tribute alike to the 'Squire of Roundway', as he was locally and affectionately known; to the soldier, and to the man of county affairs.
>
> The tribute to the 'Squire of Roundway', and in this connection we write in the wide scope and embrace Devizes and the neighbourhood, was symbolised in that great company of mourners from the neighbourhood which stood four and five deep

THE LATE LORD ROUNDWAY.

LARGE AND REPRESENTATIVE GATHERING AT FUNERAL.

IMPRESSIVE OBSEQUIES.

The scene in the Devizes Cemetery on Saturday afternoon last when the body of Lord Roundway was committed to the ground near the grave of the only daughter of his only son, the present Lord Roundway, was a striking tribute —alike to the " Squire of Roundway," as he was locally and affectionately known; to the soldier, and to the man of county affairs. The tribute to the " Squire of Roundway," and in this connection we write in the wide scope and embrace Devizes and the neighbourhood, was symbolised in that great company of mourners from the neighbourhood which stood four and five deep on the confines of the space set aside for the family mourners and those in a representative capacity; that to the soldier by that solemn single line of civilian clad veterans who had served under the deceased Peer when he commanded the old 2nd Volunteer Battalion of the Wiltshire Regiment, and who thus paid a silent and impressive tribute—by a representative contingent, in full military dress, of the 4th Battalion Wiltshire Regiment, into which the old Volunteer Battalion was merged—by officers in their uniform, and by the buglers of the Grenadier Guards, commanded by the deceased's son, the present Lord Roundway; that to the public spirit of him who served his country so well by his old colleagues on the County Council, on the Bench, and in other administrative organisations—together forming a gathering of over 2,000, the largest company assembled at a Devizes funeral for many years, and in all probability the largest ever seen at a funeral here.

Nor was this the only evidence of respect and esteem in which the deceased Peer was held. The general appearance of the town testified further to this; flags at the churches and public and other buildings were at half-mast, windows were black-boarded and blinds drawn, 'he bells at St. James's, Southbroom, and at St. Mary's tolled out their message, and the whole of the inhabitants seemed to be personally bereaved.

THE LATE LORD ROUNDWAY
In the uniform of the 2nd V.B. Wiltshire Regiment.

on the confines of the space set aside for the family mourners and those in a representative capacity ... together forming a gathering of over 2,000, the largest company assembled at a Devizes funeral for many years, and in all probability the largest ever seen at a funeral here.

Nor was this the only evidence of respect and esteem in which the deceased Peer was held. The general appearance of the town testified further to this: flags at the churches and public and other buildings were at half-mast, windows were black-boarded, and blinds drawn, the bells at St James's, Southbroom, and at St Mary's tolled out their message, and the whole of the inhabitants seemed to be personally bereaved.

Charles's body was laid out on a purple-draped catafalque in the drawing room at Roundway before being conveyed on a hand bier to the cemetery with the chief mourners following on foot down Quakers Walk.

The mourners included Charles's immediate family and staff as well as the Baynes and Murray cousins, the Duke of Beaufort, the Marquess of Bath, Lord John Joicey Cecil and Percy Hurd, the MP for Devizes. There were also hundreds of other official mourners representing different organisations in which Charles had been involved. The members of Roundway staff present were listed and reference was made to the head gardener, Mr Snelgrove, having lined the grave with ivy and flowers. The newspaper report concludes by saying that the memory of Lord Roundway 'remains as an example of a perfect English gentleman whose life was devoted to public service'.

The gross value of Charles's estate as per probate of 13 October 1925 was £145,389 (£8.7m today) and the net value after death duties was £118,194 (£7m today). In his will, Charles left his personal possessions to Rosalind and the residuary of his estate to Ted.

Charles's concern for the staff at Roundway was highlighted in an article in *The Times* of 30 October 1925 which reported the provisions of his will. He left £200 (£12,000 today) each to his butler, John Savage, and his housekeeper, Anne Davies; £150 to his head housemaid, Mary Rambridge; £50 each to his footman, Henry Robinson, his coachman, John Bond, and his estate carpenter, Henry King, and six months' wages to his other domestic servants. These were generous bequests but they were also part of a landowning tradition of providing estate staff with de facto pensions.

Rosalind continued to live at Roundway until her death in 1938, while Ted and Gladys remained in London at Hamilton House in Ashburn Terrace, Kensington, with family members living nearby, including Lilian in Walton Street and the Baynes family in Lowndes Square. London continued to play a major part in the Colston family life, just as it had done in the Victorian era when Charles and Rosalind split their time between Mayfair and Wiltshire and Louisa, Lillian and Amy's family all lived in London.

Rosalind continued to be active in the life of Devizes after Charles's death, opening the park (now without fallow

Lilian Colston's house in Walton Street, Chelsea.

Postcard of the deer at Roundway (©Wiltshire Museum).

Rosalind (centre of front row) at Hillworth House, Devizes c1930.

deer)[196] and grounds at Roundway for functions and attending them herself. She was described as being 'of a quiet, unassuming disposition: affectionate, and one with whom those of not such high social-standing were always at their ease' and she provided financial and personal support for a wide range of local organisations, not least the Conservative Party. She was president of the Devizes Division Women's Unionist Association and Dame President of the Devizes Habitation of the Primrose League.[197]

The tradition of providing supplies from the Roundway estate to relatives in London also continued. In a letter from Rosalind to Christobel of 26 July 1933, she wrote about sending bracken for therapeutic purposes: 'I am sending the bracken on Thursday by train. I don't think there is any occasion to make the whole mattress of it – I should put it on the top of the existing one and tie it round so that it can't move. Will you let the people know the day? I don't think you understand that Frank King is unable to do <u>anything</u> much less cut bracken which is rather hard work.'

Irene Cooper, who was a housemaid at Roundway between 1934 and 1939, spoke respectfully of Rosalind.[198] She remembered Ted and Gladys as being very pleasant but distant and that Ted did not get on with Rosalind, or, in Irene's words, 'did not work with his mother at all'. It is not clear exactly why although it seems from comments made by family members that Rosalind was a more robust character whereas Ted was much more easy-going. In contrast to the public perception of her being unassuming, the private persona has been described as domineering and fiery. Perhaps the truth lies somewhere in between. Whatever the family dynamics, Rosalind led a fairly solitary life in her widowhood, with only occasional visits from Ted and Gladys. Ronnie Baynes wrote of Roundway in a letter to his father, dated 22 September 1929, that 'so few of the family ever come here now, which is sad'.

Ted pursued his career as a regular officer in the Grenadier Guards. His promotion to Brigadier-General had been temporary during the war and he dropped back to the rank of lieutenant colonel afterwards. He was made a substantive colonel in 1924 on succeeding to the command of his battalion. He took it to Constantinople when there was every probability of an outbreak of war with Turkey and played a part in the escape of the ex-Sultan from the city. In 1927 he was given command of 131st East Surrey (Territorial) Infantry Brigade, a position which he held until 1931. His duties would not have been onerous and could be carried out while living in London.

In 1931, Lilian Colston died in Kensington at the age of 78, after a long illness. She was buried in the family tomb at St James's Church in Devizes. Lilian left her estate, valued at £29,801 (£1.7m) to her Baynes nephews and nieces. Her very fine china collection was bequeathed to Christobel and Dorothy. In the family papers there is a collection of touching letters written by relatives and friends, chiefly to Christobel, expressing their sorrow at Lilian's death and often thanking her for sending mementoes of Lilian: their cousin J.H. Murray wrote to Christobel on 6 February 1931 saying of Lilian: 'I have seen little of her of late years; but in my early life she was a very potent influence. With the exception of my own sister there is no woman whom I have known for so long. I think we began to meet about 1867; and I can remember dancing with her in a house in Great George Street on the night on which you were born!'

Part of Lilian Colston's china collection.

Correspondents also included servants who had worked for Lilian, such as Emma Hall who had retired from her service to Cambridge and wrote on 30 March 1931:

> I am writing to thank you for every thing you have so kindly sent me. I should have been Happier if you had kept more but hope you would have done so if you had wished to do so as I have no Right to so much as you have sent in every way.
>
> I do thank you for the Water Colour of Stoke Bruerne Rectory done by yourself and the Church by Miss Dorothy. My sister and I have quite a lot of Water Colours in our little Home that you have both given me. I do value them for they remind me of <u>very</u> <u>happy</u> <u>times</u> I have been with Miss Colston – not of the sad. I do try to think of that time more than the latter. I cannot forgive myself for being so selfish. My only comfort is I know dear Miss Colston forgave me from Her dear letter and I must try to live that I may go where we know she is. Oh the Joy for Her to be at Rest. I ought not to trouble you with my Grief but you are so kind to me I feel I cannot help myself …

In 1932 Ted retired from the army with the honorary rank of Brigadier-General. In the same year he became an exon of the Yeoman of the Guard and in 1937 he led the parade of the Yeomen in the Coronation of King George VI and Queen Elizabeth. He continued to play an active role in running the estate and fulfilling his duties in the wider community of Devizes and Wiltshire.

During his two decades as head of the family, Ted was a Justice of the Peace and Deputy Lieutenant of Wiltshire. He was also variously President of the Devizes branch of the Old Contemptibles' Association, President of the Devizes Literary and Scientific Institute, Chairman of the Devizes and District Orthopaedic Crippled Children's Clinic, Vice-president of the British and Foreign Bible Society, President of the Devizes Troop of Boy Scouts, President of the Devizes Lawn Tennis Club, President of the Devizes Rugby Club and President of the Devizes and District branch of the Junior Imperial (or 'Imps') League.

At the end of 1932 Ted's cousin, the younger Christopher Darby Griffith,

Junior Imperial League or 'Imps' Ball in Devizes: (seated left to right) Mrs Joyce Wiltshire, Lord Roundway, E. Joliffe and Miss M. Cannings: (standing) J. Wiltshire and W. T. Dyke.

Padworth House garden front
(*Country Life*, 22 September 1922).

died, leaving the Padworth estate to him. Before his death, Christopher had been told by his doctor that he needed to have an eye operation for a cataract and he was extremely worried about going blind. He became very 'nervy and upset' and started to keep a pistol under his pillow. On Armistice Day, 11 November 1932, his maid, Kate Brimpton, went to wake him in the morning with his usual glass of hot water and found him dead; he had shot himself with his pistol.[199]

In addition to concerns about his health, Christopher may also have been worried about some of his investments losing money in the Wall Street Crash of 1929–31. Ted wrote to Christobel shortly after Chrisopher's death saying: 'Yes Padworth is most worrying, his investments were, or are, truly appalling.'

It was a tragic and lonely end for someone who was remembered fondly by his family and servants. Christopher had taken possession of Padworth after his mother Arabella died in 1891, kept it in good condition and was an energetic and generous host. There is a touching record of his busy social life and kindness as an employer in the reminiscences of Hilda Hearn who joined the staff of Padworth in May 1922 as a housemaid. In her memoirs, entitled *My Life in Domestic Service at Padworth House*,[200] she recalled how:

> … the Major had large week-end parties throughout the summer months, so it was essential to be installed to learn the running of the House before the season began. He was a very likeable person, and I am sure we were all anxious to give satisfaction in our work however hard it was, because he was so appreciative. He never made the lower class feel inferior, and whenever he had occasion to make a speech, he always managed to refer to his dislike of class distinction. He never used foul language, and to my knowledge only said 'Damn' on one occasion, when a heavy curtain rod became dislodged and fell on his head.

The overall inheritance was very substantial, with a gross value of £187,604 (£12.9m today). Padworth would have been left to Ronnie Baynes if he and Cecilia (née Day), whom he had married in 1930 when he was 50 and she was 35, had been blessed with a son but unfortunately there were no children born to the marriage.[201] Ted decided to sell the main house and much of the estate, which totalled about 900 acres and included three farms, substantial woodland, the common, a mill, two pubs and various houses and cottages. He kept the Croft[202] where Josephine Creasy, who ran the Roundway Kennels in Devizes, went to live and to which the kennels were relocated.

Ted was fortunate to find a buyer given that the crash of 1929–31 had led to a deep recession and mass unemployment. Between 1928 and 1931 the value of all agricultural produce declined by a third, which depressed agricultural rents to the extent that in 1936 they were at the same level as they had been in 1800. Land prices fell to about one third of the level seen in the 1860s.[203] Demand for country houses fell accordingly; the President of the Auctioneers and Estate Agents' Institute declared in 1930 that 'the large family residences, especially of the older type, are practically unsaleable'. Some were turned

Ronnie and Cecilia's wedding in 1930.

into schools (as eventually proved to be the case for Padworth), other institutions and offices but many houses were also demolished, contributing to a total of about 130 which disappeared between the wars.[204]

Ted brought many of the treasures from Padworth to Roundway, including the paintings, which had been described in detail in a 12-page article about Padworth in two successive editions of *Country Life* in September 1922 with beautiful photographic illustrations. The pictures included portraits by Gainsborough commissioned by Christopher Griffith (who had expanded the house at Padworth in 1769) of his second wife Catherine and

The drawing room at Padworth (*Country Life*, 22 September 1922).

himself. There was also a portrait by Godfrey Kneller of Sarah Chicheley, the daughter of the Darby Griffith's ancestor Sir John Chicheley, Master-General of the Ordnance in 1674.

Ted also brought to Roundway Lord Nelson's Order Book of 1801, which had been bequeathed by Admiral Henry Darby, one of Nelson's most trusted captains.[205] The collection included several pieces of furniture by Chippendale and some fine English silver plate, which had originally come to Padworth with Arabella Darby Griffith from the Colston family. The Padworth pictures were mentioned in a letter to Christobel from her cousin June who, with William, was staying at Roundway in the spring of 1936: 'Henry welcomed us with joy and said in a loud aside "I'm very glad to see you!" When Aunt Rosie disappeared, he beckoned to me and rushed me round the Padworth pictures, lighting them up with a huge electric lamp.'

Colston's Cottages, completed in 1937.

Ted continued his father's twin traditions of attending to the legacy of Edward Colston the Philanthropist, by opening in 1937 some newly built Colston almshouses in East Sheen, Mortlake, and of generosity to Devizes. On 18 July 1936 he and the Mayor of Devizes Cllr R.P. Shepherd opened the new outdoor swimming-pool on land that Ted had made available to the town at Rotherstone. The new pool, which was designed in a 1930s style and cost £3,500 (£243,000 today), measured 100ft by 35ft.[206] It replaced the town's first bathing area, which dated from 1878 and had been located in a section of the Kennet and Avon Canal, and which was subsequently deemed unhealthy for bathing. Indeed, it had been the subject of parliamentary exchanges in 1895 between Charles Colston and the relevant Minister, Mr Campbell-Bannerman.[207]

In the same year, 1936, Sir Christopher Baynes died at the age of 88 and was buried in the Colston family tomb at St James's Church in Devizes. He may have been a difficult father when his children were young but he could not be faulted for his generous provision for them in adulthood which enabled them to pursue their careers and interests to the full. Christopher's strong financial position, after his early years of unemployment, was facilitated by his long career at the Bank of England, Amy's substantial dowry and by his inheritance from his father, Sir William, in 1897 who left effects of £62,732 (£8m today). As a result, Christopher left a fortune to his children of £127,110 gross (£8.8m today) which, even after death duties, ensured their financial independence for the rest of their lives.

Having started at a significant disadvantage financially to the Colstons, Christopher left an inheritance comparable in size to that of Charles Colston in 1925. But for Ted's inheritance of Padworth, it is very likely that his assets would have exceeded in value those of the Colstons. This not only reflected better financial management by Sir Christopher but also that his wealth was mainly in securities and possessions, which had recovered well after the Crash, rather than in land and buildings, which had continued to decline in value and were costly to maintain. Landed wealth also brought with it the maintenance of a lifestyle and local obligations which were expensive, made cost-cutting difficult and often had to be part-financed by the sale of other land and buildings at unfavourable prices. The times, therefore, were not auspicious for the long-term future of large landed estates like Roundway.

17

Loyal Service

DESPITE the challenging economic environment in the inter-war years, staffing levels were maintained at Roundway and Rosalind had the benefit of a similar number of servants as she had enjoyed as a young bride in the 1880s. The commitment and dedication of these members of staff ensured that the house ran smoothly and efficiently. It would seem that the problems of recruiting and retaining domestic staff that affected other country houses after the Great War[208] was not an issue at Roundway where the Colstons were regarded as considerate employers and had a stock of about 40 cottages on their estate.

Left: Cottages in Roundway village. *Right*: View through the Conscience Lane gates towards the house.

A strong flavour of that commitment of the staff at Roundway can be found in the story of the King family and the testament of Irene Cooper (later Bailey) and Joan Regan (later Cully) who worked for Rosalind in the 1930s. Henry King (always known as Harry) was mentioned in Charles's will in 1925 and worked as a carpenter and builder. His parents, Isaac (born 1829) and Ruth (née Swanborough), worked on the estate and lived in the Lower Lodge on Conscience Lane. Harry's eldest brother Frank was under-gardener and Frank's son Alec (1885–1958) was also a carpenter at Roundway, living in one of the estate cottages.

Harry's younger sister Mary King (1862–1945) had ten children and her grandson David Owen (born in 1927) wrote many years later about his memories of Roundway:

I was born in Devizes, Victoria Road, and my bedroom looked across the K&A Canal to Roundway Park. My mother's side of the family (Kings) were all servants of Roundway as gardeners, carpenters, footmen, seamstresses, laundry workers, serving the estate in some way … Lower Lodge, Conscience Lane is where my great-grandfather (Isaac) lived. In those days it was the frontage of two cottages, the occupants of which had to open the entrance gates when they heard a carriage arriving … A great-uncle (Frank) was under-gardener but dubbed up as a footman/butler on special occasions. As a child I remember his livery (Lincoln green) with metal buttons which had to be wrapped in tissue paper after every use. This was donated to Devizes Amateur Dramatic Society in the late 1940s …

As a boy we watched the Boxing Day procession of the harriers down Quakers Walk to the meet at the Bear in the Market Place … I remember Lord Roundway in his military uniform at Armistice Day parades, also Lady Roundway, a tall figure in a long fur coat as she walked into town down Quakers Walk. He loved country life, she the social life of the London residence. As children we were told of the tragic death of their only daughter as a result of a sleep walking accident, hence no heir to the estate.[209]

Letter from Rosalind, Lady Roundway to Irene Cooper, April 1934.

Before her death in 2009, Irene Bailey (née Cooper) provided a vivid testament of her life working at Roundway between 1934 and 1939:

> I went to Lady Roundway of Roundway Park, Devizes where I took a position of 2nd housemaid of four for two years, then I took Head Housemaid of four. It was a very big house. It was 14 bedrooms in the best side of the house, then we were 10 in staff there, so there were the servant quarters but all had to be kept clean and everything was hands and knees to clean with dustpan and brush and bees wax polish for floors and oil for all the carved oak.

Irene summarised the staff at Roundway when she arrived as follows:[210]

Butler	– Mr Robinson	2nd Housemaid	– Phyllis Strong
Lady's maid	– Mrs Robinson	3rd Housemaid	– Doris Scott
Footman	– Harold Gilbert	4th Housemaid	– Joan Regan
Cook/Chef	– Mr Pearson	Head gardener	
Cook	– Ethel Boulter	and Chauffeur	– Mr Snelgrove
Kitchen maid	– Molly Hiscock	Cow-man	– Mr Brown
Scullery maid	– Olive Nash	Carpenter	– Mr Pink
Head Housemaid	– Irene Cooper		

She provided this photograph below of the staff cleaning the carpets outside, identifying each person and commenting:

It was very hard work at spring-cleaning time for we had to take up carpets, beat them by hand then pull them up and down to bring up the pile. All paint was white and had to be washed. It was certainly very hard work – when you see them today and they still grumble! We had to just get on with it.

Carpet cleaning (from left to right): Mr Sartin, Molly, Irene, Phyllis, Harold, Olive, Joan, Doris and another gardener.

Other people worked part-time for the estate, such as the gardener Polly Hemmings who in the 1930s used to sweep Quakers Walk.[211] Irene remembered that Rosalind adored the chef, Mr Pearson, despite the fact that Irene considered him to be 'a bit of an old rogue'. Romance blossomed between Molly Hiscock, the kitchen maid, and Mr Pink, the estate carpenter, and they later married. With the exception of the chef, Mr Pearson, Irene found all the rest of the staff good to work with, helped by the wide age range between them and the strong leadership provided by Henry Robinson and his wife whom Irene thought were very pleasant. They used to eat together in the Servants' Hall, which Irene described as being 'underground' or in the basement. The kitchen maid cooked their food and they ate very well.

The servants' life at Roundway at this time was fairly predictable as there was only the elderly Rosalind in full-time residence who led a quiet existence. She went to London for a month every year, which was when the servants spring-cleaned the house. Irene described their existence as being 'self-contained'. Members of staff were not allowed into the gardens although they could go down Quakers Walk. Jack Sartin, whose family continued to live on the Roundway estate, remembered Lady Roundway giving all the estate staff a Christmas box in the 1930s with cloth, coal and meat to last the winter.[212]

Irene's working day as head housemaid started between 7.30am and 8am when she would check the dining room and make sure that Lady Roundway's room was ready for her downstairs. Then she would take up cans of hot and cold water ready for Rosalind when she woke up. Irene would then do the cleaning with the three housemaids under her – the younger housemaids cleaned the servants' quarters while Irene and the 2nd housemaid cleaned the top parts of the house. There were no vacuum cleaners, so all the work was on their hands and knees. They made their own beeswax for the polishing by cutting the wax into shreds and soaking it overnight in turpentine.

In the afternoons they cleaned silver and brass and sewed and carried out any necessary repairs. The footman and the butler cleaned the dining-room silver in the still room in the cellar. Tea was between 4pm and 5pm and the servants' evening meal was at 6pm. The day did not finish until they had turned down Lady Roundway's bed and put out water for her for the night.

Silver salver with Colston crest.

Irene's bedroom in the servants' quarters was in the top of the archway block in the quadrangle on the left-hand side as you face it from the courtyard. Three housemaids shared the room, which was freezing cold. They were supposed to be in bed by 9.30pm but Irene recalled that the 'naughty' 2nd housemaid, Phyllis Strong, used to sneak out at night and then footman, Harold Gilbert, would let her back in.

Irene had a half day per week off and every other Sunday. She would always cycle the 8 miles home to Market Lavington from Roundway. She was paid 22s 6d per week (£78.50 today) and managed to put by savings out of her wages given that she had free board and lodging. She described Roundway as a time warp even in its day. Irene's mother had been in service before her and she was used to long hours and hard work, having started her service aged 16 in 1928 as a kitchen maid in a house close to her home in Little Cheverell and then at Major Gwatkin's house in Potterne in 1930 as an under-house maid. Irene considered her job at Roundway, in her words, as a 'top notch' position.

Towards the end of her life, Rosalind suffered from breast cancer and used to go to the Hans Crescent Hotel in Knightsbridge in London for treatment. Irene was putting out the hot and cold-water cans for Rosalind in her bedroom at the moment that she died in 1938 and she remembered the distinctive sound of the death rattle and the terrible smell caused by the cancer.

A year after Rosalind's death Irene left Roundway when she married Melville Bailey. Rosalind had given her one of her dresses, which Irene adapted to become her wedding dress and which she treasured all her life. She described Rosalind as 'a real old Lady' and recalled her with considerable fondness. After the outbreak of the Second World War, Irene started working for a doctor's surgery and was still working there aged 94 in 2006 when the author met her, some 72 years after she had first joined the staff at Roundway.

HAMILTON HOUSE,
ASHBURN PLACE, S.W.7.

15 May 1939

Irene:

     I understood that you were not leaving till next Thursday when I hoped to see you.

     You are really due for a holiday so I am sending you two weeks wages in lieu (45/-) - also a pound more to buy yourself a wedding present.

     I hope you will be very happy. Thank you for your excellent services.

Left: Letter to Irene from Ted, 1939 and *right*: Melville and Irene Bailey at their wedding.

Joan Cully, née Regan, also reminisced about her time working at Roundway as the 4th housemaid under Irene.[213] After leaving school, Joan, like many of her classmates, had gone into domestic service. Roundway was her second job and, like Irene, she enjoyed working there and thought that it was 'lovely' – a friendly place with good food and seemingly the only drawback being the cold bedroom, which she shared with Irene.

As the 4th housemaid, Joan had to clean the servants' quarters and do all the washing up. She remembered the large table in the subterranean servants' quarters and Henry Robinson, who had nothing to do with the girls, wearing a large white apron. She only saw the front of the house when they cleaned the carpets on the front lawn and they were told they could not go into the gardens in case they distracted the gardeners. She remembered the 2nd housemaid, Phyllis Strong, as a 'good old London one' and that the 3rd housemaid, Doris Scott, was 'a scream' who would play the piano when no-one was about. They greatly appreciated their trips to the cinema for which Rosalind paid. The laundry in the Queen Anne section of the house, with its large coppers which used to be filled by the men servants and lit from a fire beneath, were rarely used at this time and washing was sent home to be done at the servants' houses. Joan's sister Hazel remembered bicycling up to Roundway with freshly ironed aprons.

In the main part of the house the housemaids were not allowed to polish the floors as old Lady Roundway would slip, as Joan remembered happening one day in Rosalind's study on the ground floor. Everyone screamed for Henry Robinson but no bones were broken. Like Irene, Joan was there when Rosalind died. She remembered Ted as being quiet and that he 'seemed all right'. After she left to work in the Post Office and then get married in 1942, she bumped into Ted in Devizes one day and he said: 'If you'd stayed with us, you'd have been better off.' She never went back to Roundway.

As the butler, Henry ensured that standards were kept at the highest level. In 1923 he had married Lady Roundway's maid and 'lived an essentially happy life with her'.[214] At the same time, he maintained a voluminous correspondence with various members and friends of the family. The subjects ranged from recollections of sporting events to current news of local affairs, from learned comments on portraits and other pictures to unusual aspects of family history, the latter often illustrated by genealogical tables. There are particularly good examples of this in Henry's correspondence with Sir Christopher Baynes who was similarly interested.

In the inter-war years, Henry also continued with his passion for the hound pedigrees. The Roundway pack had been sold in 1920, but hounds continued to be bred in the Roundway Kennels which moved to Padworth in the mid-1930s. One such pedigree still in existence was given to Sir Christopher and is signed 'H. Robinson, 25 years whip to Roundway Harriers' and dated 5-3-30. In the previous month, on 20 February, Henry wrote to Sir Christopher saying:

I wanted to give you some interesting details of the wonderful Beagle Major '18 which I enclose and which the greatest men in the Foxhound world of the present day have been immensely interested including the Duke of Beaufort, Lord Bathurst, Mr Isaac Bell (Master of the S & W Wilts) and the late Col Clayton Swan.

The Duke saw some of my pedigrees and wrote and asked me to write him out one or two of the famous Badminton lines which I did and he has had them framed at Badminton. He wrote me such a nice letter and presented me with a list of the Badminton Hounds from 1728 but unfortunately there is a break in the continuity of 50 years and you will see 'Major' goes back to the famous dog-hounds of the 5th Duke of Beaufort which were used at Belvoir in 1800 and the amazing thing is that no one knows their breeding as the hound list at Badminton between 1744 and 1805 are lost.

Lord Bathurst has given me both of the valuable books he has written recently and inscribed my name in each and wrote me such a nice letter having seen the Duke's pedigrees I wrote and I believe some of my work is being used for the Hunting Edition of the Lonsdale Library.

It is probable that the pedigree enclosed with this letter was a summary document which Henry then re-worked over the following fortnight into the beautifully finished document for Sir Christopher which is dated 5 March 1930. It is written on a double sheet of strong foolscap paper in his fine copperplate hand, with the pedigree on one side of the beagle Stoke Place Major 1918, and on the other a long dissertation on some of the hounds from which the beagle was descended and their owners, as well as a comment on Major's own qualities. The links with the Roundway pack are highlighted; for instance, a footnote on the pedigree says: 'This skeleton pedigree shows how Aldenham "Restless" FS1890 carried pure Foxhound blood into the Harriers & Roundway Pastime 1906 linked it with the Beagle Kennels.'

Hounds at Roundway.

The dissertation describes vividly Henry's first encounter with Major in 1927 when he followed The Pewsey Vale Beagles at Potterne near Devizes and it ends with a description of a hunting day when the old hound Major excelled himself:

> The last day of the season of 1927 was an invitation meet at Badminton and the Master of the Pewsey Vale asked me to whip in if possible and he would call for me and bring me back to Roundway. We had a great day, old Major was a shining light all day going over the Badminton walls. How interested I was to watch him, knowing that he had the blood of the famous dog-hounds of the 5th Duke of Beaufort. At the end of the day we went up to Badminton House for tea. The Kennelman and I had just put the pack into a loose-horse-box where they were all rolling in a plentiful supply of straw, when the Duke strolled out to have a look at them (he had been hunting his own hounds that day, but the Duchess and his sister had been with us).
>
> I shall never forget the Duke's tall figure, as he went into the horse-box with the little pack, old Major climbed up and when on his hind legs just reached about the tops of the Duke's hunting boots as he stroked his head. I told him that he went back to his uncle's (Lord Henry Somerset's) small Harrier blood and that he had a dash of foxhound blood that went back to the famous Badminton dog-hounds of the 5th Duke of Beaufort that were used at Belvoir in 1800. His Grace was immensely interested and having seen some of my pedigrees wrote to me afterwards to write him out some.

The death of Rosalind in November 1938 led to the expression of much sympathy in the town of Devizes. She left an estate of £40,072 (£2.6m today). There was a long obituary in the *Wiltshire Gazette* on 10 November which referred to Rosalind's illness in her last years and said that she only consented to a resident nurse after a fall.[215] The newspaper praised her dedication to local causes and how she put people at their ease, regardless of social standing. Her passing was the end of an era and Roundway's days were now numbered.

18

The Beginning of the End

AT THE OUTBREAK OF WAR in 1939, Ted and Gladys moved from London to settle at Roundway for the duration. To help run the house they invited relations to come to live with them. In the same year, the past at Roundway was conjured up by the publication of Dorothy's *Enter A Child* (using the pseudonym Dormer Creston). It was her fourth book and greatest literary success to date; it garnered a host of positive reviews, which she kept in a blue folder of paper cuttings. V.S. Pritchett, writing in the *New Statesman*, found it 'Extremely readable and amusing … An entertaining picture of her times'. The novelist Anthony Powell in the *Spectator* commended 'Miss Creston's power of creating atmosphere and character by projecting, as it were, a series of pictures'.

Dorothy's family, however, felt that she had been unfair in portraying her father in such a harsh light only three years after Sir Christopher's death. There must also have been extreme disquiet about the criticism of Christopher and Amy in some of the book reviews, the most trenchant being by Raymond Mortimer in the *Listener*: 'Miss Creston was the imaginative child of very unimaginative parents. Their cruelty was the more intolerable because it was unintended, and their daughter could not console herself with hating them … Even today the Society for the Prevention of Cruelty to Children would do well to deflect some of their attention from the slums to the schools provided for the richer classes …'

Dorothy herself seems to have had doubts as well as is shown in this record that she wrote of a conversation with an unidentified friend (probably Laura, Lady Lovat)[216] in June 1944: 'I asked her before going if she thought I was too

Dorothy with her father and her dog Peter outside Horton House in the early 1930s.

hard on my father in *Enter A Child* but had done it to save other children. She said it wouldn't save them but make it worse as it would give other fathers tips as to how to ill-treat them; they'd all read the book to get ideas how to do it.'

William, meanwhile, was author of a more prosaic publication entitled *Wages During Sickness*, which he wrote for The British Hospitals Association in March 1939. He had had to sell his farm in Somerset in 1926, after living there for five years and keeping everything in perfect order, as he could not make it pay. He had returned to the family house in Lowndes Square and became involved in charitable activities including the early orthopaedic hospitals.[217] After his father's death in 1936, William and his sisters moved to 18 Ovington Square in Knightsbridge which remained their London house for the rest of their lives. William stayed in London throughout the worst period of the Blitz and commanded No. 3 Company of the 1st London Home Guard Battalion of which one of his fellow officers wrote this light-hearted tribute to him:[218]

Major Sir William Colston Baynes
Bart, MC, late Coldstream Guards
Holds in firm hands the guiding reins –
Fights the sloth which our zeal retards.
Where could you find a better than he
To fight the battles of Company 3?

Major Baynes is a peerless knight
Sans peur et sans reproche, and so
Day after day he strives for the right –
Into the battle his energies go.
Not so much fighting the German hordes
As elderly gentlemen sitting on Boards.

Board of this and Committee of that –
Zone H.Q. and A.C.I.
Struggling with them, laying out flat
The grim obstructions that seem so high.
And even waking with ring discreet
The Sleeping Beauties of Warwick House Street.

Silhouette of
Sir William Baynes, Bt.

Most of us aren't exactly young –
Most of us aren't extremely fit –
But if and when the toxin's rung
We'll all of us try to 'do our bit'.
Come what may, be it good or ill
It's 'Follow m' Leader' while we've got BILL.

Ted joined the Home Guard when it was formed from the original 1939 Local Defence Volunteers (LDV), and was soon a battalion commander of the Wiltshire area, before being appointed Area Commander in 1941. He was always willing to lend his name to a good cause which, during the War, included the presidency of the local National Savings Weeks, the Devizes and District War Weapons Week, Warships' Week and Wings for Victory Week.

His approach to his public duties and his character were described by the MP for Devizes, Sir Percy Hurd, in a tribute to him after his death in 1944: 'He did not aspire to become a Member of Parliament as his father and not a few of his forbears had been. He was reserved by nature, and put deeds before words ... The wage earners and townspeople of Devizes had a good friend in him and never did he seem happier than when joining in their festive gatherings at the Conservatives' Bateson Club and at the popular fetes for which he was always ready to lend Roundway Park.'[219]

Ted and Togo in *Vogue*, August 1933.

A counterpoint to the deference shown to Ted in Devizes is provided by John Leech in his book of reminiscences about his upbringing as son of the Superintendent of the Wiltshire County Mental Hospital. He describes a journey with Ted in about 1940, when John was a trainee reporter on the *Wiltshire Gazette*: 'Not all my assignments were agreeable. Once, the editor got me a lift to the annual meeting of the Devizes Division Conservative Association at Marlborough, in Lord Roundway's car. His Lordship drove. The agent, Ted Jolliffe, whose sister had helped to bring me into the world, sat in the front passenger seat and said: "Yes my Lord; no my Lord" all the way to the Castle and Ball and: "No my Lord; yes my Lord" all the way home.'[220]

Letters between the Colston and Baynes cousins between 1942 and 1944 provide a vivid commentary on life at Roundway and the last years of Ted's life. Dorothy had moved, after Christobel's death from cancer in 1940, to Newton House, Kirkhill, in Invernesshire near

Beauly, and kept up a wide-ranging correspondence with family, friends and former staff.

The Baynes house in London, 18 Ovington Square, was empty during Dorothy's absence. The lease was jointly owned by William and Dorothy but William preferred to live at his club, Brooks's, or at Brown's Hotel. As he wrote in a letter to Dorothy of 22 May 1942: 'There are <u>no</u> servants in London; hardly anyone is living in their own house, and if they do they do all their own house-work. All hotels, lodgings and small flats are <u>packed</u> at present.'[221] Ronnie and Cecilia, lived 3 miles from Roundway at Horton House in Horton. They had rented the house since their marriage in 1930 and visited Roundway regularly.

Left: Horton House. *Right*: Julia Crofton (in foreground) at a show held at the Willats family home, Denton Court in Kent, with her daughters Ruperta and Ione immediately beind her.

Ted's widowed maternal aunt, the redoubtable Julia Ruperta, sister of Rosalind, was one relation who came to stay at Roundway during the war. After the death of her first husband William Willats in 1893, she married Col Morgan Crofton in 1894 but was widowed in 1916.[222] Dorothy wrote of Julia: 'She was, I realise now, the only one of my relations of that generation who looked life straight in the face: and what she saw generally made her laugh. Not only was she handsome of face and figure but she diffused an Olympian atmosphere of splendour.'[223] Julia wrote on 24 June 1942 from Roundway to Dorothy (addressing her as 'Doreen'), her goddaughter and cousin:

> Dearest Doreen
>
> I don't know that I have any news for you that would <u>interest</u> you. I've asked Ruperta to send on a paper with rather uncomplimentary Photos of your 'beloved Cat' (as I see you call him), giving Certificates & whatnots to 'Home Guards'. G carries on with her Bridge as usual & scrounching around to get more than her <u>due</u> (by getting other

people's coupons for herself) she has rather a clever if immoral trick of giving <u>us</u> <u>all</u> very old and <u>dusty</u> Tea pre-war stuff & taking all <u>our</u> tea coupons for Earl Grey Tea that she gets from Fortnums & M for her own private consumption in her suite. She really <u>is</u> a 'smart Guy' at looking after self.

... We are in the midst of haymaking & the Admirable C was pitching hay regardless of missing his dinner until 9pm last night as clouds threatened hay. The ungrateful G saying if he couldn't come to dine at the proper time they certainly needn't keep anything for him. However as he is persona grata with all the Staff he <u>did</u> get some food in the Pantry – when he'd had a wash somewhere about 9.30 & at any rate the Home field hay was saved when we got a shower later.

... My Mrs Wade has come down to do Housemaid as one has departed with crocked knees. Her beloved Boy is fighting somewhere in the East. Goodbye for the present, hope you are well & Happy?

From your aged Cousin & Godmother Julia Crofton.

This view of Ted and Gladys is backed up by William in his letter to Dorothy of 22 May 1942 reacting to her concerns about Ronnie and Cecilia's relationship with Ted and Gladys: 'I do not think you need worry about R & C and Roundway. <u>No-one</u> is popular there and they (T & G) have become almost impossible to meet. If Julia had not been there I do not think I should ever have bothered to go there at all – except for Bill [Bill Thomas, the land agent at Roundway] whom I found attractive – except for his tiresome habit of contradicting <u>every</u> one <u>every</u> time anyone opened his mouth. I had to tell him about it on many occasions, but he did not improve … Yes, I think my popularity is the more noticeable the further away I am: the only remark T ever made to me at Roundway whenever he saw me was "Hullo, Bill, you'll find the Aunt in the billiard room".'

A similar view of Ted is contained in this excerpt from a letter to Dorothy from Ronnie dated 7 September 1942, focusing on Henry and the celebrations to mark his half-century of service:

Robinson's letter will amuse you; the 'impression' to which he refers is the seal with which I sealed our letter to him, knowing his love of heraldry: it is 'my' arms, that is to say Baynes and Day together. Robinson helped me a lot when we were having it made.

Bill gave him a silver cup; Cousin Julia gave him £5, so did Cecilia and I; your letter seems to have pleased him enormously. Nobody knows what Ted gave him, but the general opinion now is that he didn't give him anything at all (fact).

Cheerio: ever thine,

Jacko

Henry's reply to Dorothy's letter of congratulation was heartfelt:

I think you will understand my feelings about a month ago when I went out and met a tiny tractor hauling the beautiful coach away to be broken up for scrap.

I had heard something about it and as it had been standing out of doors for some time I told his Lordship I should like the bars and the iron ladder so have got them.

Do you remember in the days of long dresses how careful we had to be to guide your dress up the narrow ladder?

Well as the old coach passed me with the tiny tractor puffing, I took off my hat to it and watched it out of sight.

The following month, Julia wrote again to Dorothy, this time from London where she was staying to see her two daughters, Ruperta and Ione, who were also visiting London from their home, Denton Court, near Canterbury: 'As you love your old Cat so, I enclose a letter just come from him (you can wear it or tear it, I don't want it back). I like his cheek in hoping I'll return tomorrow sober when I haven't tasted Beer, wine or spirits for over 2 years & he has run the changes daily on every form of intoxicant!!! I grew many hundred Sunflowers & have greatly added to the Poultry rations by the seed. Ted has been sweeping up Crab apples for the Hospital & stripping sweet corn during my week's absence but he is incurably lazy & idle & I don't suppose did much …'

A few weeks later, on 4 November, William wrote to Dorothy about Julia's campaign for better food at Roundway: 'I had also to write Julia a letter about my best meal so that she could flaunt it in Gladys' face – but I think G is pretty impervious by now.'

Ruperta acknowledged her mother's poor opinion of Ted in a letter to Dorothy at about this time: '… nothing that poor old Ted does, however, seems to be right'. He comes across more sympathetically in a letter he wrote to Dorothy on 29 November 1942:

I beg to acknowledge your cheque. I will of course see to what you want; luckily by Dec 5th I shall have my <u>first</u> lot of white chrysanths through, buds just breaking so they will be nice and fresh, I have told Snelgrove [the head gardener] what you want. I doubt if I shall be able to deliver myself, but that owing to HG [Home Guard] work cannot be helped. At the moment I am very short handed, two estate men away, my House chauffeur is on the sick list and also my Estate Driver, so I am working one of three, which means driving various cars under diverse circumstances. However, we get along. But my hands are nearly frozen, hence the awful writing. I am writing Sat evening and I hope to post while out on a Scheme Sun <u>morning</u>, as I have no one left to send in the usual <u>evening</u> Sun post.

HG is gaining very strong, getting stronger but that I am not preparing to talk about. You may have seen that one of my Platoon officers, Lieut Forster aged 61, has received the G Cross posthumously, as he was killed on the spot. A very gallant gentleman.

No shows for dogs, except ten mile limit nowadays, but more sales than I can manage. I never hear of Jane. I will inform Mrs Creasy, very glad to hear Peter [Dorothy's dog] is better …

I certainly miss our 'teas' or rather my nice cocktail and your 'milk'. I have a certain amount of news, but I can't pass on by letter – one never knows. I go to London on Tues (always the first Tues in month) to attend various Directors meetings which I have managed to collect on that date.

Gladys is not too bad. I get a lot of rheumatism in left leg. Aunt Julia is in bed having taken a scary toss on the flat. No one's fault but her frocks are so long in front.

Well I suppose I had better end up and put ready for my posting in the morning. Cows are milking well. You seem doing endless matters, perhaps not bad for you as long as you do not overdo it. I think I have told you all I <u>can</u>. I should like to see you my dear, but I never take more than two days off and then only to the Croft, where I can get back from by car in 1 1/4.

Well here is end.

With love. Yr loving CC.

Ted and Josephine Creasy, who ran the Roundway Kennels from the Croft at Padworth, were by this time in a relationship,[224] although it is not clear when it started. Ted's and Gladys's marriage had experienced great strain after the tragedy of Betty's death, and Ted had become over-reliant on alcohol. The Croft provided him with a sanctuary away from the stresses of Roundway life, both in terms of his family and the difficulties of managing the estate and his other responsibilities in wartime conditions. Josephine and Ted had much in common, not least a lifelong love of hounds, hunting and the countryside, interests which were not shared by Gladys. It seems that this relationship, which was pursued in a discreet way at Padworth, was accepted by Ted's family. On Boxing Day in 1942, Cecilia wrote this description of Ted: 'I met Ted in the town on Saturday in the small Morris complete with Togo [his dog]. He has very kindly given us a lump of venison, so tomorrow we hope to feast on it, though not I fear from a silver dish, but after all silver dishes are hardly in keeping with parlourmaids of 14!! And anyway ours all went to the bank directly the evacuees arrived. Ted went off to the Croft on Wednesday, where Mrs Creasy and large numbers of dogs still are and I rather gather he was staying there over Christmas.'

Unlike many large houses, Roundway was not requisitioned during the war. Requisition often involved only one week's notice of intended government use, minimal compensation, the erection of temporary buildings and substantial damage during the wartime occupation. Roundway did, however, house soldiers posted on the estate in and around Devizes. Ronnie and Cecilia took in evacuees and proved such good hosts and created such positive memories that their evacuees returned in later life to visit Horton House, long after their wartime hosts had died.

The family's nostalgia for their childhood days at Roundway at the end of the previous century is captured in this excerpt from a letter in early 1943 to Dorothy from her cousin Ruperta Willats. The letter is headed PAPER ECONOMY STUNT as it was written on the back of a letter from Kent County Police Court Mission:

> It is a comforting thought that we were fully aware of our enjoyment in the early days of Roundway visits; it must be tragic to look back on the past and feel 'we were happy then and never realised it'. Of course, there was always the fear of parental disapproval, and terrifying reproof in the background but that <u>may</u> have added spice – they say you can't have sunshine without shadows.

19

Sounding the Last Post

IN FEBRUARY 1943 Julia provided Dorothy with a typically acerbic description of life at Roundway:

> I lead an infuriatingly dull life & see practically no one even to pass the time of day to, until lunch at 1 when G & T conduct their usual squabbles over the Staff & the Food. At 1.30 G goes off to her rooms & 'out' at ¼ to 3, 4 days a week to Bridge, the remaining 3 which includes Sunday she has Bridge here & Tea (to which Ted, Bill Thomas, & Self, are <u>not </u>invited) also upstairs. I just see Ted who <u>sleeps</u> from lunch until 4 pm when he & Togo visit the Farm where he & Mr T mutter Home Guard affairs to each other.
>
> At 6pm <u>I</u> retire to my Bedchamber where I am now allowed a wood fire by Dr's orders in the afternoon. I do not attend Dinner but have a cup of Bovril upstairs, as really what with Ted being invariably 'squiffy' after dinner & Gladys' loud wireless Jazz, one got no peace at all. However, I don't see <u>them</u> again until next day.
>
> I am always longing for the end of this most tiresome War to get away to spend my only short remnant of life in my <u>own</u> Flat or House & forget all here for good & all and I daresay it is reciprocated with T & G. I miss Willie's weekly or even fortnightly, call so very much. He was such a pleasing link with the outside World.
>
> … I am glad you saw Noël Coward. I believe G goes to the 'Pictures' here sometimes after her Bridge which has had rather a lurid time as one place after another has requested her & her Club <u>to go</u>, on account of the noise they apparently make which seems to annoy the other occupants of the Pubs they rent a room at. I think there are 18 to 20 of these idle people & they quarrel a good deal.

According to Eileen Thomas, the wife of the agent Bill Thomas, Gladys asked Bill whether etiquette would permit her to invite a successful and charming owner of a cafe in Devizes to come and play bridge with her. He advised her against this plan, pointing out that she would be compelling her butler to wait on a man who was basically below his social standing. Judging from Julia's letter, Gladys heeded the advice of Bill (with whom she had a good relationship) by holding her bridge parties upstairs at Roundway and thereby excusing staff from waiting on them.

Glimpses of wartime austerity and farm life can be seen in this excerpt from a letter to 'Tabba' from Ted dated 20 April 1943 (the grammar of which Dorothy later corrected in pencil):

> We have had good sales heifers, cows and bulls at 25 gns instead of 15/-. Cow twins last time to a valuable cow ... They have taken away the Marlborough Gates, the place looks awful, but left Barby's Lodge [Quakers Walk lodge] gates as they are part of the defences of the Town. No news here I am very busy over HG we increase in strength.
>
> Aunt J is not too bad she comes down for lunch each day, I think her shoulder has mended. Scuse scrawl hands very cold. Do you know the description of a utility 'article' it has a handle and sides, and you use your own bottom. Well I will see to everything. I am getting quite a goat and hen breeder. Happy Easter.
>
> Yours with love
> The Kat.

The last letter that we have from Ted to Dorothy is from Roundway, dated 30 November 1943:

> Dearest Tabba,
>
> So sorry not to have answered before. I have been very much on the move driving solo in beastly wet & fog. Sat. I lunched at Salisbury with Col. Mitchell the Vice Chairman of the Conservative party from London. He was most interesting being in constant touch with the P.M. Then I concluded my day by driving 25 miles back in semi darkness, fog and rain. Tues. I have the annual general meeting of the Bateson Conservative Club in the town so I shall have something to talk to them about. They have had a very good financial year.
>
> Had a lot of trouble with the cows, due to abortion, which is very infectious – puts you back 9 months for cow. I am sending in about 30 galls milk per day. The pullits woke up today and produced 4 eggs instead of their usual 1 or 0.

What a very good idea turning your house into flats. I only wish it could be done here. Aunt J seems very comfortable where she is [Hove in Sussex] and far less dull than here. The U.S. troops are going to take over Rowdeford House and use the drive as a park place. The Gov. have requisitioned it months ago. I would rather have had British troops there. I have no news as beyond visiting my HG officers I don't see anyone much.

The first Tues. in every month I go to London for the board meeting of my National United Laundries and generally stop at the Croft. I do hate travelling in the blackout so much. Thank you for the 3 shillings, I have already ordered the wreath, I think it will be light yellow chrysanths, singles, unless I can find anything tougher. I shan't be here myself. I am afraid I have no news, so glad to hear the book or books are going so well. I think the handwriting is OK but the paper is very thin.

With love,

Your loving C.C.

A week after Ted wrote this letter, he had a stroke on 7 December which was reported to Ronnie in a letter from Henry Robinson:

His Lordship was going to London for the day on the Tuesday the 7th and I called him at 7.15 and he was quite bright and joked about a pair of spats he was going to wear as he had not worn any for so long …

The car was at the door and he did not turn up so I went to the Dining Room and found he had not come down so ran to his bedroom; not there then to the Bathroom and found him in a sad way sitting in a chair leaning on the bath having had his bath and shaved and nearly dressed. I said aren't you feeling well my Lord and he said 'very bad' and I ran for Mr Thomas and he got an eiderdown and blankets and laid him on the floor and phoned for Dr Renton. I then later got the invalid chair and carried him into his bedroom and lifted him into bed … In the afternoon the ambulance came and we carried him down and he put his hand on the Bannister and helped us exactly like his dear father did when poor Savage and I carried him upstairs that day in Upper Belgrave St. I have not seen him since but feared directly I found him that it was similar to his father. It is so unfortunate that there is so much difficulty in getting a nurse for it is so sad for him not to be home.

Ronnie reported a further comment from Henry as he carried Ted downstairs: 'As we went down the stairs I glanced up at the portraits of his mother and father, and grandfather, g.g. grandfather and his g.g.g. grandfather, all looking down on us. You can imagine what a Christmas we had, the usual bundles of Christmas decoration came in, but I had not the heart to put it up, and asked the odd man to take it away. Poor Henry, his <u>world</u> is beginning to crumble away.'

On 16 December, Ronnie wrote to Dorothy about Ted, explaining that he had been in hospital in Devizes for the last ten days, apologising for not telling her about the stroke earlier and urging her to keep the news to herself. It seems that Gladys was keen to let it be known that Ted was suffering from nothing more than 'gastric trouble'. Ronnie also took the opportunity to reminisce about their childhood at Roundway:

> I feel very sad, as we all must be; & I was thinking only the other day of those times when we 3 were children at Roundway & played at soldiers; each of us 3 took the name of some famous General & I think that name lasted the whole of that visit; 'Duke of Wellington'; 'General Woolfe' [sic.] & I have a sort of odd memory that one visit <u>you</u> were 'General Nelson'!

In his subsequent Christmas letter to Dorothy, Ronnie provided more information about Ted's condition:

> … he can hardly say any words; just mumbles faintly & occasionally one word or so comes out quite clearly; he is quite cheerful & smiles or grins if one tells him anything that amuses him; he seems to understand <u>everything</u> that is said to him; he doesn't seem worried or unhappy & Cecilia & I both consider that it's rather as if his brain was too sleepy or drowsy to have any sensations like that …
>
> Renton [the doctor] told me that he made Ted promise that he wouldn't touch spirits at all again (wine & champagne are all right). I asked Renton if he thought Ted would keep that promise, & he said 'ah, that's the question'; I think the general opinion is that <u>if</u> he doesn't keep off whisky etc he'll have another 'stroke', which would probably finish him. The specialist said that 50% of his ability for doing any business had definitely gone & would <u>never</u> come back; Cecilia & I both think he isn't as well as he was when we first saw him (we have each separately seen him 2 or 3 times).
>
> … I was up at Roundway yesterday fetching some venison that Robinson had got for me, I had a long talk (half an hour or more) with him in the billiard room, & when I left he said, 'I'm not putting up any holly this year; I haven't the heart to do it'; & he

nearly broke down. I think Gladys would do her best to be nice & kind to Ted, but I don't think she's very understanding. She has been very odd telling everybody not to say anything about Ted, & if they are asked, to say it's 'just a gastric attack, & he's going on well'; she told me not to write to you or Billy & nobody was to tell Cousin Julia & then it came out that on the very day that he was taken bad she herself wrote & sent Cousin Julia a <u>full</u> account of everything, & also said 'of course, this is what we've been expecting'.

The cause of Gladys's secrecy was probably an understandable desire to keep her in-laws in their place and to sideline Josephine Creasy. A further picture is provided of the situation at Roundway in this letter to Dorothy from Henry on 18 January 1944:

Thank you for your very nice letter and for your very real thoughts of our sad days here at Roundway. His Lordship I am sorry to say makes very little progress at present but yesterday he got as far as the bedroom window of his new bedroom (the Queen Anne Bedroom) where he has his own bed moved and the nurse has his former room, the Queen Anne Dressing Room. He was pleased to see the deer but the cows which he was looking for did not happen to be in the park.

We were very fortunate in obtaining a very nice nurse and we all do everything we can for her and his Lordship; he is in pain but sleeps a good deal and forgets what part of the day it is. Mr Ronald told me that he had sent my letter on to you so you know how suddenly everything happened and for a mercy it did not happen on his journey either to or from London that day.

I wonder if you remember being at Roundway 43 years ago this Christmas … Now good bye and I have written more than I started out to and I would like you to feel we are doing all we can for his Lordship.

I remain your Obedient Servant
Henry Robinson

P.S. 19th, 11 am. Have just shaved his Lordship and he seems rather better and enquired about the cows.

In spite of the good nursing and care, Ted failed to make further progress and died on 29 March 1944 aged 63. The *Wiltshire Gazette* reported his funeral at length, describing how the tenantry filed past the open coffin, which lay in state in the billiard room, to pay their last respects.

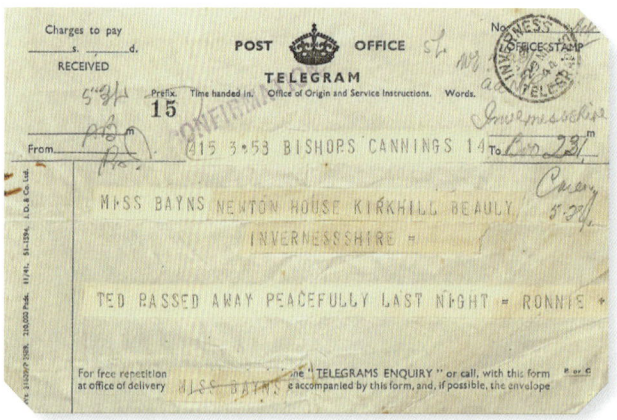

Telegram to Dorothy about Ted's death.

On the day of the funeral, the coffin was carried out of the house by estate workers and placed on a gun-carriage drawn by an armoured car, with nine Grenadier Guardsmen as bearers and the Devizes Home Guard Band playing a dead march. The funeral procession passed through the gates of Marlborough Lodge and on to Southbroom Church. After the Church service, the coffin was again taken in procession to the cemetery, with the pavements thronged with people.

Ted's coffin was lowered into the family vault, close to the grave of Betty, by men of the Grenadier Guards. Soldiers from the Wiltshire Regiment fired three volleys over the grave and a drummer of the Grenadier Guards sounded the Last Post and Reveille. Dorothy sent a wreath for the funeral and a blue envelope on which she wrote: 'Please don't open till you tie it onto wreath'. Inside the envelope is a card with string on which she had written: 'Good bye, beloved cousin, good bye'.

Obituary

BRIG.-GENERAL LORD ROUNDWAY

DISTINGUISHED MILITARY CAREER

Brigadier-General Lord Roundway, C.M.G., D.S.O., M.V.O., late Grenadier Guards, died at Roundway Park, Devizes, yesterday after an illness of several months. From 1932 he had been an Exon of the Yeomen of the Guard.

The Right Hon. Edward Murray Colston, second Baron Roundway, of Devizes, Wiltshire, in the Peerage of the United Kingdom, was born on December 31, 1880, only son of the first baron, whom he succeeded in 1925. He was educated at Eton, where he was in the houses of the Rev. S. A. Donaldson and Mr G. T. Mount, Mr. Donaldson being also his tutor. In 1900 he entered the Grenadier Guards, served with the second battalion during the South African War, in the course of which he was wounded, and gained the Queen's Medal with three clasps. Making the Army his profession, he continued to serve during the years of peace; he reached the rank of captain in 1908, and was made an M.V.O., and he received his majority in 1915. In the 1914-18 war he served with distinction, fighting throughout the retreat from Mons, on the Marne, and on the Aisne before being wounded and invalided home. The award to him of the D.S.O. was gazetted in 1916. Next he was sent to Egypt with the rank of temporary lieutenant-colonel to establish a school of technical instruction for the army stationed there, termed the Imperial School of Instruction. He was given a brevet lieutenant-colonelcy in 1917, and the same year was appointed to command the 233rd Infantry Brigade under Allenby with the rank of temporary brigadier-general. His services during the last war were mentioned in dispatches six times and in addition to his British honours he was also awarded the Order of the Nile and the Order of the White Eagle of Serbia.

After the last war he reached the substantive rank of lieutenant-colonel, Grenadier Guards in 1920, commanding the second battalion, and that of colonel in 1924. He was appointed to the command of the 131st Surrey (Territorial) Infantry Brigade in 1927, serving as such until 1931. The next year he retired with the honorary rank of brigadier-general. During the present war he had been zone commander of the Wiltshire Home Guards. In 1904 he married Blanche Gladys, only daughter of the late Mr. G. Duddell, of Queen's Park, Brighton, and Hong-kong. The only child of the marriage, a daughter, died in 1924 at the age of 14. The barony, which was created in 19--, becomes extinct.

The Times 30th March 1944.

20

The Sale of Roundway Park

TED'S WILL must have been a shock to Gladys and the family. Although the house and estate at Roundway were left to her, virtually all the rest of Ted's wealth went to Josephine Creasy. Ted left her the Croft at Padworth, his London house in Sloane Terrace, most of his shares and cash and the Regal Theatre in Southend, Essex.

The Roundway settled estate which Gladys was bequeathed comprised the Mansion House and the freehold lands and property in the borough of Devizes and the parishes of Roundway, Rowde and Bromham. This totalled 1,584 acres. She also received £1,000 (£43,500 today) and was asked to donate Ted's medals and orders to the Grenadier Guards.

There were pecuniary legacies to Ted's godchild Auriol Pratt (£100) and Gladys's cousins Lady Baddeley (£50) and Dora Pollitt (£50). Despite the problems between Ted and Gladys, it was her family alone to whom he made bequests, apart from his staff and the main beneficiaries of his will, and not to his Baynes relations whom he presumably thought were hardly in financial need and from some of whom he had become distanced in recent years. Accompanying the bequests that he made to his staff was a request to Gladys to continue the pensions that he paid to retired staff. The staff mentioned were as follows:

Manager	—	E. Brough Taylor	£50
Bailiff	—	Edward Snelgrove	£50
Chauffeur	—	Henry Hales	£50
Cook	—	Ethel Bolter	£25
Estate Foreman	—	Alfred Pink	£50
Head Herdsman	—	Frank Brown	£50

Henry Robinson was not mentioned in the will but this is probably because he was provided with free tenure in the Quakers Walk Lodge for the rest of his life.

Josephine Creasy's bequest was worded as follows: 'I give devise and bequeath to Mrs. Alice Josephine Frances Creasy who has for many years managed my business of The Roundway Kennels the following real and personal property which I regard as the assets of and capital available for such business …' In addition to the kennels, Josephine Creasy received:

Freehold of 3 Sloane Terrace
Freehold property of Padworth and all the chattels therein
Freehold property at Little Missenden, Bucks
Regal Theatre in Southend, Essex
All cash and securities in the branch of St Martins Bank, 32 Lowndes Square, London
All securities deposited at Lloyds Bank (Cox's and King's branch)
All other (if any) securities which represented part of the Padworth Estate
Ted's stamp collection

The total gross value of Ted's estate was £296,264 (£12.9m today). The net value of the personal estate amounted to £187,934 (£8.2m). Death duties of £69,326 (£3m) were paid by 6 September 1944. The will stipulated that the bequests to Josephine Creasy, Auriol Pratt, relations and staff had to be paid or made over to the beneficiaries free of all death duties. Even if Ted had left all his wealth to Gladys, it is unlikely that she would have stayed at Roundway given her estrangement from Ted, the unhappy memories connected with the house and her strained relationship with the Colston family. A letter from William to Dorothy dated 14 January 1944 indicates that Gladys had been under the impression that she would inherit everything and intended to sell up: 'The entail[225] ends with Ted and, as he has no children, he can dispose of the property by will as he pleases. According to Julia, Gladys told her she knows that Ted has left her (Gladys) everything, and also that she means to sell everything up.'

At one stage it was thought that Ted would leave the Roundway estate to William: it was later said that the family confidently expected him to be left the estate and that Ted's will was 'one of the great blows in his life'.[226] William received prior warning, however, before Ted's death that he would not inherit, as he explained in the same letter of 14 January 1944 to Dorothy quoted above: 'No, it does not come to us. Jackson, the solicitor at Devizes, mis-informed me on the subject some years ago – or else I misunderstood him. Anyhow, as the situation seemed to be critical, I wrote to him a fortnight ago to clear the matter up.'

As a trained lawyer, it is highly unlikely that William would have misconstrued the solicitor's earlier comments and it is much more likely that, when Ted changed his will in 1939, he wanted to make provision for Josephine Creasy alongside Gladys. The only way he could achieve this was to exclude William, leave the Roundway estate to Gladys and his other assets to Josephine Creasy.

William, however, put a brave face on it: 'I am not a bit worried about Roundway myself; I never wanted the house, and it is getting rather late in life even to take on the woods'. That said, he would have liked to have passed it on to his young cousin John Baynes who had been told as a boy (he was born in 1928) that he might one day inherit Roundway.

Ruperta Willats wrote to Dorothy about Ted's death in a letter from Denton Court dated 8 April 1944:

Ted Colston.

Poor old Ted's death, though expected, seems a wrench in life. I am sure you must feel it very much. The roots of old acquaintance and affection went down so deep, almost to the beginning of consciousness, and though he was greatly changed, one felt that somewhere far below the surface the little boy with a grin, and a kitten on his shoulder, still existed.

Since the news came one's spirit seems constantly to be wandering about Roundway. Most often I find myself a little way up the stairs near Aunt Rosie's portrait, also in that rather dark passage leading from the ante-room where the Colston family tree used to hang, to the billiard room, down which Uncle Charlie's cheerful confident footsteps were so often heard approaching. Poor Henry, what <u>must</u> he feel? You three are his last connection now with his beloved family. I quite expect Gladys will sell the place as soon as an opportunity arises.

Gladys, now aged 65, with her sources of income severely reduced and the continuing wartime austerity, would have struggled to carry on at Roundway even if she had wanted to do so. During 1944 Ted's secretary and friend Bill Thomas took on the responsibilities of managing the estate from the local land agency firm. Bill and his wife Eileen lived in the Swiss Cottage on the estate and found Gladys pleasant to work with and gave her all possible help. Eileen found Gladys to be graceful, friendly and kind and considered that this more attractive side came to the fore once Gladys no longer had to be on the defensive against sharp Colston critics. Bill Thomas had a reputation for irascibility, as we have seen from William's previous testament, but such determination was just what Gladys needed at her side.[227]

She also had Ronnie and Cecilia nearby at Horton House with whom William was living at this time to escape London. William described their day-to-day life in this amusing letter to Dorothy dated 19 November 1944:

As you are sometimes fond of details of other people's lives, I will tell you how we live here. I have the drawing room entirely to myself, with a large table and all my own papers and books; no-one disturbs me there and I only meet my hosts at meals and for very occasional walks. I have an oil stove which I may light at will, and every evening C lights a wood fire for me. R & C live <u>entirely</u> in R's little cubby hole all day, and how they spend their time I cannot imagine. C does a good deal of housework, and cooks meals when the maid is out; works two days a week in the Secretary's office of the Devizes Hospital and goes in once a week for a Red Cross working party; and she also keeps all my laundry mended – so I suppose <u>she</u> does have her time pretty well filled up.

But R, as all his life, seems to do absolutely nothing. He seldom goes for a walk, as he has lumbago; he wanders out to measure the water in the rain gauge, and to see what the temperature of the thermometer is and record it all in his note book, and tells me all about it at lunch; he also goes to see if any eggs have been laid 2 or 3 times a day – only they usually haven't. He only has enough petrol to go to Devizes twice a week, when he spends a happy morning, doing the household shopping and meeting his friends. Apart from all this he sits in the chair at his roll-topped desk from after breakfast well into the night – it is usually 2 or 3 am before he goes up to bed – whether he sleeps all the time or what he does is a complete mystery to me.

We have meals in the pantry which is really the nicest room in the house, except for the kitchen; also convenient for washing up after meals, which is the only household work I am allowed to do. But C is expecting to get a 14 year old for the parlour after Xmas, and then I suppose all our amateur housework will come to an end. Well, well. They were both very surprised to hear I am sometimes bored: apparently neither of them knows what it means – but then perhaps a cow does not either.

Henry Robinson retired in 1945 at the age of 71, having worked at Roundway since he arrived as a footman in 1892. The austerity of the war years continued under Clement Attlee's post-war Labour government with rationing (which was not finally abolished until 1953), strict regulation and high taxation. It is against this background that Gladys asked Bill Thomas in 1946 to make discreet enquiries about the possibility of selling the house and estate.

The parallels between Gladys's experience with the sale of Roundway and that of her mother in 1888–90 with the sale of Duddell's Villa and Queens Park in Brighton, through which Gladys lived as a young girl, are striking. Her mother, Kate, had put the property up for auction in 1888 after her husband's death and lengthy negotiations ensued with Brighton Corporation before they agreed the purchase in 1890.[228] Gladys would also have been aware of the sale and dismemberment of her mother-in-law Rosalind's old house, Whitton Park,[229] and the sale in 1945 of Urchfont Manor and 59 acres near Devizes to the County Council for a residential training centre.[230]

The Roundway estate at this time comprised:[231]

» 1,584 acres in total, which undulated from being a little over 200 feet above sea level on its west boundary and rising sharply to over 600 feet at its north-east boundary on the Downs.

» 6 farms which accounted for 1,352 acres – Iron Pear Tree; Rowdefield; Roundway; Manor, Rowde; Lower and Home – principally involved in dairy farming but with a significant increase in arable farming during the war.

» 39 cottages – 23 on the farms and 16 forming the hamlet of Roundway.

» 29 acres of allotments (proportionately larger than on most estates) and 142.5 acres of woodland (poorly maintained) were also included in the overall acreage.

The gross rent was £2,246.3 (£86,327 today) and the net (after tithe rent annuity, taxes, repairs and maintenance, insurance and management) was £1,274 (£48,967 today).

The impending sale of Roundway was a key factor in Dorothy Baynes's decision to change her surname by deed poll to Colston-Baynes in May 1946 so she could keep the Colston flame burning. In June, Bill Thomas approached the Society of Merchant Venturers of Bristol (the Society), with which the Colston family had been connected for over three centuries, to see if they would be interested in purchasing the estate at a price of £130,000 (£5.35m today). The Society conducted protracted negotiations over the purchase; it drove a hard bargain and a final agreement was not reached until 1948.

In the meantime, in November 1946, a meeting took place between Lady Roundway, Wiltshire County Council and the Society at which the suggestion was made that, if the Society bought the entire estate, it could sell the house and lease the Home Farm to the County Council as a training college for teachers in rural areas. In early 1947, before the Society had purchased the estate, the sale of the house and 38 acres was agreed directly between Gladys and the County Council for £12,500 (£480,000 today) and the Home Farm was leased by the Council. Given the bitter winter of early 1947, the coldest for three centuries, which was exacerbated by the disruption of energy supplies, Gladys must have felt very relieved to have sold the house.

In parallel with these negotiations in the autumn of 1946, Gladys started to sell the contents of Roundway. The best items were sold at Christie's in October and the remainder were sold at Roundway itself in a three-day sale. The items sold at Christie's were of such quality that they fetched at auction £9,378 (£386,000 today) which was equivalent to 75 per cent of the sale price of the mansion and 38 acres (£12,500).[232]

On 2 October 1946, in the Christie's Old Masters sale, 46 lots were sold for a total of £1,446 including *The Stag Hunt* by Jan Brueghel (£40), Gainsborough's portrait of Christopher Griffith, Esq. (£55), three paintings by William Hogarth (total of £232), portrait of Sir John Chicheley by Sir Peter Lely (£72), a 'Poussin landscape' (£11) and a still life by Simon Verelst (£78). Other highlights that came up for sale in subsequent Christie's sales over the following month were a set of ten Chippendale mahogany dining chairs, which fetched £1,550, and a James II (1688) silver-gilt cup and cover, which sold for £820. A significant number of Colston family miniatures also came up for sale in November, including Alexander Colston by Richard Cosway and one by Samuel Cotes in 1770 of Christopher Griffith, MP of Padworth.

R.P. Way, whose family were antique dealers in Bristol and Bath, recalled a clever find while cataloguing the house sale at Roundway:[233]

> I remember one find I made when cataloguing the contents of Roundway Park, the estate of the late Lord Roundway. In and around the numerous bedrooms, I noticed that several pieces of bedroom furniture had similar inlay. I had these pieces collected together and found that they formed a complete Sheraton suite. I catalogued them in one lot. As the day of the sale approached, the local dealers did not believe the inlay to be original because the furniture had at some time been French-polished. But when the suite was offered for sale, it was bought by a local woman for between £400 and £500 and a well-known London dealer was the under-bidder. I was glad that my judgement had brought such a good return for the family.

Major John Bartholomew (1920–2016) recalled how dark and very sad the house looked during the sale. His father outbid Ronnie for the Lynwood Palmer oil painting of Lord Roundway and his coach, which sold for £110 (a black and white image of this painting is on page 132). Josephine Creasy also lost out to the Major's father in the bid for this painting (which Major Bartholomew thought she should have had).[234] Nina Murray, half-sister of Rosalind and Julia,[235] also referred to the sale in a letter to Dorothy of 2 June: 'I told you we went to the sale at Roundway. The old days seemed like something one had read about, Charlie, "Little Dot", Rosie, Willie DG.'

In January 1947, Gladys reduced the asking price for the estate to £75,000 (£3.1m today) due to the publication of the Town and County Planning Act which, despite speculation to the contrary, did not loosen planning restrictions on building development on the outskirts of towns such as Devizes. The Act was based on three wartime reports and it ensured that

Rooms at Roundway empty of their furniture, paintings and other contents (photographed in 1954).
Clockwise from top: drawing room and enfilade beyond, dining room, circular room and
first floor bedroom (Historic England).

there was no incentive to landowners to raise funds by selling peripheral parts of their estates for development and it also implemented complicated valuation procedures. It effectively subjected land to stricter state control and established that, if planning permission was granted to build on land, there would be a development charge of 100 per cent on any increase in its value. This was a major blow to the many estates suffering heavy death duties which, in turn, resulted in inheritance tax payments becoming the main driver of post-war land sales (in contrast to the immediate period after the Great War when it was the agricultural depression). It also caused problems for satisfying the increased level of demand for land for housing in Devizes after the war.

In the wake of the Town and Country Planning Act, the Land Steward's 'Report and Valuation of the Roundway Estate' of April 1947 prepared for the Society valued the estate, excluding the house, at £54,000 with a further £2,500 deducted for repairing and refurbishing buildings, thereby giving a final value of £51,500 (£2m today). The Report estimated that the Society could obtain a return of 2½ per cent p.a. on the estate at this price, rising to 3 per cent p.a. after five years. Gladys was left with no option but to accept this much reduced valuation although final negotiations, conveyancing and completion on the sale would take another year.

Not surprisingly, Dorothy was extremely upset about the sale of Roundway, which she discussed with her close friend James Lees-Milne who was at this time working for the National Trust. Few owners showed interest in donating their houses to the National Trust before 1939 and the first 18 months of the war saw the Trust's activities practically in abeyance, after which there was a dramatic change in the mood of owners. The National Trust became seen as the only apparent solution to their long-term problems and James Lees-Milne spent the years between 1943, when he was invalided from the army, and 1951, when he retired as Secretary of the Country Houses Committee, travelling the length and breadth of the British Isles to visit houses and assist the families in the often tortuous process of donation to the National Trust. Roundway was not of sufficient stature to be of interest to the Trust, but James Lees-Milne later recalled Dorothy's distress at the time of its sale: 'I fancy that she adored Roundway and her heart was there. Whenever she referred to it tears came into her dear eyes.'[236] She eventually found even talking about it too upsetting: 'Doreen was so distressed that she would not discuss it'.[237]

In 1948, Gladys finally completed on the sale of the estate for £50,000 to the Society of Merchant Venturers, which made this investment in its capacity as Trustee for the H.H. Wills Charity for Chronic and Incurable Sufferers. It had an immediate 'windfall' of £6,000 (£214,000 today) from selling timber from the woods and hedgerows, given that timber prices were then at historically high levels.

After the sale, Bill and Eileen Thomas continued to live in the Swiss Cottage, supplementing their income by growing strawberries and taking in paying guests.[238] Gladys moved to London, first living in a flat in 21 Harley House on Marylebone Road where her cousin Lady Baddeley also lived and, later, at 8 Princes Gate Court in Knightsbridge where she remained for the rest of her life. Gladys's cousin Jill Hepple, née Pratt, remembers Gladys well from this time in the 1950s and 1960s. By then Gladys was an elderly lady and Jill remembers her as being frail and lying on her chaise longue but, although small and gentle with a quiet voice, she was by no means mousy. She was to remain as charming and resilient as ever until her death, aged 90, in 1969.

21

White Knight

THE MINISTRY OF EDUCATION'S plan in 1947 to use the house and 38 acres as a training college for teachers of rural subjects came to nothing. As a result, the buildings were leased to Wiltshire County Council, which used them as storage space for the Fire Brigade and other departments. By the early 1950s, it was clear that Roundway was a liability to the Council.[239] Various options were considered by the Acting Children's Officer, including for its adaptation for use as a boarding school for girls with special educational needs, but the cost of repairs and adaptation, as well as the ongoing costs of maintenance, were deemed to be prohibitive. The County Architect, Frank S. Bowden, prepared a full report on the cost, repairs and conversion, which he estimated would total £35,000 (£1m today).

Roundway Park in 1954 (Historic England).

Above: South facade in 1954 (Historic England).

Left: (Left to right) Clive Leach, who later worked for Peter White, David Phillips and Henry Sheppard, all from Devizes, at Roundway c1951.

Below: Roundway Park in 1954 (Historic England).

The county's education sub-committee then considered the possible adaptation of part of the building for additional accommodation for primary or secondary schools in Devizes but, again, concluded it would not be cost effective. The Clerk to the County Council, P.A. Selborne Stringer, checked with other council departments but found none interested in taking on Roundway. In view of these factors, it was concluded that the County Council's Education Committee should discuss the situation with the Ministry of Education in Whitehall with a view to the premises being disposed of without delay.

The issue came to the floor of the House of Commons on 16 April 1953, when the MP for Devizes, Christopher Hollis, asked the Minister of Education, Florence Horsbrugh, to make a statement on the future of Roundway. The Minister replied: 'The local education authority for Wiltshire have fully considered the future of Roundway House and have reached the conclusion that it should be sold. I have informed the authority that I am prepared to consider favourably this proposal.'

After this the County Planning Officer duly wrote to Devizes Rural Council to inform them that the house was to be advertised with vacant possession and, when disposed of, it was possible that the property would be demolished as its further use for residential or similar purposes was doubtful.

It was possible, continued the letter, that the house would be included in the list of buildings of special architectural or historic interest to be prepared for the Devizes Rural District and the matter had been referred to the Ministry of Housing and Local Government. The County Council's Town and Country Planning Committee then considered the question and the Rural District Council was asked if it wished to offer any observations on the potential listing. Brig. K.M.F. Hedges, Council Chairman, said the main building was of relatively recent origin and had no particular merit. As a result, it was decided to inform the county planning officer that the Council did not consider that Roundway House should be scheduled as a building of special architectural or historic interest.

The disposal moved rapidly and, by November 1953, the house had been sold for demolition to London firm Charles Griffiths Ltd for £6,000 (£165,000 today). A few days before Roundway was scheduled for total demolition and subsequent redevelopment of the site, Peter White, a Devizes builder, heard of the sale.[240] He approached Griffiths with an offer to buy it for £7,000 – an immediate profit of £1,000 for the demolition company, which they accepted. The purchase included not only the mansion but also two entrance lodges, the gardener's cottage and 38 acres.

Roundway House to be Demolished?

NO HISTORICAL INTEREST

ROUNDWAY HOUSE, Devizes, bought by Wiltshire County Council for £7,500 in 1947 after the death of Lord Roundway, for use by the County Education Authority as a teachers' training college, may be demolished.

The County Planning Officer in a letter to Devizes Rural Council, considered on Tuesday, stated that the house was to be advertised for sale with vacant possession and when disposed of it was possible that the property would be demolished as its further use for residential or other similar purposes was doubtful.

It was likely, continued the letter, that the house would be included in the list of buildings of special architectural or historic interest to be prepared for the Devizes Rural District and the matter had been referred to the Ministry of Housing and Local Government. The County Council's Town and Country Planning Committee were to consider the question and the R.D.C. were asked if they wished to offer any observations.

Brig. K. M. F. Hedges, Council chairman, said the main building was of relatively recent origin and had no particular merit.

It was decided to inform the county planning officer that Roundway House should be scheduled as a building of special architectural or historic interest.

MR. HOLLIS'S QUESTION

The Wiltshire News 27th November 1953.

In his memoirs, written in 1999, Peter White described his experience of Roundway as follows:[241]

'The whole property, having been vacant for at least twelve months, was in a very poor state, especially the mansion, woodlands and gardens. The mansion could be approached by the London Road entrance drive, and Quakers Walk entrance from the town. In the Roundway estate heyday, both of these drives, I am told, were kept in immaculate condition, but by now Quakers Walk was just a footpath, and it was bounded by elm trees on either side to form the avenue. The trees were very old and shedding their branches whenever the wind blew. I immediately thought this was a big public liability and decided to apply to cut down the trees and then re-plant them, and install new fences, which I did at the time. There was a very

Quakers Walk gates and lodge.

fine pair of wrought-iron gates at the town entrance, alongside the lodge, which was occupied by the butler who had retired from service at Roundway House several years earlier, with a free tenancy for life. The London Road Lodge was empty, as was the gardener's cottage.

Because of its dilapidated condition, having been occupied for about 10 years by various government departments throughout the war, I chose to demolish the main house which was riddled with dry rot. My vision was to convert the coach house

View from north of the 'new' Roundway House after partial demolition (Historic England).

into our home and develop the estate. We purchased Roundway in 1953 and in the early stages held several auctions of the fixtures and contents setting aside anything that would be suitable for our home. Our new plan was for a five bedroom house comprising a sitting-room, hall, study, and dining-room, and a garage for two cars. In addition, we converted part of the first floor over the old brewhouse into a self-contained flat for a couple who came to work for us in the house.

Sometime in 1953 I received an invitation to tender for the demolition of a large country house on the edge of the Fairford RAF station. This station had a runway that was being extended to take the new large USA bombers and also act as a possible emergency landing runway for the space shuttle which at that time was beginning to be developed. When I inspected the house I found that many of the windows, doors and interior fittings were of the highest quality and several were exactly the same style and size as the Georgian ones in Roundway House. I obtained the contract for the demolition, and extracted the materials I needed for our new home. We also sold off the stone and other materials from the external walls, which were of excellent quality, for the building of a large new house near Stow-on-the-Wold. The conversion work at Roundway took about a year and we moved in from Greenfields towards the end of 1954. The children were now teenagers and away at school so we constructed a hard tennis court. The grounds were very extensive and we were only able to keep parts in good order.

On the right-hand side of the main drive from London Road was a large narrow area of land mostly covered by small trees which appeared suitable as a housing site without spoiling the approach to our new home. We were successful in obtaining planning permission for 74 houses and bungalows on this land which included the old kitchen garden. It

Houses on the front drive of Roundway Park.

meant we had to reconstruct and light the road through the garden to public highway standards. The houses and bungalows found ready buyers almost as soon as they were finished. At the outset we put the plots on the market with planning permission at £200 each, but could not find any purchasers. We built very nice semi-detached houses and detached bungalows and sold the freeholds at the then market price of £2,600 (£67,000 today) each. To reduce our holding, we also sold the two entrance

Recent photographs from Roundway Gardens showing, *clockwise*, the road itself, the former gardener's cottage and the old garden wall.

lodges[242] and the gardener's cottage, the latter being incorporated into the housing estate. This meant we were left with the renovated part of Roundway House and ten acres of park land and gardens which were much enjoyed by all the family. It was this development, more than anything else, which probably marked the turning point in our fortunes and put me on the road to success.'

The illustrated catalogue of the sale of the fixtures and fittings of Roundway before partial demolition on Wednesday 24 November 1954 by Joint Auctioneers Ferris & Culverwell and Tilley Culverwell shows how every item possible was auctioned off, ranging from the Adam fireplace in the Large Drawing Room (£50) to 3 locks (for 5 shillings).

Fireplaces in 1954 before demolition (*from left to right*): Drawing room, library and the first floor bedroom (Historic England).

Peter White's own copy of the catalogue details in his meticulous handwriting the price realised for each item. It provides a fascinating record of the house, room by room. Over 350 lots were offered for sale of which 37 lots with a value of £697 did not sell, according to a note written by Peter White on a separate sheet of paper tucked into the back of the catalogue. He also noted that the sale raised £3,827 (£103,000 today), just over half of the cost of buying Roundway.

A further sale on 9 March 1955, of 380 lots of 'Timbers and Building Materials Resultant from Demolition of the Mansion' included two layers of lead found on the roof.[243] Again we have Peter White's own catalogue with his neatly written record of prices achieved but it does not provide a complete record so it is difficult to ascertain the total raised. The timbers sold consisted of over 380 lots of mainly flooring, partitioning, shelving, windows, shutters, doors,

Historic Fittings To Come 'Under Hammer' At Roundway Sale

A DOOR will begin to close on nearly a thousand years of history next Wednesday, when an auctioneer's hammer will clear the way for a bold new enterprise.

Roundway House, Devizes, the country seat of the Colston family for generations until the death of the last Lord Roundway is coming down.

Soon, Roundway Park, reserved in a Charter by King Henry in 1149, will be the scene of a great building operation. It is to become a big private housing estate.

Meanwhile the "appointments, fixtures and fittings" are to be sold. Where soon will be seen the fine stone mullioned bay french windows and ornamental crisscross ballustrading or the magnificent stone archway with pillared supports and scroll ornamentations?

The Colston crest appears on many items to be sold.

A carved oak overmantel, portraying the Murray-Colston arms together, to come under the hammer in the library, recalls a day in 1879 when Charles Edward Colston brought to Roundway as his bride Rosalind Emma Gostling-Murray, of Whitton Park Hounslow, Middlesex.

The wonderful panelling in the drawing-room, also to be sold, was taken from Whitton Park the home of the Murray family, and is believed to be a copy of that in the orangery at Kensington Palace, being copied at the request of the then Duke of Argyll.

What is the secret behind Lot 251 in the bathroom? It reads: Casement frame, box shutters, fitted drawers white painted skeleton cupboard.

And what famous names of history have been announced from the top of Lot 163: "The finely-carved oak staircase with magnificent wall panelling, twisted bannisters and newels, believed to date from Charles II."

Roundway Park was known from time immemorial as New Park, a name now remembered only in the titles of some Devizes streets. The change came about 100 years ago. Soon after Henry's charter of 1149 New Park was, by Royal command, "imparked," which meant that future tenants leased it direct from the King.

The present mansion was built by James Sutton, in 1780. His architect was James Wyatt, whose other work can be seen at Wilton House, Fonthill and Salisbury Cathedral. Wyatt lowered the old house by one storey and incorporated it into the north side of the quadrangle of the present mansion.

One of the features of the present house is that the reception rooms form a continuous line of 70 yards, opening into each other with fine mahogany double doors. The old or "Queen Anne" part, dates from the early 18th century and possibly earlier, the laundry was once the drawing-room and the kitchen the dining-room. Between these two large rooms are two panelled small rooms.

In 1941, the Colston family, the descendants of Edward Colston, the great Bristol benefactor, purchased New Park. He was a governor of Christ's Hospital and founded Colston School and numerous Bristol charities.

The sale will take place next Wednesday morning at 10.30, and the auctioneers will be Ferris and Culverwell, of Devizes, in conjunction with Tilley and Culverwell, of Chippenham.

One view of Roundway House and (inset) the fine old oak staircase.

The Salisbury & Wiltshire Journal 19th November 1954.

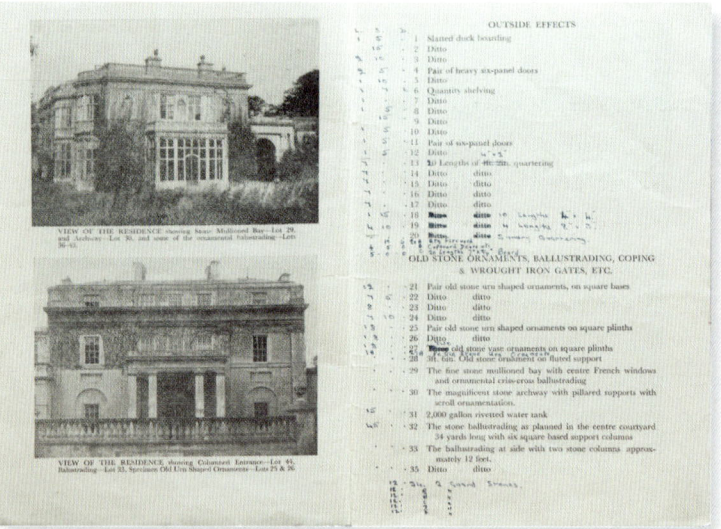

Peter White's copy of the 1954 sale catalogue of fixtures and fittings.

panelling, wooden imitation pillars, boarding, moulding, skirting boards and the odd 'stack of firewood'. Interspersed among the lots were a few non-timber items such as a large butler sink (white glazed), 500 bricks, stone slabs, piping and a large riveted water tank. In addition, the catalogue states at the end of the listed lots: 'There will be a further 100 lots of excellent Building Materials to be lotted at the time of Sale.'

Architectural salvage was nothing new and had long been a natural corollary of country house rationalisation, renovation and demolition. Roundway itself had been a beneficiary of this process when panelling saved from Whitton Park by Rosalind Colston in 1898 was installed in the enlarged entrance hall. Between the 1920s and 1950s, an estate, in the words of John Martin Robinson, was 'more valuable dead than alive, in bits rather than as a whole'[244] and Roundway was clearly no exception.

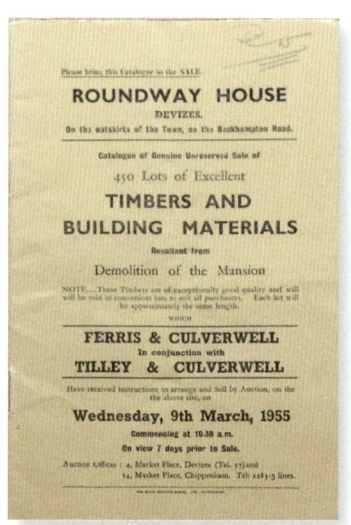

Sale catalogue 1955.

Peter White's work at Roundway led to his involvement in the controversial partial demolition of the Marquess of Lansdowne's Bowood House, near Calne, in 1955, including interiors by Robert Adam. In his memoirs, Peter White described his involvement with Bowood in this way:

During the early part of our work at Roundway we attracted the interest of the Marquess of Lansdowne, whose estate is Bowood, near Calne. Soon after I started at Blackfords I had been involved in many of the building projects on the Bowood Estate. I knew Lord Lansdowne well and he was most interested in what I was doing for my own house at Roundway, and wished to inspect the work. He told me he was considering demolishing the big house at Bowood, and if he finally came to that decision, would I do the work? This was wonderful news for me and, through his agent, Hugh Tapper, I was introduced to his architect, Freddie Samuels (of F. Sortain Samuels), who in due course designed the small houses we built at Roundway. Freddie was an assistant in Sir Albert Richardson's office. Professor Richardson was the leading expert on Georgian architect of the time, and he and Freddie Samuels had worked on the major new facade and alterations at Woburn for the Duke of Bedford. It was a most controversial project, but looked splendid when completed. Lord Lansdowne entrusted me with the demolition of the main Bowood mansion, including the Diocletian Wing.

The controversy about Bowood, which was partially demolished in 1956, marked a turning point in public attitudes towards the demolition of country houses as described by the architectural historian Giles Worsley: 'The rate of demolition remained high ... but the assumption that demolition was inevitable and acceptable began to be challenged. The Marquess of Lansdowne's destruction of much of Bowood House, Wiltshire, caused uproar in the newspapers. Demolishing a country house, formerly a private act, had become a matter of public concern.' [245]

It is no coincidence that this turning point came at a time of economic recovery and improved business confidence, which enabled people to take a more enlightened view of the country's architectural heritage. The peak of country house destruction in 1955 was thus a lagging indicator: recovery was underway but the unwinding of the financial and psychological effects of long years of war and austerity took time to play out.

The fact that Bowood and Roundway were not totally destroyed at a time when obliteration was the norm received recognition from heritage experts. Madeleine Beard observed in *English Landed Society in the 20th Century* that there was a trend in the 1950s to remodel large country houses and build new smaller ones. Thus while 200 country houses were demolished in this decade, 40 were reconstructed or built. [246] Peter White recalled in his memoirs that he received official approval for the 'rationalisation' of Roundway from a group headed by John Betjeman: 'They congratulated us on the good job we had done, and designated the newly renovated house as a grade two building.' Similarly, the Georgian Group reluctantly consented to the demolition work at Bowood in 1956, despite a public outcry and criticism from heritage experts such as James Lees-Milne.[247]

The White family much enjoyed their time at Roundway and their home has been described in this way by Brian Wilkinson:[248]

What had originally been the coach house was converted into a house. The arches were blocked in to give the appearance of relieving arches, containing the main entrance and flanked by sash windows. These relieving arches also contain decoration from the demolished house in the form of oval medallions with carved husk decoration. The main door is surrounded by a decorative carved architrave and simple pilasters, no doubt also saved from demolition; these in turn are surmounted by a semi-circular pediment which gives the composition a neo-Georgian feel. On the first floor flanking this block are two oval windows, again rescued from demolition. The ground floor bay window on the south of this block was added at the time of conversion.

View from north-west of Roundway House in 1961 (Historic England).

To the rear there has been the addition of a brick flue to accommodate a fireplace in the new drawing room and also a ground floor extension of modern brick, cavity wall construction to accommodate a kitchen. Also a large number of sash windows and casements have been inserted both at ground and first floor level, as none existed here previously. Note also that this elevation is of brick and would have originally been concealed with trees and shrubbery.

Oak floors have been laid on the ground floor to replace the flagstones of the original coach house and other salvaged materials have been used as internal doors, skirting boards and dado rails, and on the staircase the ironwork from the main house. Some internal partition walls are original, being made of lath and plaster over studwork.

View from south-west of Roundway House in 1961 (Historic England).

In retrospect, Peter White regretted what he had done at Roundway as he wrote in his memoirs: 'In 1953 it was fashionable to demolish old unused country homes, and there were no restrictions on such activity. Although it seemed right at the time, looking back 46 years later I feel the demolition of the original Roundway property – a grade two listed building – was wrong.'

Henry Robinson continued to live in the Quakers Walk Lodge until his death in 1959. The early years of his retirement after 1945 must have been extremely worrying as he witnessed the sale of the house and estate and the felling of the elm trees on Quakers Walk. In spite of this, Henry continued to cut a dash – Clive Leach remembers him from these days as a very tall figure wearing a leather coat down to his ankles[249] – and he remained active and engaged in his many interests until the end of his life. Friend and author Daphne Moore described Henry at this time:

Quakers Walk Lodge today.

His retirement was never one of rest or idleness. His unfailing zest for the chase remained with him to the end, and he would bicycle for miles to hunt with the Duke of Beaufort's, the Avon Vale and the School of Infantry Beagles. He was 77 when I first met him, out cubhunting with the Duke's; on another occasion he bicycled out to watch the bitch-pack hill-hunting in the woods round Hawkesbury, and I enjoyed a long talk with him before he left for his 35-mile journey home, in tempestuous windy weather, with two very steep hills to negotiate.

Soon after this a regular correspondence developed between us. He wrote in an old-fashioned copper-plate hand, precise and beautiful, and expressed himself with all the assurance of a well-informed mind. He used to make out hound pedigrees tracing back to the 18th and 19th centuries, exquisitely written with a fine pen in microscopic lettering of amazing clarity.[250]

On his death, Henry left Daphne Moore 'several books from his small but very interesting library. The text was liberally interspersed with corrections and comments which revealed his deep knowledge on the subject of hound-breeding'. These books along with others collected by Daphne Moore are now in the Muniments Room at Badminton (Daphne had lived on the estate in the Old Laundry for many years). In view of Henry's acquaintanceship with the Duke of Beaufort and their mutual respect, there could be no more fitting place for his library and papers to reside.

The collection includes note books written by Henry in his beautiful hand, such as 'The Roundway Harriers 1914–15', 'Pedigrees of Famous Foxhounds', 'Herd Recording Register 1939–40' and a blue hardbacked book of Colston family pedigrees.[251] There are also three large books given to Henry by Isaac Bell, MFH of the South & West Wiltshire Hunt. These were for Henry to write up his pedigrees and other notes, a reminder that Henry's diligence needed supporting financially since these great leather-bound ledgers were beyond his own financial resources.[252]

We should leave the last word about Henry to Daphne Moore:

One could write endlessly of this unique character; a striking figure, always immaculately dressed, with a square-crowned bowler hat, stiff, high collar and well-tailored suit, looking as though he belonged to an earlier age, as indeed he did. He had an almost military bearing and a quiet courteous manner rarely met with today … Henry Robinson was, indeed, a most remarkable man.[253]

A year after Henry died, the Whites decided to move and put Roundway House, set in 20 acres, on the market in 1960 at a price of £26,000 (£588,000 today). They eventually sold the property in 1962 for £17,500 (£367,000 today) to Devizes solicitor Derek Alsop and bought a house in the Royal Crescent in Bath.

~❦~ Epilogue ~❦~

IN THE 1960s William and Dorothy Baynes corresponded on a weekly basis. Their brother Ronnie had died on 22 June 1953 at Horton House so they were the only surviving siblings. Many of William's letters remain and a golden thread of reminiscence about Roundway runs through them.

Since 1957 William had been living in a beautiful Georgian house, Pythouse,[254] near Tisbury in Wiltshire, which had been converted into apartments for the elderly. There he found care and company and could live within his means. Dorothy continued to live in 18 Ovington Square in London. Her last book, entitled *The Youthful Queen Victoria,* was published in 1952, its timing unexpectedly aligned with the accession of the young Queen Elizabeth II. It was probably her most successful book commercially and garnered many favourable reviews.

William's letters to Dorothy start 'Dear Toby' (a play on Tabby) and cover a wide range of subjects, including the residents and staff at Pythouse, the wider Baynes family and current affairs.[255] The latter prompted him to reminisce about Charles Colston:

> I must often have told you how I once asked Charlie, in the innocence of my youth, why he did not take in a Liberal daily paper as well as the Morning Post, so that he could know what objections there were to Conservative views? To which he replied quite seriously: 'Oh, my dear boy, it's so <u>confusing</u> to read the arguments on <u>both</u> sides of any political question!' And that I think was the view of most M.P.s in those days except the comparatively few at the top who had more intelligence.

In November 1965, William recalled the autumnal colours of the woods at Roundway:

> The autumn tints always remind me of the Hill Wood at Roundway where I was first taught to admire them; do you remember how lovely they were, and how often we saw them, as we were nearly always at Roundway in September (for the partridge shooting) after spending August somewhere by the seaside? ... Of course the <u>Home</u> Wood at Roundway was the most perfect I have ever known; quite small as woods go, but with the most wonderful variety that I have ever come across in so small a space, and all up and down hill, which added to its enchantment.

A year later, William's fond reminiscences about Home Wood were tempered by the reality of

New Park cigarette box owned by William Baynes.

the changes he had seen at Roundway during his lifetime. He asked Dorothy if she remembered 'the wonderful show of colour all the beech trees in it made, as we used to see them more particularly from the circular room. But the whole of that wood was cut down after Gladys sold the place, and when I last saw it, the whole of that hill side was replanted with young fir trees – all of which I particularly dislike – except of course the Scotch fir, which grows quite differently. So be it old codger.'

At the end of December, his Roundway news mentions that Ronnie's widow, Cecilia, was nearing the end of her life: 'The Thomas's, from the Swiss Cottage in the Roundway Home Wood, looked in on me a day or two ago. They told me Cecilia is now in a very bad way, and in hospital again, in Bath I think. I am afraid she is very unhappy.' Cecilia died shortly after this, leaving her money to the church in Seend, which had strong links to the Wadham Locke family from whom Charles Colston bought the Rowdeford estate in the 1890s.

Roundway continued to be much in William's thoughts and, a year later, his 1967 Christmas letter contained more reminiscences:

> This is to wish you a happy Christmas Day, and I hope you will have some friend to visit you – or perhaps you will be going to have tea with Gladys Roundway, but I am not sure whether you still see her. I used to have tea with her myself on Christmas Day (if she was not playing bridge) in the later years when I was still able to go to London for the festival.

But I think the best Christmas times we used to have were in the last century when both our Baynes grandparents were still alive and lived near Wimbledon where we always used to go, until our grandpapa died [1897], and after that we used to go to Roundway, but I never really enjoyed that nearly so much – in spite of the carol singers and mummers, and snap dragon, none of which used to be provided for us at West Hill.

The summer of 1968 saw the death of Josephine Creasy at the Croft, Padworth. She bequeathed the residue of her estate to the Kennel Club, a decision of which Ted would no doubt have heartily approved.[256] In the following year, Gladys died aged 90. Jill Hepple, her cousin Lady Baddeley and two maids (who were old friends) went in a cab to the cremation in Putney. There was no one else there and the vicar called her Lady Blanche. Gladys left an estate with a gross value of £182,666. In her will she made a number of bequests to friends and staff, after which the remainder of the estate was divided between Mrs Dora Pollitt and the four children of her cousin Beatrix Pratt of Ryston Hall, Norfolk, of whom Jill Hepple was one. Jill remembers Gladys saying some years earlier, when there was a play on called 'The Millionairess', that Jill should not get her hopes up as she herself was no millionairess.[257] That said, Gladys's estate was still substantial, with a value in today's money of £2.5m before death duties and £1m after tax.

In the same year, 1969, William's increasing frailty led to his departure from Pythouse to the Old Forge at Britford, near Salisbury, where a former nurse Miss Gowers provided the full-time care that he now needed. He died in 1971 aged 95. Dorothy lived until she was 92, dying in April 1973, the last of the Colston family members to leave the stage. Her obituary in *The Times* paid tribute to her long and successful literary career. The correspondence between William and her in their later years remains a testament to their great affection for each other and for Roundway, which played such an important role in their lives.

Since the 1970s, the majority of the Roundway estate has changed very little due to the stability of its continued ownership by the Society of Merchant Venturers. In 1976 Roundway House was sold by Derek Alsop[258] to Air Vice-Marshall and Mrs Alan Frank whose family live at Roundway to this day. Two years after the Franks' arrival, I visited them and took the photographs dated 1978 which are included here in the Epilogue.

2. WILTS, Nr. Devizes
3 receptions, 6 bedrooms. Tennis court. Swimming pool. **5 ACRES. £49-54,000**
Tel. Chippenham (0249) 51231

1976 sale particulars.

Roundway in 1978: *Top row*: Rose garden, gate posts, and eagle arch; *middle row*: houses on the front drive, south facade, and entry to cellars; *bottom row*: Quakers Walk gates, Marlborough Lodge, and thatched cottage.

Close to the Home Farm is the Home Covert where John and Sarah Phillips lived from 1963 to 2010. They bought the 33 acres of woodland from the Society in 1959, having put in a bid of £4,000 (£214,000 today). They built a house on the land and, after a storm flattened the woods, planted 36,000 trees. They also developed the area around the house into a botanical garden based on the three old water gardens of the Roundway estate and ran the arboretum in order to further their conservation, educational and charitable objectives.[259]

Left: Swiss Cottage 1978. *Right*: Drive to Roundway House.

Most of the mature trees in the Roundway Hill covert were felled in the late 1940s, except for a few beech near the entrance at the north end, a few at the bottom of the slope and a few ash on top of the hill. In 1972, Mike Dunn, the Forestry Commission's chief forester, proposed the development of a countryside trail, with picnic areas, in the covert which was reopened and widened by members of the Conservation Corps (now the Wiltshire Wildlife Conservation Volunteers). Students from Devizes School also helped to develop and maintain the trail until 1996.[260] The cedar trees on the front drive, however, have continued to mature and create a splendid avenue.

The Kennet & Avon Canal, which runs under the bridge outside the Quakers Walk gates, has been restored and the Queen reopened the canal in Devizes in August 1990. This heroic rescue was achieved often in the teeth of opposition and adversity and it took until 2000 and £30m to ensure fully the canal's long-term future.

The greatest changes have been to the Home Farm and to the edge of town. The fields bordering London Road in Devizes have been developed for housing by the St

Caen locks on the Kennet & Avon Canal.

Monica Trust, which administers the Roundway estate for the Society. The development of the Society's land was controversial. For example, proposals by the police and County Council to light Quakers Walk at night and to keep the gates permanently open (on the basis that closed gates would deter residents of the new development from walking into town)[261] were both

Recent photographs *(clockwise):* New housing beside Quakers Walk, the view up Quakers Walk and the allotments.

opposed by the Quakers Walk Protection Group and by the Trust for Devizes and were defeated, thereby preserving the character of the Walk. Access was subsequently improved on either side of the gates and the latter restored in 2013 with the missing dolphin plaque from the Colston arms replaced with a newly crafted cartouche, only to be vandalised a year later. The allotments for which the Colstons donated the land along the side of the canal continue to thrive to this day.

The Society sold the neglected farm buildings at the Home Farm, which were then converted into a house. The scrap dealers had already picked over them after the war, salvaging the biscuit-making machines for the hounds, which were prized for their high copper content.[262]

Left and right: Home Farm in 1978 before conversion.

When the stables at the Home Farm were renovated following its sale in 2002 (sale particulars opposite), a child's riding hat and a small horse crop were found. These had belonged to Betty Colston whose pony had been shod there in preparation for her summer holidays at Roundway in August 1924.[263]

2002 sale particulars.

Betty's grave in Devizes Cemetery had been positioned so it looked through the trees up to Roundway. On a visit there some years ago, I was shocked to find that the stone angel on the grave was lying on its side, having been severed from its base in the name of Health and Safety. Devizes District Council, however, welcomed my offer to repair and take responsibility for the grave and, although the trees have grown and obscured the view from it to the house, the angel is watching over her little girl once more.

The statue on Betty's grave before and after restoration.

Dorothy described Roundway in *Enter A Child* through her eyes as a girl of a similar age to Betty when she died, and therefore Dorothy's words provide a fitting note on which to end this book:

Slowly I climbed the stairs, and, when I was half-way up, I stopped and leant over the bannister. Here I was almost on a level with the hanging chandelier that lit the hall with its four gas lamps. Three of these burned soundlessly, but the flame of the fourth rang a low, perpetual song. The sweetness to me of that soft, most familiar sound in the silent house! Always as far back as I could remember it had sung its lush golden song;

it was, as it were, the inner living voice of Roundway — Roundway, my childhood's Paradise, and of all places on earth most dear.

It sang of leaf-shadowed garden paths; of black grapes dropping heavily in the tropic world of hot-houses; of cold, smooth apples in the orchard among their tufted leaves; of the soft hound-puppies with their little swinging bellies; of the deer in the park giving their shrill cries at sunset; of a minute pink frog that I kept in the garden tank, whose leap was so swift that one could not see it; of the potting-shed, and the fluffy black mould left sticking inside the flower-pots; of the sound of the garden door beneath its fan of coloured glass as one opened it on the inside, and of the spacious, open-air sound as one shut it on the outside; of the enamelled laurel leaves in the shrubbery, slippery and cool against one's face as one pushed through them, but sheltering hidden twigs that tore small wounds in one's thin, hot skin; of the tiers on tiers of pictures on the dining-room walls, like a perpetually open scrap-book; of ivory-handled, gently-gliding mahogany doors; of each morning's lovely awakening to the sight of the flowered yellow curtains illumined with sunlight, that hung over my windows; of the old nurse, Mrs Turner, in her lilac-sprigged cotton dressing-gown, walking about on those early summer mornings carrying a cup of steaming tea; of the nursery passage where we always played games on 'the last evening'; of the sight of every familiar room and fireplace and landing; of the dearness of those who lived here; of the gold-powdered atmosphere of gentleness and laughter; it sang, in fact of all the outpoured sweetness of Roundway.

Roundway Park in the 1870s.

Appendix I

Key Dates

1636	Edward Colston 'the Philanthropist' born in Bristol (for a summary of Edward's life see Appendix III)
Late 1600s	Leading Devizes families Suttons and Willys acquire land locally
1700–20	Queen Anne house built at Roundway, most likely by George Willy the elder
1704	Edward Colston buys West Lydford Estate in Somerset
1721	Edward Colston the Philanthropist dies
c1730	Prince Sutton (1701–79) marries Mary Willy, daughter of George Willy the elder
1732	Suttons inherit property from George Willy
1762	Prince Sutton serves as Sheriff and Justice of the Peace for Devizes
1765	James Sutton (1733–1801) inherits London clothing business from his uncle William Willy (1702–65)
1768	James Sutton becomes MP for Devizes
1769	James Sutton serves as Mayor of Devizes
1770s	Willy family buys Nicholas's land holdings at Roundway
1771	James Sutton marries Eleanor Addington
1775	James Sutton inherits New Park from his uncle George Willy the younger (1695–1770), via his brother
1777–83	Sutton family builds New Park to James Wyatt's designs
1780	Henry Addington succeeds James Sutton as MP for Devizes
1783	New Park designs exhibited at Royal Academy
1785	James Sutton serves as Sheriff of Devizes
1794	Humphry Repton produces his Red Book for New Park
1797	Rev. William Colston starts as Rector at West Lydford
1800	Eleanor Sutton (daughter of James) marries Thomas Bucknall Estcourt Sr (1775–1853)
1801	Henry Addington becomes Prime Minister
	James Sutton dies
	Eleanor and Thomas Estcourt occupy New Park

1804	Henry Addington resigns as Prime Minister
1805	Thomas GB Estcourt Sr takes over as MP for Devizes from Henry Addington, on the latter becoming Viscount Sidmouth
1819	Edward Francis Colston (1795–1847) marries Marianne Jenkins (1792–1865)
1829	Eleanor Sutton Jnr dies
1830	Thomas Estcourt Jnr (1801–76) marries Lucy Sotheron and takes on New Park
1835	Thomas Estcourt Jnr becomes MP for Devizes
1839	George Holford buys New Park from the Estcourts
1840	Edward Francis Colston buys New Park from George Holford and changes the name to Roundway Park
1847	Edward Francis Colston dies; Edward Colston the Hussar (1822–64) inherits Roundway
1848	Edward Colston the Hussar marries Louisa Murray (1826–1900) and sells Filkins Hall
	James Bucknall-Estcourt becomes MP for Devizes
1849	Edward Colston (1849–59) born
1850	Amy Ruperta Colston (1850–1919) born
1852	Lilian Colston (1852–1931) born
1854	Charles Edward Hungerford Atholl Colston (1854–1925) born
	Rev. William Colston's Rectorship of West Lydford ends
1857	Christopher Darby Griffith (1804–85), husband of Arabella Colston, becomes MP for Devizes
1858	Christopher Darby Griffith Jnr (1858–1933) born
1859	Young Edward Colston dies (aged 10)
1864	Edward Colston the Hussar dies; Charles Colston inherits Roundway
1865	Marianne Colston dies
1868	Amy Ruperta Colston's Coming Out Ball at Padworth House
1872	Amy Ruperta Colston marries Christopher Baynes (1847–1936)
1873	Christobel Baynes (1873–1940) born
1876	William Edward Colston Baynes (1876–1971) born
	Celebration of Charles Colston's Coming of Age
	Thomas Estcourt Jr dies; statue is erected in Devizes
1877	Charles Colston becomes JP for Wiltshire
1878	Ronald Baynes (1878–1953) born
1879	Charles Colston marries Rosalind Murray
1880	Edward 'Ted' Colston (1880–1944) born
	Dorothy Baynes (1880–1973) born

1885	Charles Colston becomes High Sheriff of Wiltshire
1889	Charles Colston elected to Wiltshire County Council
1890	Setting of *Enter A Child* by Dorothy Baynes
1892	Charles Colston elected MP for Thornbury, Bristol and makes first major alterations to the Wyatt house
	Henry Robinson (1874–1959) joins the staff at Roundway
1895	Statue of Edward Colston the Philanthropist unveiled in Bristol
1897	Roundway Harriers started
1900	Louisa Colston dies
c1901	Charles Colston makes second set of alterations to the house
1904	Ted Colston marries (Blanche) Gladys Duddell (1879–1968)
1907	Charles Colston wins Coaching World Championship at Olympia
1910	Betty Colston (1910–1924) born
1914	Ted Colston wounded at Battle of the Aisne in September and invalided home
1915	William Baynes starts serving on the Western Front in France in May and Ted Colston in Egypt
1916	Charles Colston becomes 1st Lord Roundway
	William Baynes fights in the Somme
1917	William Baynes awarded MC and then wounded at Ypres
1919	Amy Ruperta, Lady Baynes, dies
	Charles Colston sells 535 acres at Rowde to Wiltshire CC for subdivision into smallholdings
1920	Charles Colston sells West Lydford estate
1924	Betty Colston dies (aged 14)
1925	Charles Colston, Lord Roundway, dies and Ted Colston inherits Roundway
1931	Lilian Colston dies
1933	Ted Colston inherits the Padworth estate from Major Christopher Darby Griffith
1936	Sir Christopher Baynes dies
1938	Rosalind, Lady Roundway, dies
1939	Dorothy Baynes publishes *Enter A Child* (under pseudonym Dormer Creston)
	Julia Crofton (née Murray) comes to live at Roundway
1940	Christobel Baynes dies
1944	Ted Colston dies
1945	Henry Robinson retires
1946	Gladys, Lady Roundway, starts negotiations for the sale of the house and estate, and sells contents
	Dorothy changes her surname to Colston-Baynes by deed poll

1947	Wiltshire County Council buys Roundway House and 38 acres
	Society of Merchant Venturers (the Society) leases Home Farm
1948	The Society buys the Roundway estate
1952	Wiltshire County Council's Education Committee sets up sub-committee to consider the future of Roundway House
1953	Sub-committee recommends 'disposal without delay'
	Devizes MP raises Roundway's future in House of Commons and Minister of Education agrees to its disposal
	Demolition firm Charles Griffiths Ltd buys Roundway House from Wiltshire County Council, then sells it on to Devizes builder Peter White
	Ronnie Baynes dies
1954	Peter White sells fixtures and fittings from the house, partially demolishes the main house and converts the coach house into his own family home
1955	Peter White sells timber and building materials
	Peter White constructs and sells 74 houses and bungalows on estate land (including old kitchen garden), and sells two entrance lodges and gardener's cottage
1956	Peter White carries out demolition work at Bowood
1957	Sir William Baynes starts living at Pythouse, near Tisbury in Wiltshire
1959	Henry Robinson dies
1962	Derek Alsop buys Roundway House from Peter White
1963	John and Sarah Phillips buy the Home Covert
1969	Gladys, Lady Roundway, dies
1971	Sir William Baynes, Bt, dies
1973	Dorothy Colston-Baynes dies
1976	Air Vice-Marshall and Mrs Alan Frank buy Roundway House
1978	Author visits Roundway for the first time
1990	Kennet & Avon Canal reopened by the Queen
1995	The Society, through the St Monica Trust, begins housing developments on the estate

Appendix II

A Brief History of the Ownership
of New/Roundway Park

1777–83	New Park *built* by James Sutton incorporating Queen Anne house
1801	Inherited by Eleanor Sutton (wife) and lived in by James's daughter Eleanor and her husband Thomas Estcourt
1830	Lived in by Thomas Estcourt Jnr and his wife Lucy (née Sotheron)
1837	Inherited by Thomas Estcourt Jnr and his aunt Charlotte 'Sarah' Matthews
1839	Bought and *improved* by George C. Holford
1840	Bought and *renamed* Roundway Park by Edward Francis Colston
1840s	*Improved*
1847	Inherited by Edward Colston the Hussar (son)
1864–75	Held in trust for Charles Colston on death of his father Edward Colston the Hussar
1875	Inherited by Charles Colston, later 1st Lord Roundway (son)
1892	*Enlarged and improved*
1901	*Further enlarged and improved*
1925	Inherited by Edward 'Ted' Colston, 2nd Lord Roundway (son)
1944	Inherited by Gladys, Lady Roundway (wife)
1947	Mansion house and 38 acres bought by Wiltshire County Council and renamed Roundway House
1948	Estate bought by the Society of Merchant Venturers
1953	House bought by Charles Griffiths Ltd and then by Peter White
1953	House *partially demolished*
1962	House bought by Derek Alsop
1976	House bought by Frank family

Appendix III

Slavery and Philanthropy: The Life of Edward Colston

THIS CHAPTER is not intended to excuse Edward Colston for his slave trading activities which are rightly a subject of condemnation in Bristol and beyond. Instead it is an attempt to provide a factual account of the different activities in which he was involved in a long and active life.

Edward Colston was born in 1636 in Temple Street, Bristol, the eldest child of William and Sarah Colston who are thought to have had 11 children.[264] The Colston family had lived in the West Country for 300 years since Thomas Colston, a mercer or cloth-merchant, came south from Lancashire to Bristol in about 1340 to take advantage of the city's thriving wool trade. The family prospered, trading and owning ships operating in many parts of the world. Edward's grandfather, Thomas Colston was Sheriff of Bristol in 1561 and Mayor in 1577 and his

father, William, was Sheriff and also Deputy-Lieutenant of the city. A strong sense of the world in which they lived can be gained by visiting the Old City of Bristol today with its cobbled streets, remains of the Old City walls, narrow streets, fine churches, beautiful buildings (albeit many are Georgian or later), St Nicholas Market, proximity to the river and the general bustle of people.

Edward's staunchly Royalist father William (1608–81), who entertained Charles I at his house in Wine Street in 1643, left Bristol for London in 1645 when the city was taken by the Parliamentarians in the Civil War (1642–51). As a result, Edward was educated in the City of London at Christ's Hospital (of which he later became a governor in 1680). The family only returned to Bristol in 1661, after the Restoration of the monarchy, from where they resumed their trading activities – including in wine, oil, fruit and sugar – with Spain, the West Indies and elsewhere.

The Philanthropist.
Pub. by
C. MITCHELL,
38, College Green,
Bristol.
EDWARD COLSTON, ESQ.,
Founder of Colston's
School.
Entered :
Stationer
Hall.

Portrait of Edward Colston, 1722.

Edward's career benefited from the rapid development in overseas trade and colonisation by Britain in the first part of the 17th century, which saw the foundation of colonies in New England, Virginia and the West Indies as well as the establishment of the first trading stations in India. In 1654, aged 17, he was apprenticed for a term of eight years to Humfray Aldington, a member of the Mercers' Company of London, and it is thought that he spent some time in Spain as part of his training. In 1673, at the age of 37, Edward was admitted to the Mercers' Company in London.

As a result of the East India Company's monopoly of eastern trade, Edward's business was conducted with merchants in the west in places ranging from Virginia to Naples. He traded in a wide range of commodities, including textiles, carpets, wrought silk, wine, sherry and Newfoundland cod. A colourful story about how Edward came to adopt the dolphin as his family crest relates how one of his vessels sprang a leak which then mysteriously stopped. It was discovered that a dolphin had forced its way into the hole and saved the captain, crew and merchants on board.

Colston coat of arms by Henry Robinson.

Until the 1680s, Edward's trading activities had been principally conducted from London. In 1680 he became a member of the Royal African Company, based in London, which had the monopoly between 1672 and 1698 of slave trading between the west coast of Africa and the Americas. He took an active part in the planning and financing of slave trading ventures to Africa. His name was present in the Company's records for 11 years and he was Deputy Governor of the Company in 1689–90.

After his father's death in 1681, Edward began to be involved actively in Bristol again, which was then the second city to London due to its maritime trading. William had originally left his Bristol business to his younger son Thomas but the latter died shortly after his father and bequeathed his brother Edward the Bristol ships and business as well as his house in Small Street. In 1683 Edward became a Freeman of Bristol and was elected a member of the Society of Merchant Venturers, being described as a 'free Burgess and St Kitt's merchant'. The Society, founded in the 14th century and granted a Royal Charter in 1552, effectively controlled all shipping entering and leaving the Port of Bristol so no-one in Bristol could engage in commerce beyond the seas unless they had first been admitted to the Society.[265]

In 1689, Edward sold his ships in Bristol and took a long lease on Cromwell House by the River Thames in Mortlake, Surrey.[266] This remained his principal home for the rest of his life. The area was then rural, well away from the coal smoke pollution and insanitary conditions of central London. The house was named after Thomas Cromwell who, for a time, held the manor of Mortlake. It was fairly plain inside, with oak panelling in the Puritan style, but the garden was more ornate with a magnificent catalpa tree, orange trees and evergreens such as

Left: Old Cromwell House c1855 and *right*: Gate posts to Cromwell House today.

Portuguese laurel, ilex, yew and myrtle (as mentioned in his will). There was also statuary and a summer-house by the Thames, which he particularly enjoyed. The late Elizabethan and Stuart eras saw not only the development of the flower garden but also the introduction of trees, flowers and plants from abroad including some of those mentioned at Mortlake and others such as the tulip, laburnum and nasturtiums.

Edward continued with his overseas trading activities until his retirement from business in 1708 at the age of 72, although he continued to pursue various commercial and financial interests, including the acquisition of land in various parts of England, some of which remained in the family until the 20th century.

Edward never married and when encouraged to do so is said to have replied: 'Every helpless widow is my wife and her distressed orphans my children.' His philanthropy was reputed to have originated from an experience in Spain as a young man, which was described many years later in the *Devizes Advertiser* of June 1858:

'While there he was taunted by some Roman Catholics with the remark, that the Protestant religion had produced no examples of great charitable benefactions. He replied, that if this were true, he trusted God would one day permit him to wipe off the stain, and to exhibit to the world the vital power of the protestant faith. God so blessed his efforts that he lived to endow the school at Bristol, which bears his name, with a sum of £40,000. Another school, on a smaller scale, almshouses for the poor, various contributions to the noble foundations of London also testified to his liberality ... When advised to buy an eligible house for his own use, he replied, 'Ay, ay, I must first house those who have made me what I am,' referring to the blessing of the poor.'

Edward was a High Churchman, as reflected in the large donations that he made for the repair of various churches such as All Saints' Church in Corn Street, Bristol, where he dedicated a monument to his parents and six of his deceased siblings after his mother's death aged 93 in 1701. When in Bristol, he attended daily service at the cathedral and each Sunday he used to stand at the door to observe the boys from the school he founded enter the church. In 1704 he became a member of the Society for the Propagation of the Gospel and in 1708 he was elected a member of the Society for Promoting Christian Knowledge.

Colston memorials in All Saints' Church, Corn Street, Bristol.

He was also a staunch Tory and was elected as the senior MP for Bristol in October 1710 at the age of 74. Edward had a peremptory manner and made many enemies who misrepresented him and spread rumours about his private life. Part of the motivation for Edward's philanthropy was no doubt to demonstrate that the Tory party was equally concerned about social reform as the Whigs who had dominated the city's corporation since 1696. His parliamentary activities were focused on presenting petitions on matters which concerned the commercial interests of Bristol rather than playing an active role in wider parliamentary affairs. Petitioning was vital for Bristol given that, since the Civil War, its position as the second city and port to London had been in relative decline. He did not seek re-election on the dissolution of parliament in 1713, probably due to his age.

Edward took a very close interest in the charitable organisations that he endowed and was prescriptive about the way in which their affairs should be conducted, particularly the requirement for hard work, observance of Anglicanism and avoidance of Whiggism. His brusque manner and exacting demands meant that he sometimes had serious disagreements with the charities and organisations that he sought to help such as Christ's Hospital, the Corporation of Bristol and the Mortlake Vestry.

His charitable donations were extensive, totalling £63,940 (£13.5m today) in his lifetime in public benefactions but probably considerably more if his smaller private donations are taken into account. His charity was mainly focused on Bristol but he was also active in supporting causes elsewhere, particularly in Mortlake and London. They ranged from small donations (such as for the relief of debtors in Ludgate Prison and the Marshalsea) to large benefactions such as the endowment of Queen Elizabeth's Hospital, Bristol (a school for orphan boys), and the foundation and endowment of Colston's School (initially called Colston's Hospital) at a cost of £40,000.

Colston's School was opened in 1710 after Edward became disenchanted with the City Corporation's attitude towards Queen Elizabeth's Hospital, given that they considered such an institution to be 'a nursery for beggars and sloths'. Colston's School was housed in a Tudor mansion Edward had acquired in 1707 called the Great House in the centre of Bristol where Queen Elizabeth I had once stayed. He then placed the school in the charge of the Society of Merchant Venturers, which administers the school to this day. In 1857 the school moved to Stapleton, Gloucestershire, and in 1861 the Colston Hall Company bought the Bristol property from the boys' school and demolished the Great House in order to build a concert hall, called Colston Hall, which was opened in 1867 and, after several re-builds, continues to thrive to this day. In 1891, the Society of Merchant Venturers opened a sister school called Colston Girls' School, which is now in Cheltenham Road, Bristol.

Left: Original Colston's School in the Great House in Bristol and *right*: recent photograph of Colston Hall.

In his old age at Old Cromwell House in Mortlake, Edward was looked after by his unmarried sister Ann, then by his great niece Sarah and finally by a kindly neighbour Mrs Elizabeth Beavis. He was active in supporting causes in London as well as Bristol, particularly St Bartholomew's Hospital where his portrait, painted by Godfrey Kneller in 1693, hangs to this day. He died at Mortlake in 1721 aged 85 and was accorded a magnificent funeral (more elaborate than the low-key service that he requested in his will) in which his hearse was accompanied by eight horsemen and three mourning coaches with six black-plumed horses each.[267] The bells of the Bristol churches tolled for 16 hours and he was buried in All Saints'

Church, Bristol, where the effigy on his tomb, designed by James Gibbs, was executed by sculptor John Michael Rysbrack from the portrait by Jonathan Richardson in the Council House.[268]

Rysbrack tomb to Edward Colston in All Saints' Church, Bristol.

Edward had executed his last Will and Testament a year before he died. It was a lengthy document 'in thirty and three sheets of Paper' containing many bequests to relatives as well as to charities. As an illustration of his meticulous care and attention to detail, he prepared an itemised estimate of the cost of his funeral, which amounted to £207. 17s. 2d. The benefactions bequeathed in his will totalled £12,385 (£2.6m today).[269] There is a footnote to this summary of benefactions: 'The Reader is requested to observe, that Mr Colston's public Bounty was not by any Means oppressive to his Family – as it is well known that he bequeathed sufficient Fortunes to his Relations.' The latter amounted to £100,000 (£21m today) of which his great niece Sarah inherited £60,000 (£12.6m today). His fortune included land in the West Country (including the West Lydford estate in Somerset), Northumberland and Lincolnshire.

He is commemorated in Bristol by John Cassidy's 1895 bronze statue in Colston Avenue, a stained-glass window in the north transept of Bristol Cathedral (placed there by the Dolphin Society in 1890) and another window in All Saints' Church designed in 1907 by Henry Holiday. Colston Hall and other institutions and streets were named after him. A number of societies were founded after his death, which gave money to the poor: the Colston (1726), Dolphin (1749), Grateful (1759) and Anchor (1769) societies. There were later societies such as the Bristol University Colston Society, founded in 1899, with funds for scientific research. There is also a Colston bun, and Colston Day has been traditionally commemorated annually on 13 November with the ringing of the bells of St Mary Redcliffe Church and a dinner held in aid of local charities.

John Cassidy's 1895 statue of Edward Colston in Colston Avenue, Bristol.

The descent to Edward Francis Colston who bought New Park in 1840 is explained as follows. Edward the Philanthropist's great niece Sarah died a year after him in 1722 and the inheritance reverted to her aunt Mary, Lady Hayman, née Colston and sister of Edward. She had married Sir William Hayman in 1670. He was a Bristol Knight and Mayor of Bristol in 1684. The following year he was indicted for kidnapping felons for transportation and sale as slaves in the West Indies, which gave rise to his description as a 'white slave trader'. He was a pugnacious character who, as High Sheriff, quarrelled with the notorious Judge Jefferies and there were rumours that he had ensured the 'removal' of Sarah Colston so that her share of £60,000 of Edward's fortune reverted back to his wife. It is also alleged that he insured the death of Sarah's parents just before the latter's demise.[270]

The Haymans' daughter Mary married Thomas Edwards[271] of Filkins Hall, Oxfordshire.[272] He was a successful lawyer in Bristol, having studied at the Middle Temple, and was MP for Bristol (1715–19) and then for Wells (1719–35). His father was also the attorney who had managed most of Edward Colston's estates. Thomas and Mary Edwards had two daughters who were co-heiresses. One, Mary, married in 1723 Francis Willoughby, second Lord Middleton, of Wollaton Hall, Nottinghamshire. The other daughter, Sophia, was the ancestress of Edward Francis Colston of Roundway Park. She married Alexander Ready in 1737.

Sophia and Alexander lived in Filkins Hall where they had four children: Mary (born in 1738) who died in infancy; Alexander (born 1742); Thomas (who was buried in 1746) and Edward (born 1749). In 1754, Alexander and Sophia petitioned parliament to change their surname to Colston in a Bill which was passed and became an Act in March 1755.

Alexander and Sophia Colston.

This had been necessitated by a clause in Edward's will of 1720, which requested that any husband of his female heirs must change their name to Colston in order to inherit, although it is not clear why Sophia and Alexander did not petition much earlier. The Colston fortune meant that Sophia brought £20,000 (£4.4m today) to the marriage (as cited in the *Universal Spectator* of February 1737) and she was also the beneficiary of coal mines around Bristol: Coalpit Heath, Serridge, Westerleigh and Winterbourne to the north east and Clapton to the south west.[273]

Alexander died aged 89 in 1775 and there is a memorial to him in Fairford Church, near Filkins Hall. His life had proved to be a fine example of the social mobility that characterised the 18th century. The son of a cordwainer, he rose to the ranks of country squire through a sound education, a lucrative career and three financially advantageous marriages.

Sophia continued to live at Filkins Hall until her death in 1790. She left most of her fortune in trust to her son Alexander Jnr and his children. Alexander Jnr had been educated at Trinity College, Oxford, and became Rector of Broadwell in 1765 and of Henbury in 1786. He married Louisa Elers in 1744 and they had at least seven children. These included Edward who married Arabella Clayfield of Bristol and it was their son, Edward Francis Colston (1795–1847) who bought New Park in 1840.

Appendix IV

A Portrait of Dorothy Colston-Baynes

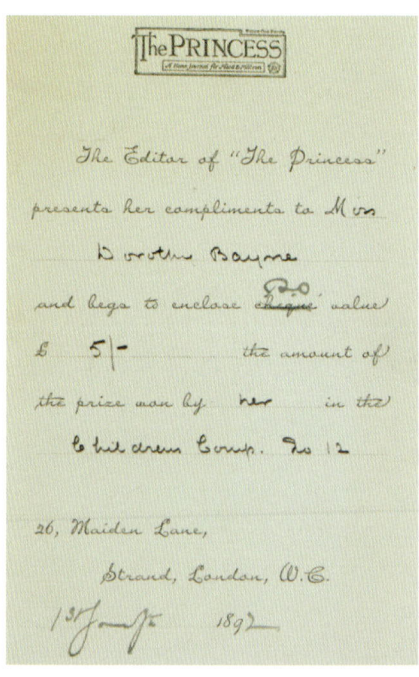

BORN IN 1880, Dorothy Baynes mainly grew up in London, which she describes in detail in the first part of *Enter A Child*. Before recounting some upsetting scenes from her childhood, chiefly linked to her difficult relationship with her father, she is at pains to show that her parents were doing their best within the constraints and customs of their time as was commented on in more detail in Chapter 8: Family Life.

Dorothy illustrates the dreariness of her life by describing dull lessons with her governess: 'During term-time, and term-time naturally covered the greater part of the year, I spent nearly all day shut up with my governess in a little back-room. This forced incarceration of middle-aged and childhood was a dreary affair for both. That confined, sunless room was soaked in boredom.' She did, however, see the amusing side of the governess-pupil relationship as a teenager in this spoof photograph taken in 1896 of her with her governess, Miss Thorpe. And there were early signs of her literary talent with her prize from the *Princess* magazine, aged 12.

Miss Thorpe and Dorothy in 1896.

Dorothy's *Princess* certificate.

Later, Dorothy attended the Slade School of Fine Art in London (1905–08) where she was a few years older than most of the other students. In her mother Amy's diaries of both 1906 and 1908 there are references to Dorothy going to her studio, usually on a Saturday. Her cousin Keith Baynes, who was also at the Slade at this time, remembered Dorothy dressing, in his words, 'ostentatiously', but failing to make much of an impression.

She was already suffering from ill health and depression, which would recur throughout her life. Amy recorded in her diary entry of 21 October 1908: 'Dorothy and I drove to see Dr Russell who thought she should be 5 weeks at the Home … Christobel took Dorothy to the Home near Haslemere where she is to have a "Rest Cure" with massage and electricity.' She returned home on 2 December: 'Dear Dorothy returned from her 6 weeks rest cure, looking very well and strong; she and Christobel went to see Dr Russell who thought D. wonderfully improved.' Dorothy was also prone to hypochondria, which perhaps helps explain why, despite her medical problems, she lived to the great age of 92.

Few examples of Dorothy's paintings exist but there is a catalogue for an exhibition by members of the Friday Club in London in February 1915 in which she exhibited a painting entitled *A Profile* alongside works by artists such as John Nash, Bernard Adeney, Nina Hamnett, William Rothenstein and Paul Nash. Unlike her cousin Keith Baynes, who went on to make a successful career as a painter, she decided to abandon painting and concentrate on writing instead.

Her literary career started at the age of 39 with the publication by Heath Cranton Ltd in 1919 of a collection of her poems entitled *The Clown of Paradise* under the pseudonym of Dormer Creston.[274] She used this pen-name throughout her literary career and it had the advantage of being gender neutral in a world where female writers were not necessarily taken seriously, particularly at the start of her career. At the time of publication, Dorothy and her sister Christobel, both unmarried, lived at home with their father in Lowndes Square in London, their mother Amy having died at the beginning of the year. The sisters were determined not to be victims of the 'enforced idleness'[275] of middle-class women which characterised their mother's generation. They were typical of the Edwardian generation of women in that they combined conventional activities, such as charitable works, with a more emancipated approach to developing their own skills and talents.[276] In their case, they were fortunate in being supported by their parents in doing so.

Amy with Christobel and Dorothy at
Roundway in Edwardian times.

Dorothy's book of poetry was particularly influenced by her wartime correspondence with Alec Agar-Robartes, the son of Viscount Clifden, who sent her some moving poems from the Front. The inspiration for her next work, *My Ancestress, Charlotte de la Trémoille*, probably written in the early 1920s but unpublished, was the Murray family. Charlotte was an inspirational character, the granddaughter of William the Silent, Prince of Orange, and the great-times-seven grandmother of Dorothy through the Murray family. The manuscript recounted her part in the English Civil War on the Royalist side, supporting her husband the Earl of Derby whose loyalty to the Royalist cause and Charles I, in spite of the latter's contrary and distrustful attitude towards him, led eventually to the Earl's beheading in 1651 by the Parliamentarians. Charlotte's portrait was painted by Rubens and Vandyke and in 1644 she had shown great courage, resourcefulness and leadership in successfully defending the family's fortified house, Latham in Lancashire, from the Parliamentarians while her husband was fighting on the Isle of Man.[277]

Another more substantial work (100,000 words) from this time was *Jeanne La Pucelle* about Joan of Arc, which Dorothy completed in 1925 but again for which she did not find a publisher although it elicited some good opinions from the Century Company in the US.[278] Her fluency in French was vital in researching this biography and provided the basis for her next book, a translation of Verlaine's poems entitled *Poems from Paul Verlaine*, which was published in 1928 by Selwyn & Blount.[279] It received a glowing review in the *Mercure de France* on 15 August 1928, which praised its fidelity to the original in terms both of its felicitous and careful choice of words and its musicality. '*Ce poète suit l'original de très près, avec souvent des trouvailles singulièrement heureuses ... Parfois, la transcription se rapproche étonnemment du chant de l'original, les images sont finement transposées, et le choix de mots est d'un artiste.*' Dorothy also wrote poetry in French of which examples remain.

Dorothy writing in Lowndes Square.

She kept a record of the books she read and paintings she saw between 1925 and 1939. She also started a diary in 1928 which ran, with gaps, until 1935. It records events, thoughts, books read and literary quotations. Dorothy's periodic illnesses (particularly from colitis) and depression are catalogued and there are vivid descriptions of London life, activity in Lowndes Square and visits to galleries and the theatre. Some well-known people pass through the diary, from Sacheverell Sitwell to the Royal Family at a Buckingham Palace Garden Party in July 1933.

In 1929, Dorothy had her first major literary success when Eyre and Spottiswoode published her book *Andromeda in Wimpole Street,* a collection of the love letters of Elizabeth Barrett and Robert Browning during their engagement. It was received with critical acclaim: for instance, *The Times Literary Review* said: 'Miss Creston has been struck with rather a happy idea … the story which these letters tell … is best told in the words of the lovers themselves. Miss Creston has told it so … Those who do not know the story and the two long volumes of letters will find her book a good introduction to the subject.'

It sold well in both Great Britain and the US[280] and ran into two further editions in 1937 and 1943. Many years later, Dorothy's friend James Lees-Milne wrote of her: 'She was not unlike Elizabeth Barrett before she became Mrs Browning. Perhaps if Doreen had met her Mr Browning she would have changed. But she was a darling, hyper-sensitive person with a strong sense of humour.'[281]

For her next book Dorothy turned again for inspiration to her Murray forebears who were at Court during the Regency period. In an article for *Blackwoods Magazine*, Dorothy later recalled that as a child she used to be told anecdotes of her great-great-grandmother Lady George Murray and her life at Court. Lady George Murray was a lady-in-waiting at the court of George III while her daughter Amelia (1798–1884) was a lady-in-waiting to Queen Victoria and published her reminiscences entitled *Recollections of the Early Years of the Present Century* in 1868.

Dorothy's new book, *The Regent and his Daughter*, was published in 1932 by Thornton Butterworth and describes the lives of the Prince Regent and his daughter Princess Charlotte and her tragic inability to bear a son and heir to the English throne. The book won critical acclaim: James Agate said 'She writes beautifully … maximum wit' while Lord David Cecil included her as one of only four women writers in his *Anthology of Modern Biography*.

Dorothy's family were similarly enthusiastic; Rosalind wrote from Roundway to congratulate Dorothy on the book on Christmas Eve 1932: 'My heartiest congratulations to you on your book which I have been reading with the greatest pleasure. What wonderful criticism you have had and it must be very interesting getting the American ones now.' The book quickly went into a fourth impression and was recommended by the Book Society. The celebrated historian and biographer Philip Guedalla wrote the introduction and the book inspired

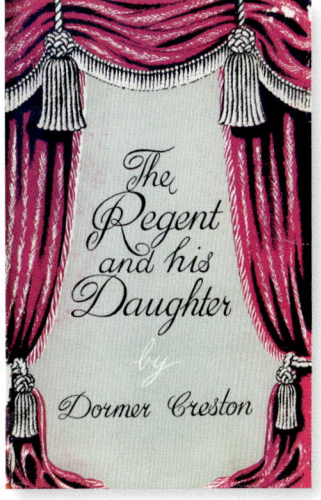

Book cover of
The Regent and his Daughter.

Noël Coward in 1933 to write his musical *Conversation Piece*, which ran in the West End at His Majesty's Theatre before transferring to Broadway.

Christobel helped Dorothy with her historical research and also wrote and illustrated her own book in the early 1930s on the subject of colour-music, the art of combining music with colours with correlations of harmonic and emotional effect, which was explored by early 20th century composers such as Arnold Schoenberg and Alexander Scriabin.[282]

Its preparation entailed correspondence with Sir Walford Davies who at the time was organist of the Chapel Royal at Windsor Castle and made regular broadcasts on the radio on classical music entitled *Music and the Ordinary Listener* (later in 1934 he succeeded Elgar as the Master of the King's Musick). Sir Walford wrote an encouraging letter to her on 24 September 1932: 'I have spent some interesting time this morning reading the Colour-Music book, and imagining the children's enjoyment of it … What I admire is the kindness you so deftly, lovingly and ingeniously show to our babes learning their notes in making what is often associated with drudgery so interesting and romantic. All success to the venture.'

The book appears to have been printed privately[283] and there is a letter from Roundway dated 26 December 1933 in which Rosalind Colston thanks the sisters for 'the delightful book which I shall much enjoy reading …'[284] Alongside her literary activities, Christobel kept up her musical studies as a pianist, corresponding with Miss Penrose in Holland Park, who was a sight-reading specialist, and regularly attending concerts.

The two sisters were enthusiastic users of the British Museum Reading Room and many of their book request slips survive, revealing that they ordered books ranging from *John Nash* to *Hay Dieting*, from *Decorative Patterns of the Ancient World* to *Lip Reading*. They were also interested in the new and fashionable pursuit of Theosophy and spiritualism.[285]

Christobel ran the household at Lowndes Square after Amy's death in 1919, and then from 1936 in Ovington Square, thereby enabling Dorothy to concentrate on her writing. Christobel carried out her duties with great efficiency and her papers provide a wonderful record of the varied aspects of her role in running a large townhouse. Among her notebooks

is one entitled 'Housekeeping – 27 Lowndes Square'. It has a multitude of pencil entries recording the purchase of household items, from golden syrup to black linen aprons, from a banister brush to pumpkin jam. There are also many receipts for household items, careful records of holiday expenditure, gardening information and a red-covered notebook which records Dorothy's weekly expenditure on items ranging from leads for her dog Peter (5/-) to nail polish (1/6d). It is all signed off by Christobel with a horizontal line and her initials C.R.B. across the page.

The sisters' holidays were carefully costed as well and Christobel kept a record of holiday expenditure in a red notebook with daily costings itemised. Christobel and Dorothy spent a number of summer holidays in Folkestone including staying in 1932 at 'Southcliff', 25 The Leas, where the bill itemises charges not only for their apartment for the week (£5 15/- 6d) but also servants' board (£1 10/-), sitting-room firewood (6/-) and the potential for payment for the electric light in the sitting-room and the use of the piano. There were also holidays abroad, particularly in the winter, and one envelope contains a piece of paper headed 'British Consulate General, Tangiers' with a list of exotic local flowers.

Much the largest section of the collection of Christobel's papers from the 1930s relates to health matters including several letters from Matthias Alexander relating to what became known as the Alexander Technique. It seems that most of the medical treatment was focused on Dorothy rather than Christobel herself. It is ironic that Dorothy referred to her Aunt Lilian's self-immolation to Louisa Colston in thinly veiled critical terms in *Enter A Child* given that Christobel seemed to have been manoeuvred by Dorothy into fulfilling a similar role for her sister 20 years later, albeit willingly. Their aunt Agnes Osborne, née Baynes (whose watercolours were featured earlier in this book), had suffered a worse fate, as she was forbidden by her father, Sir William, from marrying Jere Osborne and reduced to looking after her parents. After Sir William's death, however, Agnes was emancipated and married Mr Osborne on 28 January 1908.

In a letter of 15 September 1936, Dr George Bray wrote to Christobel about Dorothy in these terms: 'I do not think her dropped feet have anything to do with the drops or Health tea, which she has been taking, and it would be quite useless to test her for that. Probably she wants some supports built into her shoes.' There are numerous other letters to Christobel about her sister's health such as one dated 19 February 1937 from a doctor named G.W.B. James of 124 Harley Street: 'Your sister is of course a life long neurotic – and will probably remain so more or less. But the nervous disease ought to be enormously benefited by the new treatment, <u>which has not been discussed</u> very long – and gives us new hope.'

In 1935 Dorothy gave a lecture entitled 'The Regency Period' in aid of Lady Clodagh Anson's Welcome Canteen at 23 Princes' Gardens in London. In March 1936 she gave another lecture at the same venue entitled 'The Bright and the Dull Young Things of the Seventies' which raised money for the Victoria Hospital for Children in Tite Street (tickets were priced at 10/-). Later that year she published her next book *Fountains of Youth,* a biography of Marie Bashkirtseff, a Russian noblewoman who practised naturalistic painting in Paris. The book was well received by the critics, including *The Times Literary Supplement*, which wrote: 'With sure and skilful hand Miss Dormer Creston has constructed this highly entertaining biography.'

Dorothy's burgeoning literary career led to her meeting a wide range of well-known people and she recorded some of these encounters in the diary she kept intermittently between 1937 and 1951. An entry for 1937 recorded that Osbert Lancaster told her how the Duke of Richmond, while attending the Coronation service of King George VI in Westminster Abbey, managed to sell four cars to his fellow members of the peerage. An entry for 1939 relates an anecdote told by her friend Peter Coats who heard a fellow guest at a New Year's Eve party in Monte Carlo attended by the Duke and Duchess of Windsor say loudly: 'I must just have one look at that bitch who nearly ruined the Empire.' Nancy Mitford (or Rodd, her married name) told Dorothy in July 1939 that Max Beerbohm was very proud of his knighthood and, when someone asked him his opinion of James Joyce's writing he replied, 'I don't think it is the kind of writing that will lead to a knighthood!'

Dorothy's capacity for friendship found expression in her being a mentor to young writers including Eddy Sackville-West, James Lees-Milne and James Pope-Hennessy, the younger son of her childhood friend Dame Una Pope-Hennessy.[286] There is a letter from James Pope-Hennessy to Dorothy dated 16 March 1938 which captures this early stage of their friendship, when he was 22 years old and Lees-Milne was aged 30. James thanked her for a very enjoyable lunch party at Ovington Square and commented on the friendly people he met there including Midi Gascoigne and said how lucky he was 'having you and H. Nicolson for friends!' Lees-Milne also attended and 'was quite bouleversé by his conversation with you – "charming", "amusing", "delightful", "a real person", "perfectly sweet", and much more that I had already discovered long ago myself!'

Christobel appears to have been a casualty of the literary lunch-parties Doreen liked to hold at Ovington Square, as is described by James Lees-Milne in a diary entry some years later:[287]

To Doreen Baynes for a talk. When I told Eddy [Sackville] West that I considered her nearly a saint he laughed me to scorn. He said she used to lock her sister (Christobel) up in a cupboard when her friends came to the house because she was so ashamed of her. Indeed I do recall a luncheon guest before the war going to the lavatory in her house, finding the door unlocked and the sister on the seat, a Pekinese on her lap, reading a novel. But I attributed this to her sister's intense shyness and reluctance to meet Doreen's friends.

William also had a book published at this time, namely *St Joseph of Arimathea – The Glastonbury Legend*. It was handsomely illustrated with line drawings by Honor Howard-Mercer and printed by the De La More Press in London.

After the publication of *Enter A Child* in 1939 and the outbreak of war, Dorothy and Christobel moved out of London to avoid potential bombing and at the end of 1940 Christobel was confined to a nursing home in Warleigh near Bath suffering from terminal cancer. Dorothy wrote movingly about the last days of her beloved sister's life, which she spent by her side. Christobel left Dorothy her entire estate, valued at £25,464 net (£1.4m today). After Christobel's death, Dorothy went to live in Scotland on the Lovats' Beauly estate. In a letter to James Lees-Milne she wrote how: 'Maurice Baring, Laura Lovat and Veronica Phipps are still my living delights up here. I think I told you all about Maurice, didn't I? How, partly paralysed, he lies all day in his pyjamas with a blue budgerigar perched on his shoulder? Now, for the spring and summer, Laura is taking him back to her house on the island in the middle of the Beauly River [Beaufort Castle], the house where the grandsons of Prince Charlie lived.'

Dorothy's wartime correspondence contains many letters not only from her family but also from friends such as Lady Anne Hill (wife of Heywood Hill, the bookshop owner in Curzon Street) and Mary, Duchess of Devonshire (widow of the 10th Duke), who addressed Dorothy as 'Dearest Zelide' and signed off with her childhood name of Moucher. Mary's brother Lord David Cecil also kept in touch with Dorothy, as did her close friend Lady Sarah Cumming-Bruce.

Ava Wigram's correspondence included a letter of sympathy on Christobel's death and, not long after this, in October 1941, Ava married Sir John Anderson, the Home Secretary, who later became Viscount Waverley. Midi Gascoigne, mother of the writer and broadcaster Bamber, was another close friend of whom Dorothy said: 'Directly I say her name I think of daffodils and crocuses adazzle with sunshine – she has that kind of quality about her.'[288]

Other war-time correspondents included Dame Una and James Pope-Hennessy (James came to visit her in March 1943[289]), Honor Pilkington, Betty Wiggin and Selina Kay-Shuttleworth (née Bridgeman) whose two sons Richard (2nd Baron Shuttleworth) and Orlando (3rd Baron) were killed in the war. Angela Giffard described in one letter in the autumn of 1942 the rapid courtship of her daughter and only child, Diana, and Anthony (Airey) Neave, which led to their marriage on 29 December 1942. (Diana later became a life peeress in 1979 a few months after her husband was tragically blown up by the IRA). Dorothy also corresponded with Angela's sister Sylvia who wrote a long letter about her wartime life in Cairo in the summer of 1943, where she was working.

At the end of 1942 James Lees-Milne sent news from London: 'Nancy [Mitford] is still working at Heywood Hill's shop and is likely to be in sole charge as Heywood is being called up and Anne is having a baby. Midi [Gascoigne] is living with her children in one of my father's cottages in Worcestershire, and I am staying with her for Xmas. Jamesy has got a new flat in Camden Hill, very beautiful specially printed wall papers, the whole of considerable elegance.'

Shane Leslie, with whom Dorothy was at one stage romantically involved,[290] was a regular correspondent and shared Dorothy's interest in spiritualism, which is referred to frequently in Leslie's letters, such as this one of 12 May 1942:

> I am glad to hear your experiences of Dr Lascelles as I have known others who went there. Record all your own experience ... Last Sunday I spent the afternoon with a most interesting Mrs Dowden who does automatic script. As Mrs Travers Smith she took down the famous messages of Oscar Wilde. These I was interested to see as they reproduced his script exactly and I recognised the genuine signature and the Greek letters alpha and epsilon he was fond of interweaving out of his Classical erudition.

> This is to me astonishing and I cannot doubt the evidential proofs ... I am hearing of spiritualist manifestations from the other side almost every day. There seems so much evidence that the trees overshade the wood ... I am always keeping notes and I urge you to record all that you have gleaned in the years so that we can pass on our data to the brilliant investigators of the future.

Dorothy's first cousin Keith Baynes also wrote to Dorothy on Christmas Day 1942 from his home in Iden near Rye:

> I was so pleased with your Christmas card. Thank you very much for sending it. Also it makes me write to you again. Letters become more and more important as we see our friends less and less. I go to London every two months and try and see everyone I can but as I only stay a night or two I do not have much time. I see Willie every time I go and dine with him and make the most of what food there is left in London. I think I have seen more of him than I have ever done before. I saw Eddie Sackville-West the other day. He has a job at the BBC and I believe likes it very much ...

> I am quite happy in the country and am able to work. There is always light here which was difficult in the winter in London. I have been able to read a lot. I still see something of Duncan Grant, Vanessa Bell and Clive. I exhibit with them at a little gallery at Lewes. They have organised some very good exhibitions. We have all been doing decorations for a theatre which have been shown at Lewes and are now going to be shown at the Drama League in London. We have been a prohibited area here

> since the fall of France and can have no-one to stay. We are very close to France and are now having raids again and the village machine gunned … I do not think I could stand it all unless I was painting every day.

Wartime news also reached Dorothy from her close friend Eva Agar-Robartes, sister of Alec, who wrote from Lanhydrock, Cornwall, on 5 May 1943 about the experiences of her brother Gerald, Viscount Clifden, and herself:

> We have just had Dame Beryl Oliver here – a 'Queen' of the Red Cross, and Gerald and I had to take her round for inspections. She loved talking about the Royal Family and told us one or two amusing stories – how Maggie Wyndham fainted at Badminton and Queen Mary said 'Bother' and went on watching – and that when she went to see the young Kents, the little boy was heard to say as he came down the stairs 'I hope Grandmama won't stay very long', and then the children proceeded to have a fight with each other upsetting flower vases. Queen Mary said they were the worst children she had ever known (or something to that effect) as she drove away …
>
> We are getting on well with our occupational Parcels for Prisoners of War; the patchwork cushions, and wool-bordered belts and slippers have turned out well. We have at last got some materials for rug making which I am told will be extremely popular. The war news looks better, don't you think? We are threatened with an influx of Americans in the near future in Bodmin, we hope for the best.

Left and middle: Dorothy's photographs of the Agar-Robartes at Lanhydrock in 1898.
(*Left*): Constance, Violet, Victor, Eva and Gerald. (*Middle*): Violet, Constance, Cicil and Alec.
Right: Dorothy playing on stilts at Wimpole Hall with the Agar-Robartes.

At the end of the war, Dorothy returned to London and began to meet up with her friends again, having been out of the capital since 1939. Picking up again after such a long absence proved challenging for her and countless others as James Lees-Milne found at their slightly strained first post-war meeting on 7 August 1945.[291] A month later, however, the old friendship was back on track, as he recounted in his diary:

> This evening I had a glass of sherry, South African and rather hot, with Doreen Baynes, once again in her drawing-room in 18 Ovington Square, with the alcove, the peach satin sofa, the satinwood Sheraton furniture on spindly legs, the fragile Chelsea shepherdesses, and the very same wax magnolias not even dusted since 1939. It was a more satisfactory meeting than our last in Brown's Hotel. We both poured out confidential chat. She told me she goes through such agonies over reviews of her books that she often retires to bed for a week, with blinds drawn, silently weeping.[292]

That autumn saw the publication by Macmillan of Dorothy's next book *In Search of Two Characters*, about Napoleon Bonaparte and his son Napoleon King of Rome, to widespread acclaim. The reviews were numerous and overwhelmingly favourable and Dorothy pinned them into a school exercise book which captures the spirit of her busy and fulfilled life.

In Search of Two Characters marked the pinnacle of Dorothy's literary career. She received the Heinemann Award from the Royal Society of Literature in 1946 and was elected a Fellow of the Society. In mid-June she received a letter from Harold Macmillan on behalf of her publishers (he was temporarily out of parliament and working in the family business) in which he congratulated her on her prize and said: 'It is a great pleasure to us, as your publishers, that this additional recognition should be made of the merits of your work.'

The presentation of awards took place on 26 June and was made by the President of the Society, the Earl of Lytton. He not only described *In Search of Two Characters* as a book of 'outstanding originality

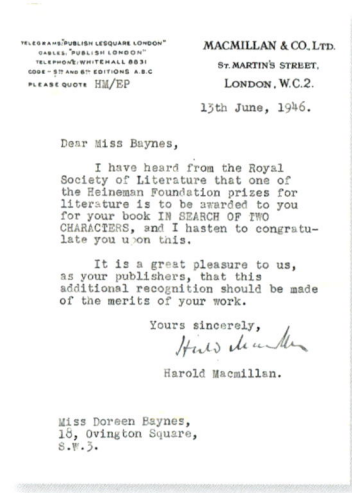

Letter from Harol Macmillan to Dorothy June, 1946.

Book cover of *In Search of Two Characters*, 1946.

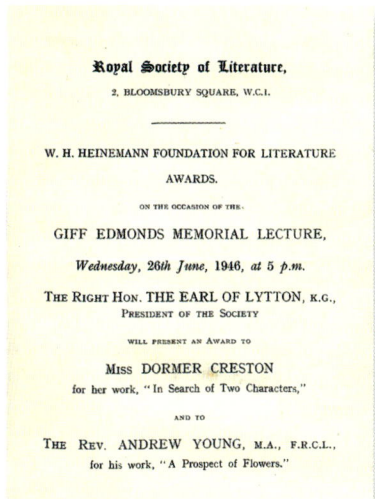

Programme for RSL Heinemann Awards in June 1946.

and merit' but also summed up two key aspects of her writing which help explain the success of her overall literary career: her ability to portray her subject from a new angle and the cinematic quality of her writing, which draws the reader into the story.[293]

Dorothy had long had an interest in writing for the stage, as shown by a play she wrote during the First World War and *Many and Various – A Ballet Revue* from the early 1940s, which consisted of about 20 short ballets (she sent it to publishers in 1943 complete with her own descriptive paintings of costumes but without success).[294] After the publication of *In Search of Two Characters*, however, she was approached by the theatrical agents Daniel Mayer in a letter of 21 April 1947: 'We produce plays, and I would enquire if you have written a play or would consider doing so? If you have already written a play I would very much like to read it, and equally so should you feel, as the result of this letter, that you would wish to embark on this type of writing.'

Dorothy's renown as a historical biographer led to invitations such as a lunch given by the Duke of St Albans in the winter of 1945/6 about which she later wrote: 'I first met Eddie Marsh at a luncheon party of about 8 people at Brown's given by the Duke of St Albans. I was put one side of Eddie and Miss Rose Macaulay on his other side. No sooner were we all seated than our host turned to those nearest him and exclaimed "Now we must all keep silent and listen to the 3 authors". The faces of the three slowly turned each to the other and for a noticeable period complete silence reigned.'[295]

In April 1946, Dorothy mentioned in a letter to Ronnie that: 'Sir Edward Marsh took me to see Lady Antrim aged 91 who was lady-in-waiting for 10 years to Queen Victoria – the idea being that she should give me various lights on the Queen for my new biography.' Dorothy was at this time working on her next book about the young Queen Victoria, and Eddie Marsh kindly read it through before publication.

In November 1947 James Lees-Milne gave a lunch party so Dorothy could meet Roger Fulford who had written a

Book cover of *The Youthful Queen Victoria*, 1952.

book about Prince Albert. The diary entry is worth quoting at some length as it captures the quirky literary world which Dorothy inhabited at this time:

Sunday 23rd November 1947

Gave an enjoyable luncheon party of Doreen Colston-Baynes, Roger Fulford and Ivy Compton-Burnett. Doreen wanted to talk to Roger about Queen Victoria whose young life she is writing. Roger is now publishing a life of the Prince Consort. I could see how happy Doreen was. They all stayed until twenty to four. Roger said to me afterwards, for we walked together to St. James's, that he feared from what Doreen had told him, the Royal Family were not opening their records to her, and questioned whether it was not because of the trouble he has got into from Queen Mary who gravely resented Roger's imputations that Prince Albert interfered in British politics.

Ivy was very characteristic, speaking volubly in her breathless, sharp manner, and often being very amusing. She began by saying that she never read the sort of books Roger and Doreen wrote and knew nothing of the subjects, implying that she cared less. Then she repeatedly interjected observations, which were very much to the point, while they were confabulating, which they did at length over coffee.

The four of us then discussed how we wrote: Doreen never at a writing-table, which gives her claustrophobia, but preferably in bed, or sitting on a stool at the fire, or in a field on the grass, a pad and paper on her knee; Ivy always at her table at the window with an electric fire the other side of her; Roger always at his writing-table, with piles of notes, carefully docketed around him, and several bottles of differently coloured inks; I at my little Empire bureau, if the weather is warm, or in my armchair as close to the fire as possible, if the weather is cold, papers balancing on the arms of my chair, a small table, a bookstand and the floor.

Dorothy continued to have an active social life throughout the rest of the 1940s and the 1950s, holding regular lunches in Ovington Square (usually on a Thursday) and keeping in touch with not only relations but also friends such as Mary, Duchess of Devonshire (who, on 14 January 1950, wrote saying she was 'delighted with Debo', her new daughter-in-law), Viscountess Broome, Violet Trefusis, Airey Neave, Chips Channon, Princess Galitzine, and writers including Vita Sackville-West, Noël Coward, and, from 1957, Anne de Courcy who became a very successful historical biographer.[296]

The diaries also record Dorothy's illnesses, including colitis, and, particularly in 1950, her depression, which was sometimes severe and at other times steady and continuous. She also mentioned in 1957 and 1958 visits from the society osteopath Stephen Ward (who would later figure so notoriously in the Profumo affair). Her correspondence also showed her continuing quest for health and psychological remedies.

By the 1960s, she was beginning to suffer from dementia and her young cousin John Baynes became her Official Receiver under the Court of Protection in 1967. He helped find a tenant for the basement flat in Ovington Square, namely the Byrne family who provided back-up help if needed. In 1966, a nurse, Miss Molloy, came to live on the top floor to help look after Dorothy. Miss Molloy later married Dr Vignoles who joined her in living in Ovington Square and also made beneficial improvements to Dorothy's medical care.[297]

The gradual onset of dementia is seen in her blue note-book from 1962–63 which shows firm handwriting at the beginning but by the end the script is deteriorating and the content is becoming less coherent.[298] In Dorothy's papers there are two letters and two postcards from James Lees-Milne in 1965–66 who continued to visit her regularly at Ovington Square, as did John Baynes.[299] Lees-Milne later recalled one of the last times he saw her:[300]

> The penultimate time I went to see her she gave me tea – or rather it was not tea exactly. She was very particular to have a silver teapot, silver kettle, sugar basin, cream jug, etc., in fact the whole correct bag of tricks. I was directed to pour hot water into the tea pot from the kitchen kettle which I did, bringing the tea pot into the drawing-room. Doreen in a moment of aberration (this was long after the days of the megaphone [nickname for her manservant], when she was practically servantless) had put, instead of the Earl Grey tea leaves, into the pot, two or three spoonfuls of Goddard's pink silver powder. I took one gulp, and was very nearly poisoned. The extraordinary thing was that Doreen drank her cup, professing it to be very good. She was quite cross with me for not finishing mine. I wonder she ever survived those final fifteen years.

Dorothy died in London aged 92 in April 1973. Lees-Milne later wrote of her to John Baynes: 'I was extremely fond of Doreen, as we were instructed to call her, who was a wonderful friend, affectionate and sympathetic. And if at times we laughed at her it was always in a loving way.'[301] And in a letter to the author he said of Dorothy: 'I only hope you did not think I was making mock of her. That is the last thing I mean to do, because I was totally devoted to her. She was an angel of goodness, sensitivity and sympathy. And those many evenings I went to drink a glass of sherry at Ovington Square will remain among the most cherished of my life.'[302]

Endnotes

1   Introduction to *Lost Country Houses of Norfolk – History, Archaeology and Myth*, Tom Williamson, Ivan Ringwood and Sarah Spooner (2015).

2   Lorna Haycock, 'The elite and the dynamics of power in late Georgian Devizes', *Wiltshire Archaeological & Natural History Magazine*, vol. 102 (2009), pp. 262–74.

3   *Victoria County History (VCH), Wiltshire*, vol. 10 (1975), p. 256; James Sutton of Devizes married Anne Palmer in 1677 and their son, also James, was born in 1678. J. Waylen, R.D. Gillman et al, *The Annals of the Royal and Ancient Borough of Devizes, 1102–1900* (Devizes, 1908), p. 14.

4   *VCH, Wiltshire*, 10, p. 247.

5   The name is variously spelt as Willey or Willy during the 18th century. Both families raised trade related petitions to Queen Anne: James Sutton in 1707 and Thomas Willy in 1709. British Library, Add. 61619, ff. 24–26b; Add. 61620, ff. 127–128b.

6   The will of George Willy the elder, dated 1732, left trusts endowing his widow, and son-in-law Prince Sutton and grandson Willy Sutton, but left his land and built property between Hugh Gough and James Sutton (Prince Sutton's father, the Mayor of Devizes, b.1678). The will said: 'I give and devise to Mr James Sutton and Mr Hugh Gough … all my messuages, lands, tenements, and hereditaments …' Copy of the will of George Willy the elder, 1732, Wiltshire Records Office (WRO), Sutton Papers, 248/83.

7   K. Dore, *Map of Devizes*, 1759, British Library Maps. K. Top. 43.33.

8   James Waylen and Henry Bull, *A History, Military and Municipal, of the Ancient Borough of the Devizes* (London, Devizes, 1859), p. 405, gives his date of death as 1765, but the Willy pedigree in Devizes Museum and Library gives his dates as 1702–63. I have settled on 1765 as this is corroborated from other sources such as the records of the East India Company of which he was a Director.

9   The 1832 Reform Act extended the vote to male property owners who earned more than £10 per year, roughly 18 per cent of the adult male population.

10 Haycock, op. cit. (2009), pp. 262–74.

11 William Sutton had been tried at the Old Bailey for the murder of Ann Bell in 1761. – Pamela Colman, *The Baker's Diary: Life in Georgian England from the Book of George Sloper, A Wiltshire Baker, 1753–1810* (Wiltshire County Council, 1991), pp. 88–9.

12 WRO, Sutton Papers, 574/116.

13 William Hague, *William Pitt The Younger* (Harper Perennial, 2004), pp. 25–6. Dr Addington's relationship with Pitt the Elder went further than purely medical matters as he played a central role in the failed negotiations for a coalition government with Lord Bute in 1778. Dr Addington alienated many politicians with his published account of the negotiations entitled: *An authentic Account of the Part taken by the late Earl Chatham in a Transaction which passed in the beginning of the year 1778*.

14 Gloucestershire Record Office (GRO), Estcourt Papers, D1571/F641, p. 92.

15 Jenny Uglow, *In These Times – Living in Britain Through Napoleon's Wars 1793–1815* (Farrar, Straus and Giroux, 2015), p. 96.

16   Lorna Haycock, *Devizes – History and Guide* (History Press Ltd, 2000), and *VCH,Wiltshire,* 10, p. 245.

17   *Wiltshire Books, Pamphlets, and Articles* (from Devizes Museum & Library), p. 100.

18   *VCH, Wiltshire*, 10, pp. 246–7.

19   *Wiltshire Gazette*, 30 March 1944, in a report on the death of the 2nd Lord Roundway.

20   Plan of Roundway Farm, the Property of Edward Richmond Nicholas, M.P. temp. Geo. II, n.d., Papers of the family of Nicholas of Roundway in Bishops Cannings, co. Wilts, 1559–1754, British Library, Add. 34008, f.1. The map has annotations which are probably of a later date.

21   *VCH,Wiltshire*, 7 (1953), p. 191. The Nicholas tenancy is illustrated in a remarkable series of private deeds lodged in the British Museum and the WRO. BM Add. Chart. 37460-616; Add. MSS. 34008 and WRO.

22   *VCH, Wiltshire*, 7, p. 191.

23   Such evidence includes plans of the ground and first floors recorded in 1952 (*Survey of Roundway House, Devizes, March 1952* by Frank S. Bowden, ARIBA, County Architect, County Hall, Trowbridge, WRO 1954/8), 19th and 20th century photographs, and the sale catalogue of fixtures and fittings (*Roundway House, Devizes, Sale of Appointments, Fixtures and Fittings of the Mansion, 24th November 1954*, Ferris and Culverwell, Tilley and Culverwell).

24   *Wiltshire Gazette*, op. cit., 30 March 1944.

25   Ferris and Culverwell, Tilley and Culverwell, op. cit.

26   The fact that only two panelled rooms on the upper floor, the staircase and kitchen/dining room ceiling are recorded in photographs taken in 1954 for the National Monuments Record (now Historic England Archive) would support the assumption that these two panelled rooms were on the first floor.

27   John Martin Robinson, *The Wyatts: An Architectural Dynasty* (Oxford University Press, 1979), p. 66.

28   Ibid.

29   Ibid., pp. 56–89.

30   GRO, Estcourt Papers, D1571/F641, Account books 1765–91.

31   Peter Lindley-Jones, *Restoring the Kennet & Avon Canal* (History Press Ltd, 2002).

32   GRO, Estcourt Papers, D1571/F641, 1765–91, p. 91.

33   Ibid., pp. 92, 93.

34   Ibid., pp. 91, 109.

35   George Carter et al., *Humphry Repton, Landscape Gardener, 1752–1818* (Victoria & Albert Museum, 1982), p. 17.

36   Brian Wilkinson, *Roundway House, Devizes,Wiltshire*, Foundation Course essay, Birkbeck, London University, 2001 (with monetary value updated using the Bank of England's Inflation Calculator).

37   Ibid.

38   Prof. Mark Girouard, *Life in the English Country House* (Penguin, 1978), p. 214.

39   GRO, Estcourt Papers, D1571/F656.

40   Ref. from Dr John Martin Robinson, 2003.

41   Ref. from Eileen and John Harris, 2003.

42   Howard Colvin, *A Biographical Dictionary of British Architects, 1600–1840*, 3rd edition (Yale University Press, 1995), p. 1115.

43 Carter et al., op. cit., p. 19.

44 Dorothy Stroud, *Humphry Repton* (Country Life, 1962), Introduction, p. 69.

45 *Draft Bill for inclosure of land in Roundway, Bedborough, Chittoe, Bishops Cannings and Marden*, c1793 (Act of 1794), John Lord Bishop of Salisbury in right of his see is Lord of the Manor of Bishops Cannings and James Sutton Esq is the lessee thereof under the said Bishop and the said James Sutton in his own right is Lord of the Manor of Marden; GRO, Estcourt Papers, D1571/E395, p. 2.

46 Carter et al., op. cit., p. 163.

47 GRO, Estcourt Papers, D1571/E396.

48 Stephen Daniels, *Humphry Repton: Landscape Gardening and the Geography of Georgian England* (Yale University Press, 1999); Timothy Mowl, *Gentlemen and Players: Gardeners of the English Landscape* (Sutton, 2000), p. 180.

49 Carter et al., op. cit., pp. 38, 42, 45.

50 Ibid., p. 16.

51 Ibid., pp. 43, 49.

52 All illustrations of the Repton Red Book for New Park are by kind permission of Gloucestershire Archives (reference D1571/E396).

53 Carter et al., op. cit., p. 61.

54 Ibid.

55 Michael Mansbridge, *John Nash: A Complete Catalogue* (Phaidon Press, 1991).

56 Carter et al., op. cit., p. 62.

57 Girouard, op. cit., p. 218.

58 Ibid.

59 The updating of monetary values throughout the book is calculated by using the Bank of England's Inflation Calculator which shows how prices have changed from 1209 to 2018.

60 Haycock, op. cit.(2009), pp. 262–74.

61 Ibid.

62 Ibid.

63 Ibid.

64 James Sutton to Addington, 9 June 1789 – Devon Record Office, Sidmouth Papers 152M/1789/F59.

65 *Wiltshire Books, Pamphlets, and Articles* (from Devizes Museum and Library), p. 100.

66 Haycock, op. cit. (2009), pp. 262–74.

67 John Girvan, *Devizes: Hidden Secrets* (Girvan Publications, 2006), pp. 99–100.

68 Haycock, op. cit. (2000), p. 53–4.

69 Uglow, op. cit., p. 85.

70 Haycock, op. cit. (2009), pp. 262–74.

71 GRO, Estcourt Papers, D1571/F637.

72 GRO, Estcourt Papers, D1571/F208.

73 WRO, Sutton Papers, 248/125.

74 The name of the house went through several variations: the house was designated as Park House on *Andrews*

and Dury's Map of Wiltshire (1773), and in the publications: John Cary, *Wiltshire* (1787); Archibald Robertson, *Road from London to Bath* (1792); John Rennie, *A Plan of the Proposed Navigable Canal between the River Kennet and the River Avon*, 1793 (1810). But William Tunnicliff's *New Map of Wiltshire* of 1791 shows it renamed as New Park (Fig. 75).

75 Waylen and Bull, op. cit., pp. 553–4.

76 GRO, Estcourt Papers, D1571/F43. The net income of £3,200 resulted from the gross income of £4,000 from the manor of Bishops Cannings from which the reserved rents of £800 of the Bishop of Sarum had to be deducted. In the mid-18th century George Willy had purchased the lease of the manor of Bishops Cannings Manors; *VCH, Wiltshire*, 7, p. 189.

77 Estcourt Park, Shipton Moyen, Gloucestershire, had its origins in a manor house of the 14th century, rebuilt in the 16th century and then demolished in 1802. A new house had been built by Thomas Estcourt in 1776–79 on a site about a mile away. This house was modernised in the 1820s, when some payments were made to 'Wyatt', probably Lewis Wyatt, and again in the 1850s. It was demolished in 1964. – Nicholas Kingsley, *The Country Houses of Gloucestershire, Volume 1, 1500–1660* (Phillimore & Co., 2001), pp. 97–8; *Volume 2, 1660–1830* (Phillimore & Co., 1991), pp. 136–7.

78 The extent of the park at New Park is delineated on an undated map of the Manor of Bishops Cannings of c1800. Estcourt land is marked on the same map (coloured beige) to the south. – WRO, Sutton Papers, 574/110 (Fig. 78).

79 *Dictionary of National Biography*.

80 Girvan, op. cit., p. 42.

81 'New Park – a Lost Estate' in *Trust News – The Newsletter of The Trust for Devizes*, issue 115 (February 2009).

82 WRO, F348, 1817.

83 Brian Wilkinson, letter to the author, 2 July 2004, outlining his argument about Estcourt's work and backed by examples of local and estate maps dating from about 1800 to 1838.

84 Ibid.

85 *Dictionary of National Biography*. Thomas Sotheron-Estcourt left Estcourt Park on his death in 1876 to his younger brother, the Rev. Edmund Hiley Bucknall Estcourt, and Darrington Hall to his nephew, George Thomas Sotheron-Estcourt, who was created Baron Estcourt in 1903.

86 GRO, Estcourt Papers, D 1571/F438, Family Records and Diary, 1737–1806, memoranda, diary extracts, entries by T.G.B. Estcourt and T.H.S.S. Estcourt.

87 WRO, D1571/F438, 1839, and GRO, Estcourt Papers, D1571/F438. Thomas Jnr records in his diary: 'January 1835. Father sleeps at New Park for the Devizes election', which is when the younger Thomas was first elected as MP for the town.

88 GRO, ref. from Brian Wilkinson.

89 *Chronicle of Devizes 3* from Devizes Museum & Library.

90 GRO, Estcourt Papers, D1571/E404.

91 Edward Bradby, *The Book of Devizes* (Buckingham, 1985), p. 95.

92 Haycock, op. cit. (2000), p. 68.

93 Waylen and Bull, op. cit., pp. 558–9. 'May 19th 1838 ... In the presence of Lord Sidmouth, the deeds were signed by which the entirety of New Park estates (valued at £54,000) was conveyed to me from £30,000' – GRO, Estcourt Papers, D1571/F2, pedigrees of Gloucester and Wiltshire branches of the Estcourt and

Sutton families compiled by T.G.B. Estcourt and T.H.S.S. Estcourt, 13th–19th century.

94   Girvan, op. cit., p. 100.

95   James Lees-Milne, *A Mingled Measure – Diaries 1953–1972* (published in 1994): diary entries for 6 September and 16 October 1971.

96   WRO, F438, 1839.

97   Newspaper cutting in Scrapbook in Long Street Museum, Devizes.

98   Marianne's portrait was found in an antique shop in Bristol in 1985 by John and Heather McOmie's younger daughter who is an artist, based in the US. She also wrote a piece on the internet about Marianne Colston. Heather McOmie had an aunt called Marianne Colston and is descended from the sister of Edward Colston the Philanthropist. Information from the McOmies from a meeting with the author in 2012 in Bristol.

99   We do not have a full picture of William Jenkins' landholdings but we know from *VCH, Somerset,* 9, that he bought part of West Pennard Manor in 1807 from John Paget, which had been part of Glastonbury Manor at the time of the Domesday Book and was in Royal ownership from the Dissolution of the Monasteries until 1628. He also bought Barton Farm in 1809, the demesne farm of Barton Manor, south-east of Street and described in the late 18th century as 'low, fruitful, well-wooded and sufficiently watered …' He added to it with Callows Farm and other land so that it finally consisted of three farms and totalled 223.5 acres.

100   Marianne's journal is contained within two hardbacked volumes and a large bound folio-sized book with the 50 lithographic prints. The latter illustrate places visited within the central part of their travels, namely between May 1820 (starting with the Temple of Minerva Medica near Rome) and October 1821 (finishing with the Haute Garonne). The periods of time either side of these dates (November 1819 to May 1820 and October 1821 to the New Year 1822) still saw Marianne sketching and painting but not with a view to producing a finished lithographic print. The books were published in 1822 by the Paris-based English language publisher A. & W. Gagliani with the lithographs by Francois Le Villain based on drawings by Marianne. They were published again in 1823 by the London firm G. & W. B. Whittaker. Information in part drawn from *Database of Women's Travel Writing: Marianne Colston* by Dr Benjamin Colbert (2015).

101   There are relatively few paragraph breaks in the original text so extra ones have been inserted in this chapter at appropriate stages for ease of reading.

102   From the document entitled: *The London Newbury and Bath Direct Railway – Proof of F. Fuller Esq. Mr Colston's Case* (1846).

103   *The Civil Engineer and Architect's Journal*, vol. 4 (1841), p. 223.

104   It is likely that these statues are casts as explained by Hugh Honour in a letter to Dr Ruth Guilding dated 20 May 2006: 'I was interested to see the photographs of the drawing room at Roundway Park with the two statues of Dancers obviously derived from those by Canova, either copies in marble or far more probably plaster casts many of which were produced by Canova's formatore. Documentation for the sale of casts is patchy and I can find it in no reference to an Estcourt or a Colston. Although casts reproduce Canova's work more faithfully than the many copies carved at Carrara, they have until recently been neglected and many were destroyed in the last century.'

105   WRO, Map 861/22.

106   *VCH, Wiltshire*, 7, p. 192.

107   It survives today, though it has since been whitewashed, and is located on the south side of the close of new houses erected in the 1960s. At the end of this close, part of the old kitchen garden wall survives.

108   Barry Barrett, conversation with the author, 8 February 2003.

109 Girvan, op. cit., pp. 106–8.

110 Fuller described the proposed route in this way: 'That he has made a careful examination of the Roundway Park Estate which is situate near the Town of Devizes and has ascertained the manner in which the same will be affected by the London Newbury and Bath Direct Railway which enters Mr Colston's Estate by the Lodge on the London Road, makes a curve to the private Carriage Road called the Quakers Walk in a deep cutting, then to the high ground above the waterfalls and so on North West into Mr Hughes' Land called Belvidere.'

111 Haycock, op. cit. (2000), pp. 71–3.

112 *VCH, Somerset*, 9, pp. 195–6.

113 Ibid.

114 Ibid., p. 209.

115 Ibid.

116 Sir John Baynes, Bt, observations from a visit.

117 Louisa Murray's diary for 1845 is in the possession of the author's family.

118 Lord George Murray died in 1803 aged 42 leaving his widow Anne-Charlotte (née Grant) with five children and debts of £13,000. He is perhaps best remembered for his work in developing Britain's first optical telegraph, which began relaying messages from London to Deal in 1796, a few years after Claude Chappe's system began operation in France. He was Bishop of St David's from 1801 until his death two years later. Lady George Murray was a lady-in-waiting at the court of George III while her daughter Amelia (1798–1884) was a lady-in-waiting to Queen Victoria.

119 Information partly drawn from a letter from Col Ian Murray to Sir John Baynes, 6 March 1981. Portrait of Sir George Wright, Bt, is in the possession of the author's family.

120 Research carried out by Sir Christopher Baynes about the descendancy from Prince Rupert, contained within documents in the author's possession entitled *Wright Baronetage*.

121 *VCH, Somerset,* 9, pp. 195–6.

122 *Particular of the will of William Jenkins Esq.*, held at the Devizes Museum and Library (Box 127).

123 Filkins Hall in Oxfordshire was originally built in 1646 but redesigned in the mid-1700s as a square double structure, retaining part of the original building. In 1876, a fire gutted the house and it was not rebuilt until 1910. The new house was built in a Jacobean style for Colonel Fenwick Bulmer de Sales La Terriere. In the 1980s it was converted into ten apartments. Information from an article by Helen Peacocke, *Witney Gazette*, 21 May 2008.

124 Girvan, op. cit., pp. 110–14.

125 The cruelty to some sufferers is shown in the treatment of Viscount Milton, the heir to the immensely wealthy Earl Fitzwilliam of Wentworth Woodhouse, by his own family in the mid-19th century as detailed by Catherine Bailey in *Black Diamonds: The Rise and Fall of an English Dynasty* (Viking, 2007).

126 Glanoysk continued to be held in affection by Louisa's descendants even after it had been sold by the family as is demonstrated by a letter to Lilian Colston dated 12 September 1916 from the Castle, Sennybridge, from a member of staff called A. Powell about the death of Miss Agnes Maskelyne of Glanoysk. Born in 1830, Miss Maskelyne had lived there from 1879 after the death of her father, Anthony, who had bought the estate. Enclosed with the letter are press cuttings about the life of Miss Maskelyne and all the work she had done for the local community.

127 In 1844 the Crammer pond was reduced in size and the Colston tomb was created on part of the reclaimed land.

128 *Particular of the will of William Jenkins Esq.*, op. cit.

129 *VCH – Somerset*, 9, p. 132.

130 Obituary in *The Times*, 23 March 1885.

131 The family history is documented by Joseph Lucas in *Historical Genealogy of the Family of Bayne of Nidderdale*, which was commissioned by Christopher Baynes and published in 1896. The book is described thus by Christopher and Amy's son William Baynes late in life (in a letter to his sister Dorothy of 21 June 1964): 'You will remember our parents employed one Lucas to write a book on our family history, and that he first traced us back to the Scotch clan of "Bane", and it was not until I was bicycling through Normandy and found the village of Baynes (pronounced now Benss with a very sharp double 's') a few miles from Bayeux, and told Lucas of it, that he at once turned our genealogy from a Scotch into a Norman one. He showed that William de Bayeux (brother of Odo Bishop of Bayeux) had enormous possessions in Yorkshire and that old deeds, about 1200 or 1300, showed the name gradually changing from Bayeux to Baynes, and therefore that we came over with the conquest. But of course it is all pure myth, but a very agreeable one.'

132 Atlas Assurance provided insurance for a wide range of businesses such as the Fire Department, distilleries, sugar houses, mercantile property in the docks, shipping in harbour and farming stock, and also included members of the Royal Family among its names of Lives Assured (past examples being King William IV and the Duke of York).

133 Daniel Stuart's pamphlet is in the British Library in a leather-bound book which starts with a pamphlet of 1793 entitled *Remarks on the Crown & Anchor Association vs Republicans and Levellers*. The second part of the book is Daniel Stuart's 160-page exposition on his arguments in favour of parliamentary reform, which was published in 1794.

134 Coleridge wrote of Stuart as follows in 1816: 'It is far, very far, from hyperbole to affirm, that you did more against the French scheme of Continental domination, than the Duke of Wellington has done; or rather Wellington could neither have been supplied by Ministers, nor the Ministers supported by the Nation, but for the tone first given, and then constantly kept up, by the plain, unministerial, anti-opposition, anti-jacobin, anti-gallican, anti-Napoleonic spirit of your writings, aided by the colloquial good style, and evident good sense, in which as acting on an immense mass of knowledge of existing men and existing circumstances, you are superior to any man I ever met with in my life time.'

135 Now 106 Harley Street.

136 Analysis of the Marriage Settlement was provided by Andrew Cameron, Partner, of solicitors Charles Russell Speechlys, 24 September 2014.

137 The Marriage Settlement also said that on Amy's death a fund of £5,000 (£555,000 today) was to be created from which Christopher had the income during his lifetime and then, on his death, the proceeds would go to their children. There was provision for the children's portion of the trust (up to a share of 50 per cent) to be accelerated in its dispersal for education and training after the age of 16 and for accommodation on coming of age (18 years old).

138 This incident is described in detail in *Enter A Child*, pp. 7–8.

139 The Baynes family lived at 5 Arthur Road in Edgbaston.

140 Charles's full name was Charles Edward Hungerford Atholl Colston. Hungerford related to Charles's great-great-great-great-grandfather Edward Hungerford of the prominent Wiltshire family which owned Farleigh Hungerford Castle and also had seats at Corsham, Down Ampney and Black Bourton. There was

also a Hungerford connection through the Duke of Atholl whose name Charles carried in honour of his great-great-grandfather John, the 3rd Duke of Atholl (1729–74). *Wilts Obituary* (from Devizes Museum and Library), p. 221.

141   Thomas Knyfton had bought Uphill Castle in April 1832 and lived there with his first wife who died of puerperal fever. Thomas celebrated his second marriage to Georgie Colston by commissioning the architect J.G. Crace to design a magnificent new drawing room and Octagon Hall in the High Gothic style. The furniture was specially made for Uphill to Pugin designs, which appear in his book *Gothic Furniture* published in 1835, and the wallpaper, 'Small Gothic', was also designed by Pugin and was used in the Palace of Westminster, amongst many other places. Information taken from the 'Guide to Uphill Manor' which is available to guests staying at the house which is now onwed by the Kennedy family and provides accommodation. (The author stayed there on 5 November 2013.) Thomas Knyfton died on 2 February 1887 aged nearly 90. His only child by his first wife was a boy who did not survive so the Uphill estate was left to Thomas' nephew Reginald Benett Graves (who came of age in 1894); his wife Edith changed the name to Uphill Manor in 1898 and had the panelled room installed in 1907. On Reginald's death in 1918, the Manor was inherited by his eldest daughter, Marjorie (her mother Edith lived until 1964), and then by her son Colin Firth who died in 1995, at which point it was sold to the current owners, the Kennedys.

142   Rosalind Murray's maternal great-grandfather, George Gostling (1714–82), a successful lawyer, bought Whitton in 1765 for £3,010 (£522,000 today) and converted the orangery (also referred to as the Green House), designed by James Gibbs in 1725, into a mansion soon after 1766, and sold the villa to Sir William Chambers, who improved it. The divided estate was later reunited and the now redundant villa was demolished in c1847, from which time the house that was developed from Gibbs's orangery took the name of Whitton Park. – Mary Cosh, 'Lord Ilay's Eccentric Building Schemes: Two Dukes and their Houses, II', *Country Life* (20 July 1972), pp. 142–5.

143   Research from local sources by Rachel Multon in July 2007.

144   Amy's diary entry for 8 June described the strict precautions taken in their new home of 2 Burlington Street in Mayfair (recently built next to the Bank of England branch of which Christopher was Sub-Agent between 1881 and 1895) after Christobel's fever had been diagnosed: 'The 4 maids all moved down from the upper floor and Trotman came and pasted up the doors of the unused room and cupboards up there and took all the stairs and landing carpets up, and put several sheets with carbolic acid near Christobel's room.'

145   The election was being fought on the new constituency boundaries arising from Gladstone's 1884 Reform Act, which had further increased the adult male franchise. The inter-connected 1885 Redistribution Act focused on equalising representation among constituencies by redistributing seats. This involved the abolition of smaller borough seats such as Devizes, which was now incorporated into the new single member Wiltshire East county constituency.

146   Charles Colston's County Council positions included being Chairman of the Roads and Bridges Committee.

147   Georgie Knyfton had previously benefited from a substantial legacy from her aunt Penelope Brice, as recorded in the local history publication *Victoria's Uphill*.

148   *VCH, Wiltshire*, 7, p. 192.

149   Brian Wilkinson, pers. comm.

150   *Enter A Child* (1939), pp. 136–9.

151   Clive Leach and David Colcomb of Devizes, pers. comm., July 2007.

152   Clive Leach, pers. comm., 23 July 2007.

153   As mentioned previously, it is likely that this is a portrayal of her grandmother Louisa Colston but Dorothy

wanted to disguise her identity in case it offended her Colston and Murray relatives when the book was published in 1939. As with the portrayal of her father and of Dame Una Pope-Hennessy (née Birch), Dorothy clearly saw the book as a way of settling some childhood scores.

154 Barry Barrett, information provided to the author on 8 February 2003, and, with regard to the auction in 1899, information from a local newspaper report (exact newspaper not specified) in Vol. 2 of the Press Cuttings at the Devizes Museum and Library.

155 Information from a local newspaper report (exact newspaper not specified) in Vol. 2 of the Press Cuttings at the Devizes Museum and Library.

156 Madeleine Beard, *English Landed Society in the 20th Century* (Routledge, 1989), p. 9.

157 *Enter A Child*, Parts III, IV and V. Although the text is presented as an unbroken quotation, parts have been missed out for the sake of conciseness and in order to concentrate on the descriptive passages about Roundway and the Colston family. As a result, parentheses or elipses are not employed to indicate excluded sections of text. In a few places, a short narrative link of no more than three words has been inserted into the original text in order to facilitate the flow.

158 Daphne Moore, 'Whipper-in and butler – a double role', *Shooting Times & Country Magazine* (17–23 May 1979).

159 Reference to the Eton College Beagles is from Henry Robinson's large red ledger entitled 'Herd Recording Register 1939–40'. The reference is contained in a section headed 'Some Notes and Skeleton Pedigrees of Beagles'. The ledger resides in the Muniments Room at Badminton House, visited by the author on 14 November 2011.

160 Although Henry's hand-writing and spelling were almost faultless, his punctuation was minimal so a few commas have been added to the extract from his letter.

161 Information from newspaper article by Keith Gardner.

162 *Roundway House, Devizes, Sale of Appointments, Fixtures and Fittings of the Mansion, 24th November 1954*, Ferris and Culverwell, Tilley and Culverwell. In 1892, Whitton Park had passed to Rosalind Colston and her sister Julia on their father's death. His will, however, had provided for a jointure of £30,000 (£3.7m today) for his widow, the sisters' stepmother, so the estate had to be sold by the heirs to fund this. It was sold at auction in 1898, which was presumably when the panelling was removed and brought to Roundway. The house with 45 acres was sold at auction by Messrs Cobb at the Mart, Tokenhouse Yard, in the City of London. – P. Foster & D.H. Simpson, *Whitton Park and Whitton Place* (Borough of Twickenham Local History Society, 1999).

163 Not long after this, the Astleys leased Chequers to Arthur (later Viscount) Lee and then sold it to the Lees in 1912 who later gave it to the nation as a retreat for the prime minister of whom the first to use it was Lloyd George in 1921.

164 Fouriesberg was the temporary capital of the Orange Free State for the Boers during the war.

165 Tabitha Prickett's father was the Recorder of York. Henry Robinson makes reference to the link in a letter of 20 February 1930 to Dorothy's father Sir Christopher Baynes, having visited the Baynes family's house in Lowndes Square in London and seen the portrait of Tabitha: 'I often wondered what was the origin of the name Tabitha which his Lordship and Mr Ronald have sometimes addressed Miss Dorothy by, so was especially interested in the portrait when I saw the name.'

166 Adrian Tinniswood, *The Long Weekend* (2016), p. 209.

167 Sir Charles and Lady Wyndham Murray lived at Froyle Place, Hilton, in Hampshire.

168 Historian Heiner Gillmeister wrote in *Tennis – A Cultural History* (Leicester University Press, 1997) about the 1901 Tennis Championship: 'Toupie Lowther's victory (in 1901) was believed to be "a foregone conclusion". Her victories over Miss Matthews of the Edgbaston Cup and Miss Duddell, in the penultimate round and in the final were triumphs "of patience and perseverance", the results being 6-0, 6-0 in both cases. That the unfortunate Miss Duddell should have been punished so severely was, perhaps, pardonable. She had been invited to the tournament committee with a view to looking after the ladies' matches. This was a novelty and imitation of this emancipatory act in England and elsewhere was recommended, but it must have distracted her from her game.'

169 Duddell Street is famous for its four gas-powered street lamps, the only working gas ones left in Hong Kong. Both the lamps and the granite Duddell steps at the end of the street, which were built between 1875 and 1889, are listed monuments.

170 This was a housing development established by Attree. The Villa and the Pepperpot, which housed the water supply for the Villa, had been built in 1830. By Attree's death at the age of 85 in 1863, however, the buildings on the development were limited with only Attree's Villa, the Spa, W.S. Cowell's Villa, the Pepperpot, the gateways and gazebo having been constructed.

171 When George Duddell came to live in Brighton he was unmarried and brought his niece Sophy (she was his eldest brother's daughter) to live in the villa with her four young children as both her parents had died and George had been her guardian since she was 16. Although the children took the surname Vernon, it is believed that George was the father of Sophy's children although there is no written evidence to substantiate this. His elderly mother was also living with him and his illegitimate son George Minza, known as his 'adopted son', from Hong Kong. By 1868 his great niece Kate Dubois was also living at Duddell's Villa after George had offered her a home on the death of her parents. Sophy, who had had two more children by then, cannot have been best pleased by this new arrival. In 1870–71, both women had children by George – Sophy's seventh and Kate's first. Kate's child, William Du Bois Duddell, was born in 1872 and George was named as the father. Not surprisingly, this was too much for Sophy who took her seven children to London where George supported her financially and she married a clerk by whom she had more children. Kate's and George's second child was (Blanche) Gladys, born in 1879.

172 Gladys had four female cousins on her mother's side of the family to whom she was close during her life and with whom Ted also had a good relationship. They were two sets of sisters: Angela and Beatrix Thynne, and Dora and Gwen Pollitt. The elder sister in each case was astringent and the younger gentle and there was no shortage of rivalry between them. Angela married Sir Vincent Baddeley who was Secretary to Winston Churchill; Beatrix married Roger Pratt of Ryston Hall in Norfolk and had four children; Dora married Mr Pollitt, a dentist, and had two boys, Jeffrey and Dick; Gwen did not have children.

173 Viscount Mahon (1880–1967) entered the House of Lords as Earl Stanhope on the death of his father in 1905, and sat as a Conservative. He enjoyed a long ministerial career which started in 1918 and culminated in his membership of the cabinet in 1936–40 as, inter alia, First Lord of the Admiralty (succeeded by Churchill in 1939), Leader of the House of Lords and Lord President of the Council. Like the Lees with Chequers, he left his country seat, Chevening, to the nation.

174 *Wiltshire Telegraph*, 15 June 1907.

175 Much of this description of Devizes at the turn of the century is drawn from *A Devizes Century*, written and published by the Devizes Local History Group in 1999 to mark the new Millennium.

176 Beard, op. cit., p. 12.

177 John Martin Robinson, *Felling the Ancient Oaks: How England Lost its Great Country Estates* (Aurum Press, 2011), pp. 9, 28–9.

178 William may have been in part inspired by the careers of his uncles Gilbert and Kenneth Baynes who had both served in Egypt as soldiers. His correspondence with his mother and siblings is preserved from this period and shows his dry sense of humour and closeness to his family, particularly the post-cards in which he excelled as a correspondent given his natural brevity: 'Looking forward to hearing shortly what is the latest state of your mind' is the full text of a post-card to his sister Christobel in January 1906. In another post-card to his mother he asked her to keep the cards as he did not have a camera with him. Hence the numerous packs of unused post-cards which he kept as a record of his travels including many different French towns, Vienna, Dubrovnik, Venice, Florence (some in the colour 'Oilette' series: 'Veritable Miniature Oil Paintings of Picture Post-Cards') and Egypt.

179 Marion Ruperta Murray Lawes was born on 28 September 1863 and was the only child of Louisa Colston's sister Emma Murray and Robert Lawes. She grew up at Old Park near Dover and married Geoffrey Cecil Twisleton-Wykeham-Fiennes, 12th Baron Saye and Sele, on 20 February 1884. They had seven children and Marion died on 27 July 1946.

180 This letter and the others from William to his mother are currently lodged in the Liddle Collection at Leeds University and run from 27 April 1915 to 29 September 1917. They formed part of the primary source for two articles in the *Guards Magazine* by Lt Col Sir John Baynes, Bt, entitled 'Life in France 1915–1916' and 'Life in France 1916–1917' and this chapter draws extensively on both the letters themselves and Sir John's commentary in these two articles. The other subject of these articles was Lieutenant William St Leger MC who was 19 years younger than William but served in the Coldstream Guards at the same time and kept a detailed diary (590 type-script pages) from 21 September 1916 to 27 March 1918, which is now in the Imperial War Museum.

181 Reproduced by kind permission of HM The Queen.

182 Professor Sir David Cannadine, *The Decline and Fall of the British Aristocracy* (Penguin, 1990), pp. 197–8.

183 Major John Bartholomew, conversation with the author, 21 July 2006.

184 Girvan, op. cit., p. 113.

185 *London Gazette*, 26 September 1917.

186 See Simon Greaves, *The Country House at War* (National Trust Books, 2014), Chapter 2 'Women at War'.

187 Beard, op. cit., p. 25.

188 The 1919 edition of *Debrett's Peerage and Baronetage* brought home the family's relative good fortune as it listed all the sons of peers and baronets who had been killed during the war. Overall, six million men in Britain served in the war of whom 723,000, one in eight, were killed (the total rises to 888,246 if soldiers from the Empire are included). In the first year of the war, one in seven officers died fighting, compared to one in seventeen of non-officers. The proportion was even higher for British and Irish peers (of whom there were about 750) and their sons of whom one in five died in combat during the course of the war.

189 Adrian Pearse, letters to Sir John Baynes, 10 September 2003 and 12 October 2004. In the latter Pearse said that other Colston properties in Somerset had descended to Dame Madalene Sabine Jenkyns of Botley Hill, Botley, Hants, comprising real estate in West Bradley (Lottisham), East Pennard, Baltonsborough, Hombolton and East Lydford, and was sold by public auction at Shepton Mallet on 27 June 1919.

190 The problems that Alec Agar-Robartes experienced in resuming civilian life were shown in three letters he sent to Dorothy after the war: one from the ship out to India in October 1920 to take up his role as an ADC to the Viceroy Lord Chelmsford, one on the return journey in 1921 and an exuberant letter in between from the Viceroy's Camp in Kashmir in which Alec declares his affection for Dorothy and his love of India: 'England is the land of prose and India is the land of poetry'. The letter from his return journey, however,

hints at a deep malaise due to psychological problems caused by his wartime experiences, particularly gassing, which in the end led to his suicide.

191 Jill Hepple, conversations with the author, 19 March 2003 and 1 November 2012.

192 Jill Hepple, conversation with the author, 19 March 2003.

193 Irene Bailey, conversation with the author, 21 July 2006.

194 Major John Bartholomew, conversation with the author, 21 July 2006.

195 There was an exhibition of Ted's lead soldiers at Slopers Shop in Devizes, which is now Boots, according to Clive Leach, pers. comm., 23 July 2007.

196 William referred to this many years later in a letter of 4 February 1968 to Dorothy, adding '... and what is a park without deer in it!' Probably a lot less trouble would be a logical answer.

197 Obituary of Rosalind, Lady Roundway, *Wiltshire Gazette*, 10 November 1938.

198 Information about the views and work of Irene Bailey result from an interview with the author, 21 July 2006.

199 Information on the death of Christopher Darby Griffith from *The Last of the Darby Griffiths – Padworth House in the 1920s*, edited by Angela Wilson (c1995), p. 51.

200 'My Life in Domestic Service at Padworth House' in *The Last of the Darby Griffiths*, ibid. The booklet provides considerable detail about life at Padworth, including reminiscences by Douglas Lawrence whose father, Frank Lawrence, was head gardener. The Major came in for criticism from the writer, Richard Aldington, who lived for a time in The Malt House in Lower Padworth, in his autobiography but Hilda Hearn strongly refuted Aldington's version of events as described in *The Last of the Darby Griffiths*.

201 Cecilia Baynes, as told to Sir John Baynes, Bt. Cecilia née Day was the only child of Major Charles Day of the Oxfordshire Light Infantry and Katherine née Scott Chad of Thursford Hall and Pynkney Hall, both in Norfolk.

202 Information about the Croft from Debrett's history of the house written for the Cross family after 1983.

203 Dr Simon Thurley, *Men from the Ministry: How Britain Saved its Heritage* (Yale University Press, 2013), p. 102.

204 Beard, op. cit., p. 61.

205 Admiral Darby's son Matthew Darby, a distinguished soldier, inherited the Padworth Estate in 1801 from his maternal aunt Catherine, widow of Christopher Griffith and the subject of the Gainsborough portrait.

206 Girvan, op. cit., pp. 60–2.

207 Hansard (9 May 1895, vol. 33) recorded this question to Mr Campbell-Bannerman by Mr Charles Colston: 'I beg to ask the Secretary of State for War whether, for the past twelve months and upwards, the sewage from the Le Marchant Barracks, near Devizes, has, owing to a complete breakdown of the sewerage system provided there, been discharged in a crude state into the Kennet and Avon Canal, about a mile from the town; whether he is aware that the canal flows downwards from that point through the town, and supplies the water for a public bathing-place for the inhabitants; and, whether, having regard to the serious danger to health and the annoyance that has arisen, he will forthwith take such measures as are necessary to abate the nuisance?'

208 In 1918 the Ministry of Reconstruction had asked a Women's Advisory Committee to look into this issue and its report in the spring of 1919 made a broad range of recommendations including limiting the working day and drawing up a scale of weekly wages. –Tinniswood, op.cit., p. 306.

209 David Owen (in Hinckley, Leics), letter to the author, December 2003, which was accompanied by a family

tree of the King family and some photographs.

210 Information in this chapter from Mrs Irene Bailey, conversation with the author, 21 July 2006.

211 Clive Leach, conversation with the author, 23 July 2007.

212 Barry Barrett, pers. comm., 15 November 2011.

213 Joan Cully, conversation with the author, 21 July 2006.

214 Moore, op. cit.

215 Obituary of Rosalind, Lady Roundway, *Wiltshire Gazette*, 10 November 1938.

216 From DJC-B Notebooks 2 (blue and red covered Century notebooks). Although the friend probably was Laura, Lady Lovat, the identity is not clear as the handwritten record in which this and other such visits are recorded never names the person whom Dorothy is visiting.

217 William's charitable activities also included legal aid work, helping to establish the Queen Elizabeth Foundation and typing braille manuscripts for the Society for the Blind. He was also very keen on chess (an envelope of chess problems, cut from daily newspapers, remains in his papers) and classical music (his record collection was that of a connoisseur with the late Beethoven quartets a particular feature). He also kept meticulous household accounts, detailing every item of his personal expenditure on a monthly basis, testament to his need to live within his unearned means and the accounting skills he acquired as the head of the statistics department in the Ministry of Justice in Cairo in 1908.

218 The rhymes are contained in a blue card-covered booklet entitled 'Company Orders' with typed pages inside. The inscription is: 'W.E.C.B. from Mark, who made the verses, and from Joan, who made the lovely book. March 1943.'

219 Tribute by Sir Percy Hurd MP in the *Wiltshire Gazette* 1944 after the death of the 2nd Lord Roundway.

220 John H.B. Leech, *Inside-Out – The View from the Asylum* (Leech, 1995), p. 98.

221 In the same letter, William commented on the situation at 18 Ovington Square: 'I have not added up the year's cost of Ovington Square yet; it is all in a pretty rocky state, but your Surveyor does not recommend doing anything drastic about it until we want to live in it again ... I will go over No. 18 with Mrs Fear on Wednesday and send you a report. The only thing I know at present is that the boiler is broken beyond repair, and to have any hot water in the house we must have a new one – probably unobtainable at present.'

222 Julia had two daughters who did not marry: Ruperta and Ione.

223 From an unbound handwritten note book.

224 Information about Padworth is from a history written for the current owners by Debretts. Major John Bartholomew, former Chairman of Wadworth Brewery, confirmed that Josephine Creasy was Ted's mistress in a telephone conversation with the author in May 2003.

225 The entail to which William referred was a legal system which evolved in the late Middle Ages to ensure the long-term survival of an estate by avoiding it being broken up on inheritance. The entail involved the property being granted to trustees who ensured that it remained intact in the male line. In the 17th century the system evolved into the 'strict entail', which settled an estate on the senior male heir for three generations at a time. It was repeatedly renewed until the 20th century when more tax-efficient trusts were introduced although the Settled Land Law of 1882 enabled indebted owners to raise funds by breaking the entail in order to sell certain assets such as works of art.

226 'An appreciation of the late Sir William Baynes', *Salisbury Journal*, 30 September 1971.

227 John Phillips of Roundway Covert, conversation with the author, 21 July 2006.

228 There were then lengthy negotiations with Brighton Corporation over the proposed housing development on the land and the retention of 17 acres as a public park, including the Spa's one acre and the Pepperpot. In the end, the park was bought by the Brighton Corporation in December 1890 for £13,500 (£1.7m today) with £9,500 (£1.2m today) paid to Kate and the rest paid to the town for work that it had carried out on her behalf.

229 At Whitton, in 1909, there was a determined effort by local residents to preserve the estate as a public park but this failed. In 1910 most of the park was sold to the British Freehold Investment Company while the gothic tower was demolished and the house soon met the same fate. The lead on the roof of the house was sold for £500 and some remains of the building survived until 1928. Development of the land proceeded steadily although there was an attempt by some local councillors in 1928 to buy the 25 acres of Whitton Park that still remained to be developed. This failed as did a last chance in 1931 and a petition from Whitton residents in 1934. Thus, by the time Rosalind Colston died at Roundway in 1938, Whitton had been demolished and the land largely developed.

230 The original 15th century house at Rowdeford was rebuilt by Sir William Pinsent in about 1680 and became the manor of Urchfont in 1767 following its acquisition by the Duke of Queensbury. Urchfont Manor remained a residential training centre until its sale by the County Council in 2012 at a guide price of £2.7m.

231 This summary comes from the Society's report of 24 April 1947 by its Land Steward, Mr P.E. Tyhurst, in which he also describes in detail the lengthy negotiations with Lady Roundway.

232 Information from Christie's sale catalogues collated by Brian Wilkinson (sent in a letter to the author, 25 July 2004).

233 R.P. Way, *Antique Dealer* (Michael Joseph, 1957), p. 175. The book was found in 2012 by Brian Wilkinson in a second-hand bookshop.

234 Major John Bartholomew, pers. comm., 21 July 2006.

235 Nina, born in 1889, was know in the family as Nini and was a painter of equine subjects. She married Major Harry Colmore.

236 James Lees-Milne, letter to Sir John Baynes, Bt, 14 June 1997.

237 James Lees-Milne, letter to the author, 3 September 1979.

238 John Phillips, pers. comm., 14 November 2011.

239 *Wiltshire Gazette*, 9 April 1953.

240 Peter White, conversation with the author, March 2003.

241 Peter White, *Memoirs* (1999).

242 The Marlborough Road lodge and the piece of land behind it were sold to the Card family who ran coaches in Devizes (Wilkinson, op. cit., c2000).

243 John Phillips, conversation with the author, 14 November 2011.

244 Robinson, op. cit. (2011), p. 31.

245 Dr Giles Worsley, *Daily Telegraph*, 15 June 2002, in an article to accompany his book *England's Lost Houses: From the Archives of Country Life* (Aurum Press, 2002) and an exhibition based on photographs from the book at Sir John Soane's Museum, London, from June to September 2002.

246 Beard, op. cit., pp. 110–12.

247 As described by Giles Worsley in an article in the *Georgian*, 2002, which accompanied the publication of his

book *England's Lost Houses*: 'In the years after the Second World War the task of protecting country houses was central to the Georgian Group, but it must have seemed an impossible task … At times it must have been easy to compromise. In 1956 the Group reluctantly agreed to the demolition of the greater part of Bowood, Wiltshire, with its wonderful Adam interiors, which the Marquess of Lansdowne considered impractical. "No-one", explained Lord Lansdowne in a letter to 'The Times', "would deny these days that a reduction of 90–100 rooms might be considered a practical improvement to a private house … I have found comfort in the painful decision that I have made from the fact that both official and unofficial men and women of good taste and experts in architectural matters who have been kind enough to study the details of the problem thoroughly have accepted my decision". It was a letter that drew a stinging response from the architectural historian James Lees-Milne: "That guardian bodies such as the Holford Committee and the Georgian Group do not even register regret, not to say disapproval, that another of Robert Adam's houses is to be sold in 316 lots seems both feeble and shocking." But the sale (of fixtures and fittings) went ahead and the dining room, which made £5,000 (£123,000 today), eventually ended up at Lloyd's of London, now sitting incongruously in the middle of Lord Rogers's Hi-Tech structure.'

248 Wilkinson, op. cit., c2000.

249 Clive Leach, conversation with the author, 23 July 2007.

250 Moore, op. cit.

251 The collection was viewed by the author in the Badminton Muniments Room on 14 November 2011.

252 The first is inscribed: 'In grateful appreciation for so many interesting notes and beautifully written pedigrees' and dated May 1929. The second large book is entitled: 'Henry Robinson – Extended Pedigree Book from Isaac bell MFH 18th July 1944' while the third is entitled 'Female Ancestry' and was given to Henry by Isaac Bell in January 1945 with the following inscription: 'Oh perish the thought! May the day never come when the gorse is uprooted and the Foxhound is dumb!'

253 Moore, op. cit..

254 Pythouse was owned by Mutual Householders Ltd and was one of the first country houses to be converted into apartments in the UK.

255 William's views were far from stereotypical. For instance, he supported both Home Rule for Scotland and the student uprisings (on the basis that such expressions of discontent would bring about much needed improvements to the country's education system); he was intrigued by pop music and voted according to the merits of each political party rather than on tribal lines.

256 Josephine Creasy's will also made provision for some of the residents of her house (presumably paying guests): Edward Brough Taylor was left £2,000 (£34,000 today), the furniture in his room, a share of the kitchen equipment and 'all my useful wire fox terriers and miniature schnauzers' and Miss Marjorie Baynard was bequeathed £1,000, the furniture in her room, a share of the kitchen equipment and 'my Kerry blue terriers'. W. O'Brien was left £1,000, the furniture in his room and the sitting room, a share of the kitchen equipment 'and also the television set'. Mrs Elsie Williams of 39 Avenue Road, St Albans, was bequeathed Josephine's 'portait in oils if she wishes to have it and any books on kennel subjects which she may choose'. Josephine's love of the sporting world was also seen in her splendid bequest to Neil W. Gardiner of Great Auclum, Burghfield, Berkshire, of £1,000 'on condition that he shall use the same to buy a horse for hunting and for keeping it as long as such money shall last or to be used by him to lease a gun in a shoot or a rod for fishing provided it shall be for his own personal use'.

257 Jill Hepple, in a meeting with the author and her son, Tim Hepple, 1 November 2012. Jill and her husband, Norman, bought some of Gladys's pieces which were auctioned at Druce's in Baker Street shortly after her

death. Lady Baddeley auctioned off the Reynolds/Romney portrait but it went for too little.

258 Simon Awdry, partner of Wood & Awdry, was President of the Grateful Society in Bristol in 1979, which was founded in 1758 in memory of Edward Colston (documents in possession of the author). He was also solicitor to Sir Rory Baynes, Bt, and to Mrs Isla Fitzgerald (née Baynes), sister of Sir Rory and first cousin of Sir William Baynes, Bt, and Dorothy Colston-Baynes.

259 John Phillips (then aged 82), telephone conversation with the author, 16 February 2003, and meeting with the author, 21 July 2006.

260 Beatrice Gillam, *Roundway Hill Covert c1820–2001* (2001). She was awarded an MBE for her work as a naturalist.

261 'New Park – a Lost Estate', op. cit.

262 Clive Leach, conversation with the author, 23 July 2007. There is a photo of Clive with his friends David Phillips and Henry Sheppard at Roundway in about 1950 when they were teenagers. Bill Thomas often used to chase them off the land! Clive was apprenticed to Peter White's building firm in 1950–55, then did his National Service (1955–57) and then worked for him again. He enjoyed working for White and said that he was a very shrewd businessman.

263 Barry Barrett, meeting with the author, 8 February 2003.

264 Main sources on Colston family history pre-Roundway: pamphlet by Kenneth Morgan, *Edward Colston and Bristol* (Bristol Branch of the Historical Association Local History Pamphlets, 1999); F. Mattingley, *Edward Colston 1636–1721* (Barnes and Mortlake History Society, 1971); *Dictionary of National Biography, The Church and Parish of All Saints, Bristol: A History*; and W. Phelps, *The History and Antiquities of Somersetshire, vol. 1* (1839).

265 Throughout the 18th century the Society's members profited greatly from the slave trade but the decline of Bristol as a major port in the 19th century led to the Society losing much of its influence.

266 The house was demolished by the Mortlake brewer James Wigan in 1865.

267 John Hargrave DD, *Riches Rightly Improved – A Sermon Preach'd at the Funeral of the Great and Charitable Benefactor Edward Colston Esq.*, reprinted by H. Green in Bristol in 1721 and included in a small maroon, leather-bound and gold-tooled book at the London Library entitled *Biographies Etc 1609–1888*. (Other biographies in the volume include those of Pope John VIII in Latin and Cardinal de Richelieu in French.)

268 There was a grisly postscript when repairs to the church in the mid-19th century led to the discovery of Edward Colston's remains. The coffin was opened and his corpse was found to be unusually well preserved. It was put on display and fragments of the garments were taken as relics until it was re-interred.

269 From *Sermon of William Embrey Edwards preached on Colston Day 1783*.

270 Moira Maidment, a past Chairman of the Temple Local History Group in Bristol, provided information about Sir William Hayman and the size of Sarah's inheritance in a meeting with the author, 30 October 2012. Moira is descended from the Colston family through her paternal grandmother and an expert on the history of the Colstons.

271 Information about Thomas Edwards and Alexander Ready is largely from Chris Hobson, *Alexander Ready, Alexander Colston: The man with two names* (Fairford History Society Monograph 6, Sept. 2010).

272 For more information, *see* Endnote 123.

273 Although the expansion of the coal industry was much greater in Britain in the 19th century than in the 18th century, it still increased from 2.5m tons in 1700 to 6m by 1770 and to 10m by 1800. The collieries were usually on land belonging to landowners such as the Colstons, who maximised profits by leasing the land for a rent or royalties on production. Examples include the articles of agreement made between Alexander

Colston and William Jones of Gloucester in 1754 and 1762 to mine coal in the manor of Clapton (and lead and iron in the 1762 deed).

274 This was quite possibly derived from an idealised name for herself of Doreen Colston, with the altered letters between this and the nom de plume spelling 'mere' in a tribute to her much-loved mother who had died at the beginning of 1919.

275 'Enforced idleness' is a phrase in Clare Tomalin's biography *The Invisible Woman* (1990) of Charles Dickens' mistress, Ellen or Nelly Ternan. The phrase is used to describe Ellen's sister Maria Ternan's escape to Oxford in 1873 to become a journalist. See pp. 152–3 and 212–13.

276 Amy's diary for 1908 records the family's charitable work such as the 'Happy Evenings' that Christobel and Dorothy helped to organise for disadvantaged girls. For instance, on Saturday 21 March Amy wrote: 'Christobel and Dorothy had 8 of the "Happy Evening" girls (who are taking part in Competitions) to tea here, and to dance, sing and make pinafores.' Christopher was also involved, supporting Boys Clubs in the East End, and Christobel looked after people from her Bible Class such as the girl she took to the Franco-British Exhibition on 17 October.

277 Other unpublished works by Dormer Creston in her literary estate include *Shakespeare Anthology* and *Valentines on St Valentine's Day*, both of which are undated.

278 The Authors' Alliance wrote to Dorothy on 30 March 1925: 'We recently cabled our New York Manager urging him to return your MS. at once, and today we receive a letter from him, of which the following is an extract: "Please ask Miss Baynes to be a little patient about JEANNE LA PUCELLE. Mr Sturgis, the Book Editor, The Century Company, talked with me about the matter yesterday, he told me that his head reader is wildly enthusiastic and has said that it is the best MS. that has come to them in fifteen years. However, his other readers are not so strong for it and it seems that the material has caused no end of office discussion, with the result that Mr Sturgis is reading it personally this week and he will give me final word within ten days."'

279 Selwyn & Blount (through no fault of Dorothy's) went into liquidation not long after publishing her book and she received two letters dated 29 March 1929 about the sale of 42 copies of her book and the royalties due to her of £22 11/-.

280 As this excerpt from a letter dated 22 April 1931 from John Macrae Jr, Vice President of her American publishers, E.P. Dutton & Co. Inc., shows: 'You will probably be interested to know that although theatre program advertising has never paid before with us (or, as far as we know, with any other publisher) it apparently has worked out very well with your book … This, with the advertising we have been doing in the papers and magazines, has, in conjunction with the play [*The Barretts of Wimpole Street* starring Katharine Cornell, which opened on Broadway in January 1931 and proved a huge hit, later being made into a film by MGM starring Norma Shearer], stirred up a sufficient interest in your book to start it selling again and keep it selling – a very difficult thing to do with any book these days when the tendency of the bookseller is to keep his stock down to a minimum and order nothing but the newest and best-selling books.'

281 James Lees-Milne, letter to the author, 31 August 1979.

282 Christobel's book was intended as one of a series of six or seven books for children on music. Her manuscript is contained in a blue exercise book with beautiful hand-painted colour illustrations and a clear copper-plate handwritten text.

283 That the book was printed privately is deduced from letters of 16 January and 4 February 1933 to Christobel from the European Art Publishing Society in London in which the whole project and the cost of printing blocks at £100 are discussed.

284 In the following year, there was a demonstration of Colour-Music between 9 and 13 April 1934, hosted by Harrods. It overlapped with painting as seen in the catalogues retained by Christobel of art exhibitions by Wyndham Tryon in 1934 and 1935, which were described by an art critic as 'interpretations in colour of music and poetry'.

285 A catalogue of books published by the Theosophical Publishing House is among Christobel's and Dorothy's papers and Amy recorded in her diary for 11 October 1908 that the sisters went to a Theosophical Lecture in Albemarle Street. With regard to the sisters' interest in spiritualism, their cousin June wrote to one of the sisters on 29 December 1935 from the Ranelagh Club and ended the letter with these words: 'Now it is time to go, and I must stop; but be happy Dearest – happiness is ours for ever, so rejoice with me who am now living at the heart of happiness and am doing all I can to draw you into the same state of Cosmic Consciousness that is now mine.'

286 Dame Una Pope-Hennessy was the daughter of Sir Arthur Birch (1837–1914) who worked for the Bank of England between 1878 and 1913. Christopher Baynes was his deputy at the Burlington Branch of the Bank of England and the two families lived next door to each other in Burlington Street. The Birch family is portrayed as the Wystons in *Enter A Child* to whose house Dorothy as a five-year-old goes for a tea party in the opening chapter, entitled *Chinese Masks*. It proves a horrible event riven with bullying by the two Wyston children, Oliver and Marcella. The latter is the portrait of Una and she is described in these terms: 'Marcella was tall and thin, and so fair that her flickering lashes looked almost white. Cleverness was wedged within her small watchful face, and this made part of her supercilious charm.' James Lees-Milne in a letter to the author wrote: 'Dame Una was very astringent, very blue-stocking, very high-brow and rather exclusive and very forbidding. Doreen was clearly terrified of her. It was because of her contempt for people, like Doreen and myself, whom she considered middle-brow. All the P-Hs were as highbrow as could be, and well aware of it.' The portrayal of the Wystons was Dorothy's revenge.

287 James Lees-Milne, diary entry, 9 July 1949.

288 Dorothy Baynes, letter to James Lees-Milne, 17 March 1942.

289 James Pope-Hennessy's visit was described in this way by Dorothy in a letter to James Lees-Milne on 26 March 1943: 'I expect you know that Jamesy and I had a date together last week in Inverness? As I came near the Caledonian Hotel, which was our rendezvous, a watching, elegantly slim figure on the doorstep rushed towards me, and we embraced with the ardour of two friends who have not met for five years. It seems unbelievable that it can be so long. He has not changed in the least, except to have become more dear than ever, and his mind still gentler. We penetrated into the Town Hall in search of Raeburns and Ramsays, then to the second-hand bookstalls in the covered-in fish market (do you know Inverness? I expect you do.) Then we investigated various back alleys (places to which, in old towns, I am always drawn). Finally, we had tea and talk, talk, talk. And then came the bald moment of parting at a 'bus stop amid the Invernessites stern – scattered on the pavement. There I left him, and went off back to the Station Hotel to wait for my car.'

290 James Lees-Milne, pers. comm., 1979.

291 James Lees-Milne, *Prophesying Peace: Diaries 1944–1945* (Michael Russell Publishing Ltd, 1977), containing extracts from his diaries.

292 Ibid.

293 From the Reports for 1945/6 and 1946/7 of the Royal Society of Literature, Bloomsbury Square, London.

294 A letter dated 5 November 1943 from Herbert van Thal of publishers Home & van Thal Ltd (the Home being Lady Margaret Douglas-Home) refers to the plays and also to the fledgling nature of the publisher in

their hope that the next months would see the publication of their first book.

295 This piece is in a red Century note book and has been compressed for ease and concision of reading. It also contains these comments: 'No one could be easier to talk to than Eddie but his only remark that I can call to mind was his admission that a mutual friend, Violet Trefusis, frightened him because she always made him feel she expected brilliant conversation. I learned afterwards that he often helped young artists by buying their pictures, and I myself experienced his great kindness of heart by his offering, purely as an act of friendship, to read the proofs of my then forthcoming book *The Youthful Queen Victoria*. One winter's day in Walton Street I met him looking very smart on his way out to luncheon. "Oh what a beautiful scarf Eddie!" I exclaimed. "Given me by Ivor Novello" he cried in his high voice. This was said with a note of triumph and his eyes gleamed. I never saw him again.'

296 In her 1950 red Sloane Lightweight Diary she recorded that 212 people came to tea or sherry during 1949 and that, between November 1949 and July 1950, she received 27 invitations to lunch. The list of engagements gradually diminishes in succeeding diaries during the decade but 1959 (when Dorothy was 79) still shows regular engagements, even if they consist more of people visiting Ovington Square than her venturing out.

297 John Baynes, reference written for Dr Vignoles (probably in 1974).

298 DJC-B Notebook 3, blue cover: Winfield.

299 References drawn from a letter from James Lees-Milne to Dorothy Colston-Baynes, 24 January 1965.

300 James Lees-Milne, letter to the author, 23 January 1980.

301 James Lees-Milne, letter to Sir John Baynes, Bt, 16 June 1997.

302 James Lees-Milne, letter to the author, 23 January 1980.

Acknowledgements

I would like to thank Dr Ruth Guilding who carried out much of the research concerning the building of New Park and the Sutton family. Lee Garton and her mother, Jessica Frank, who have lived at Roundway House since 1976, and their late husbands Robin Garton and Alan Frank, have been very hospitable and helpful on several occasions when I have visited Roundway. The late Eileen Thomas, who lived in the Swiss Cottage and with whom I stayed on my first visit in 1978, was delightful and informative in equal measure.

Rachel Multon has been a frequent companion on my research visits to Devizes and has not only carried out research herself but also introduced me to a number of people locally who have been of great help in piecing together the past. These include the late John Bartholomew, former Chairman of Wadworth Brewery; the late Beatrice Gillam MBE; the late Mrs Irene Bailey (née Cooper) and Mrs Joan Cully (née Regan), both of whom worked at Roundway between the wars, and Clive Leach, who used to work for Peter White. Rachel also introduced me to the late John and Sarah Phillips whose arboretum at the Home Covert encompassed the old pleasure gardens of Roundway.

Jill Hepple (née Pratt) and her brother Michael Pratt have been very helpful on information about their cousin Gladys, Lady Roundway. I am also indebted to Devizes historian John Girvan whose books *Devizes Hidden Secrets* and *Under Devizes* have been invaluable. He has also been very generous in sharing his amazing photographic collection, amassed in collaboration with Mike Thomas, which has greatly enhanced the illustrations in this book. I would also like to thank Barry Barrett as well as two local railway specialists: David Colcomb and Bill Crosbie-Hill. John and Sue Hawkins shared with me their impressive collection of Devizes post-cards. David Owen provided valuable information about the King family, to whom he is related, who worked at Roundway for several generations. Jonny and Rachael Rider allowed me to visit their home, Horton House, and, likewise, Peter and Delia Allfrey showed me Dolphin Lodge on Conscience Lane where they live; I was also made very welcome by the staff at Padworth House in Berkshire.

Ian Bradley has provided expert photographic skills throughout the writing of the book, and in 2003 Colin Kearley provided me with images from the 10 x 8 inch Victorian plates that belonged to Charles Colston and were found a century later in the offices of the *Wiltshire Gazette & Herald* in Devizes.

Moira Maidment was of great assistance with research into the Colston family in Bristol and likewise Dr John and Heather McOmie, who is related to the Colstons. Adrian Pearse was of considerable help on the Colstons' West Lydford estate and other Somerset interests. I am also grateful to the National Trust for information about the Agar-Robartes family when I visited Lanhydrock in Cornwall.

The author and publisher would also like to thank a significant number of people and organisations who have given permission to reproduce material in the book including the Wiltshire, Gloucestershire and Devon Records Offices. Brian Wilkinson's thesis on Roundway Park, written in 2001 when he was studying at Birkbeck College, London, has been an invaluable source of information, and he has continued to help me to this day. The late Peter White, to whom I was introduced by the late Joyce Wiltshire (pictured on page 167), was generous in not only allowing me to quote from his Memoirs and giving me his auction catalogues but also in talking at length to both my father and me about his time and work at Roundway.

It was a great pleasure to meet Daphne Moore in 1980 when I visited her at home in Laundry Cottage at Beaufort House and we are very grateful to be able to quote from her writings about Henry Robinson. We would also like to thank the Society of Merchant Venturers for permission to quote from their Land Steward's Report of 1947.

The Wiltshire Museum has been an invaluable source of information and I am very grateful to them for being able to quote from their historical records and for hosting the launch of this book. The former Librarian, Dr Lorna Haycock, kindly gave permission to quote from her work as the leading historian on Devizes and I am also very grateful to her for reading the relevant chapters of this book before publication. It is very sad that she died earlier this year before seeing this book published.

I am very grateful to a number of people who have read and commented on the book at various stages of its development: Brian Wilkinson, Rachel Multon, Dr John McOmie, Andrew Lownie, Matthew Dennison, Gillian Williamson and Sophie Smith. Bronwen Riley provided expert editing which was of great help. The encouragement of Professor Sir David Cannadine has been greatly appreciated.

It has been a great pleasure to work with Quiller Publishing who have not only produced a handsome book but have also given me expert guidance and advice throughout: Andrew and Gilly Johnston, Clare Grist Taylor, Arabella Ainslie and Becky Bowyer.

Last, but by no means least, I would like to thank my family. As I have mentioned, my father was an inspiration and co-conspirator on the project but my mother too has been of great help, particularly as she knew, as a young woman, some of the older family members mentioned in the book. My wife Maggie has been my support throughout the process of writing the book and our daughters, Clemmie and Francesca have grown up hearing stories of Roundway Park as I did from their grandfather a generation before.

Index

Note: page numbers in italics refer to photographs and illustrations

A Map of Roundway Park, formerly called New Park 47–8
Addington, Dr Anthony 6–7
Addington, Eleanor 6, 7, *28*, 34
Addington, Henry 6, 18, 28–9, *28*, 33
Addington, William Wells 35
Agar-Robartes, Alec 156, 236, 243, *243*
Agar-Robartes, Eva 243, *243*
Agate, James 237
AID (artificial insemination by donor) 161
Aisne, Battle of the (1914) 140
Albert, Prince 246
Alexander, Matthias 239
Allenby, General Sir Edmund 149
Alsop, Derek 212, 215
Andromeda in Wimpole Street 237
Anson, Lady Clodagh 239
Anthology of Modern Biography 237
Antoinette, Marie 108
Antrim, Lady 245
Atlas Assurance 64
Attlee, Clement 196

Baddeley, Lady 193, 200, 215
Bailiff's House 20, *20*
Baring, Maurice 241
Barrett, Eli 49
Barrett, Elizabeth 237
Bartholomew, Major John 161, 198
Bashkirtseff, Marie 240
Bateman, John 77

Bath and Wilts Chronicle and Herald 163
Bathurst, Lord 177
Baynes, Amy Ruperta
  birth of 55
  character of 154–5
  children of 72–3, 74
  class consciousness of 137–8
  death of 153–4, 235, 238
  diary of 69, 71–3, 74, 86–9, 90–1, 96–7, 134, 235
  financial independence of 67–8, 73
  health of 89–90, 153–4
  inheritance of 59
  marriage to Christopher Baynes 62–3, 65–7, 68
  photographs and illustrations of *55, 63, 72, 88, 104, 135, 153, 235*
  Ted's involvement in Boer War 124–5
Baynes, Cecilia 168, *169*, 182, 186, 190, 195–6, 214
Baynes, Christobel 91, 114, 134, 159, 166, 240
  birth of 72–3
  death of 181, 241
  in Egypt 136–7
  health of 87, 239, 241
  at Lowndes Square 238–9
  photographs of *72, 73, 74, 99, 235, 238*
  thankyou letter *86*
Baynes, Christopher (1753–1837) 64
Baynes, Christopher (1847–

1936)
  in Amy's diary 71, 72, 87, 88, 91, 97
  Amy's funeral 154
  Amy's health 89–90
  at Bank of England 73, 74, 170
  bicycling 96–7
  children of 72–3, 74
  class consciousness of 137–8
  death of 170, 179, 180
  in Egypt 136–7
  hound breeding 176–7
  hunting and shooting 88–9
  marriage to Amy Colston 62–3, 65–7, 68
  period of unemployment 73–4, 170
  photographs and portraits *63, 135, 143, 179*
  relationship with Dorothy 86, 137, 179–80, 234
Baynes, Christopher (son of John Baynes) xi
Baynes, John xi, 156, 194, 247
Baynes, Julia 64, 69
Baynes, Keith 235, 242–3
Baynes, Rev. Malcolm 154
Baynes, Margaret 63, *63*, 65
Baynes, Mary 63
Baynes, Mrs Neil 149
Baynes, Ronald 74, 154, 183–4, 213
  engagement to Ruby 137–8
  and First World War 141, 143
  at Horton House 182, 186, 195–6

marriage to Cecilia Day 168, 182
photographs 74, 99, *169*
Ted's stroke 189, 190–1
Baynes, Rory 135, 139, *139*, 141–2
Baynes, Simon xi
Baynes, Tabitha 125
Baynes, Tim xi
Baynes, William (1719–98) 63–4
Baynes, William (1789–1866) 64
Baynes, Sir William (1820–97) 63, *63*, 64–5, 67, 73
Baynes, William Edward Colston (son of Christopher Baynes) 74, 88–9, 91, 183, 194, 215, 241
  1960s correspondence with Dorothy 213–15
  and Coldstream Guards 141, 142, 146–8, 156–7
  in Egypt 135–7, 139–40, 156
  and First World War 139–40, 141, 142, 143–4, 146–9
  at Horton House 195–6
  impact of war on 149, 153, 154, 156
  photographs and illustrations of 74, 99, *118*, *135*, *142*, *148*, *157*, *180*
  and Second World War 180–1, 182
  Somerset farm 157, *157*, 180
  wounded in action 144, 146, 149
Baynes, William (son of John Baynes) xi
Beard, Madeleine 209
Beaufort, Duke of (5th) 177, 178
Beaufort, Duke of (8th) 58
Beaufort, Duke of (10th) 119, 164, 212–13
Beerbohm, Max 240
BEF (British Expeditionary

Force) 139, 140, 142
Betjeman, John ix, 209
bicycling 96–7, *96*
Blackwoods Magazine 237
Blancourd ('Blenco'), Henry 55, 56–7
Boer War 121, 124–6
Bond, John 164
Bowden, Frank 201
Bowood House 208–10
Bray, Dr George 239
B. R. Cant & Sons 159
Brimpton, Kate 168
British Hospitals Association 180
Britton, John 18, 26
Browning, Robert 237
Brueghel, Jan 198
Bryant, Rev. A. S. 154
Bucknall-Estcourt, James 35
Byron, Lord 43, 44

Cannadine, Sir David 145
Canning, Lord 29
Canova, Antonio 41–2, 47
Cecil, Lord David 237, 241
Charles Griffiths Ltd ix, 203
Charles I, King 226, 236
Chequers Court 79, *79*, 124
Christie's 197–8
Churchill, Lord Randolph 100
Cipriani, Giovanni Battista 16
Civil Engineer and Architect's Journal 45
Clifden, Viscount 243
coaching 97–8, *97*, *98*, 131–2, *131*, *132*, 133
Coats, Peter 240
Coldstream Guards 141, 142, 146–8, *148*, 156–7
Coleridge, Samuel Taylor 65
Colston, Alexander 232–3, *232*
Colston almshouses 170
Colston, Betty 130
  death of ix, 159–62, 172
  grave of *161*, 219, *219*
  photographs of *130*, *158*, *160*,

162
Colston, Charles 55, 61, 78, 85–6, 99, 128, 145, 159
  in Amy's diary 71, 87, 96, 134
  awarded peerage 144–5
  coaching 97–8, 131–2, *133*
  Coming of Age celebrations 74–6, 99
  death of 163
  electoral defeat 133–4
  financial concerns 99–100, 155–6
  funeral of 163–4
  improvements to Roundway Park 93–4, 121–2
  inheritance of 59, 60, 77, 83, 93, 100
  as Justice of the Peace 84, 90
  marriage to Rosalind Murray 66, 77
  as MP 62, 87, 90, 92, 93, 99, 121, 133, 213
  photographs and illustrations of *55*, *77*, *83*, *85*, *89*, *93*, *99*, *132*, *145*, *152*, *163*
  railway enthusiast 95–6
  Ted's Coming of Age celebrations 126–7
  Ted's involvement in Boer War 124–5
  Will of 164, 171
  and Wiltshire Volunteers *84*, 84–5, 88, 145
Colston Day 90, 231
Colston, Edward ('the Philanthropist') 37, 51, 53, 99, *226*, 226–33
  philanthropic work of 37, 228–30
  slave trading of 37, 226, 227
  statue to 37, 99, *231*
Colston, Edward Francis (1795–1847) 35, 37, 40, 51
  battles railway speculation 50–1
  children of 43, 45, 52

death of 53–4

Grand Tour 38–44, 47

improvements to Roundway
  Park 45–6, 48, 49

marriage to Marianne Jenkins
  37, 38

Colston, Edward ('the Hussar')
  45, *52*, 54, *54*, 58

children of 55–7, 59

death of 59–60

health of 57–8, 59

in Louisa's diary 57–9

marriage to Louisa Murray
  52, 54

Colston, Edward (son of Edward
  Colston, the Hussar) 55–7,
  56, 59, 146

Colston, Edward ('Ted') 78,
  130, 166, 167, 170, 176, 186,
  192

Betty's death 159–61

and Boer War 124–6

character of 183–5, 187

childhood of 88–9, 103–4,
  106, 107–8, 109

Coming of Age celebrations
  126–7

death of ix, 192, 195

and First World War 139,
  140–1, 143, 149

and Grenadier Guards
  116–117, 124–5, 139, 166,
  192, 193

health of 113–15, 189–92

and Henry Robinson 111,
  112, 113–14, 115–18

and Home Guard 181, 182,
  185, 187, 192

inheritance of 60, 164,
  167–9, 170

marriage to Gladys Duddell
  128, 129–30

and North Staffordshire
  Militia 112–13, 115–18

photographs and illustrations
  of *96*, *102*, *112*, *115*, *117*,
  118, *124*, *139*, *149*, *158*,
  162, *181*, *195*

relationship with Josephine
  Creasy 186, 191, 193

and Roundway Harriers 112,
  118, 158–9

suffers stroke 189–92

thankyou letter *86*

wartime at Roundway Park
  179, 183–5, 187, 188–9

Will of 193–4

wounded in action 126,
  140–1

Colston, Gladys 130, *158*, 179,
  186, 191

Betty's death 159–60, 161,
  162

bridge parties 187–8

character of 182–3, 187

death of 200, 215

marriage to Ted Colston 128,
  129–30

sale of Roundway Park and
  contents 195, 196–200,
  214

Ted's will 193, 194

Colston Hall 230, *230*

Colston, Isobel 59

Colston, John Morris 59, 67

Colston, Lilian 55, 58–9, 124,
  159, 163

in Amy's diary 71, 72, 87–8,
  134

Amy's illness 153–4

death of 166–7

Dorothy Baynes on 78–9,
  106, 107, 108, 109, 239

inheritance of 59, 68

photographs and illustrations
  of *55*, *78*, 99

Ted's Coming of Age
  celebrations 126–7

Colston, Louisa Ruperta 71–2,
  98, *99*, 124

character of 98, 101

children of 55–7, 58, 59

diary of 57–9

Dorothy Baynes on 98, 101,
  239

as head of the family 60, 61,
  62

marriage to Edward Colston
  52, 54

Will of 67–8

Colston, Marianne 37, 54, 58,
  60

children of 43, 45, 52

faith of 40, 58

Grand Tour 38–44, 47

improvements to Roundway
  Park 45–6, 48, 49

journal and art of 38–44, *39*,
  42, 47, 48

marriage to Edward Francis
  Colston 37, 38

Colston, Rosalind 78, 85–6,
  125, 127, 159, 164, 166

in Amy's diary 87–9, 91

Baynes sisters' literary
  activities 237, 238

character of 165–6

death of 164, 175, 176, 178

health of 175, 178

Lady Roundway rose 159, *159*

marriage to Charles Colston
  66, 77

music and singing of 88, 108,
  109

photographs and illustrations
  of *77*, *96*, *99*, *108*, *125*,
  145, *165*

relationship with staff 172,
  174, 175, 176

and Whitton Park 77, 196,
  208

Colston, Samuel 45, 54, 60

Colston, Sarah (great niece of
  Edward 'the Philanthropist')
  230, 231, 232

Colston, Sarah (mother of
  Edward 'the Philanthropist')
  226, 229

Colston, Sophia 232–3, *232*
Colston, Thomas 226
Colston, William (father of
    Edward 'the Philanthropist')
    226, 227
Colston, William (son of Edward
    Francis Colston) 45, 54, 58,
    60
Colston, Rev. William (uncle of
    Edward Francis Colston) 51
Colston-Baynes, Dorothy ix,
    x, 114, 129, 182, 192, 197,
    234–5, 241
    1960s correspondence with
        William 213–15
    Betty's death 160–1
    birth of 74, 234
    on Charles and Rosalind
        Colston 85–6
    coaching 97–8
    day in the life of Roundway
        Park 101–9
    death of ix, 215, 247
    Enter A Child ix, 74, 78, 85–6,
        95, 97, 101–9, 137, 154–5,
        179, 219–20, 234, 239
    health of 235, 236, 239,
        246–7
    on Lilian Colston 78–9, 106,
        107, 108, 109, 239
    literary career 213, 235–8,
        240, 244–6
    on Louisa Colston 98, 101,
        239
    at Newton House 181–2
    photographs of *74, 99, 101,
        179, 234, 235, 236*
    relationship with father 86,
        137, 179–8, 234
    sale of Roundway Park 200
    and spiritualism 242
    Ted's involvement in Boer War
        125–6
    wartime correspondence
        241–3
Colston's Cottages *170*

Colston's School 230, *230*
Connop, Herbert 118
Conscience Lane Lodge 21, 31,
    31, 94, *95*, 171–2, 267
Conversation Piece 238
Coombe Wood 63, 64–5, *65*
Cooper, Irene 161, 166, 171,
    173–5, *173*, *175*
Copley, John Singleton 33
Corn Production Act (1917)
    155
Correggio, Antonio 47
Cosway, Maria 42
Cosway, Richard 198
Cotes, Samuel 198
Country Life 169
Coward, Noël 238
Crammer pond 60, *60*
Creasy, Josephine 169, 186,
    191, 193–4, 198, 215
Creston, Dormer *see* Colston-
    Baynes, Dorothy
Crofton, Col Morgan 182
Cromwell House 227–8, *228*

Daily Courier 65
Daily Express 128
Daily Graphic 129
Dancer statues *46*, 47, 108
Darby, Admiral Henry 169
Darby Griffith, Arabella 43, 45,
    54, 58, 59, *61*, 169
    death of 60, 93, 168
Darby Griffith, Christopher 58,
    61–2, *61*
Darby Griffith, Christopher
    (son of Christopher Darby
    Griffith) 61, *61*, 167–8
d'Arpino, Cavaliere 47
Davies, Anne 164
Davies, Sir Walford 238
de la Trémoille, Charlotte 236
Devizes
    castle 3, 7
    close links to Roundway Park
        ix, x, 58–9, 66–7, 71,

83–4, 131, 144, 167, 170,
    178, 217–18
cloth trade 3, 4
funeral of Charles Colston
    163–4
Georgian period 3–4, 6, 7
government and politics 4,
    28, 29, 30, 34–5, 61–2, 87,
    165, 181, 203
hunting parties 88–9, 112,
    118
photographs *4, 29, 93, 152*
railway speculation 51
as self-sufficient market town
    131–3
St James's Church 56, *57*, 60,
    124, 166, 170
toy shop 91, 105
Devizes Advertiser 65–6, 228–9
Devizes Cottage Hospital 83
Devizes Gazette 124
Devizes Loyal Volunteers 28
Disraeli, Benjamin 62, 79, 87
Duddell, George 128–9, 196
Duddell, Kate 128–9, 196
Dunn, Mike 217

East India Company 6, 63, 64,
    73, 227
Edward, Prince of Wales *93,
    93*, 111
Edwards, Thomas 232
Elgar, Edward 136
Elizabeth I, Queen 230
Elizabeth II, Queen 213, 217
*English Landed Society in the 20th
    Century* 209
Enter a Child ix, 74, 78, 85–6,
    95, 97, 101–9, 137, 154–5,
    179–80, 219–20, 234, 239
Estcourt Park 32–3
Estcourt, Thomas 18, 20, 30–1,
    32–3, 34
Estcourt Jnr, Thomas (son of
    Thomas Estcourt) 32–3,
    34–5, 35

Farrar, Frederic 63
Felling the Ancient Oaks 83
Festubert, Battle of (1915) 142
Finden, Thomas 45
First World War 139–49
Forest Lodge 73, *73*
Fountains of Youth 240
Fragments on the Theory and Practice of Landscape Gardening 15
Frank, Alan 215
Fulford, Roger 245–6
Fuller, Francis 50–1

Gainsborough, Thomas 33
Galsworthy, John 65
Gardner, Keith 118
Gascoigne, Midi 241–2
General Sir Ronald Thynne, 129
George II, King 64
George III, King 6, 64, 237
George IV, King 64
George V, King 144, 167
George VI, King 240
Gibbs, James 231
Girvan, John 17
Gladstone, William 87, 92
Glanoysk (Glanusk House) 57, *57*, 59
Gostling, Emily 59, 77
Gregson's 63, 64, 66, 73
Grenadier Guards 116–117, 124–5, 139, 144, 166, 192
Guards Magazine 156
Guedalla, Philip 237–8

H. H. Wills Charity for Chronic and Incurable Sufferers 200
Hague, William 7
Hall, Emma 167
Hancock, John 56
Harcourt, Sir William 93
Harefield Place 64, *64*
Haycock, Dr Lorna 3–4
Hayman, Sir William 232
Hearn, Hilda 168

Hedges, Brig. K. M. F. 203
Hemmings, Polly 174
Hepple, Jill 161, 162, 200, 215
Hill, Heywood 241
Hill, Lady Anne 241
Hiscock, Molly 174
Hogarth, William 198
Holford, George Charles 34, 35
Hollis, Christopher 203
Home Covert 216
Home Farm x, 20, 146, 197, 216, 217–19, *218*
Home Guard 181, 182, 185, 187, 192
Home Wood 213–14
Horsbrugh, Florence 203
Horton House *179*, 182, *182*, 186, 195, 213, 267
Howard-Mercer, Honor 241
Hudson, George 50
Hunt, Henry 6
Hunter, Mr 159, 161
Hurd, Sir Percy 181

Imperial School of Instruction (Cairo) 143
Imperial Twilight 64
'Impromptu' 62
In Search of Two Characters 244–5
Independent Order of Oddfellows 83–4

Jeanne La Pucelle 236
Jenkins, Sarah 37
Jenkins, William 37, 54, 60
Jolliffe, Ted 181
Jones, Inigo 10
Journal of a Tour in France, Switzerland, and Italy 38–44, *39*, *42*

Kauffmann, Angelica 108
Kennet and Avon Canal 27–8, *27*, 96, 217, *217*
King, Henry 164, 171
Kitchener, Lord 136

Kneller, Godfrey 230
Knyfton, Georgie 76, *76*, 93
Knyfton, Thomas Tutton 76

Lady Roundway rose 159, *159*
Lancaster, Osbert 240
Lansdowne, Marquess of 209
Leach, Clive 96, *202*, 211
Leech, John 181
Lees-Milne, James 200, 210, 237, 240, 241–2, 244, 245–6, 247
Lely, Sir Peter 198
Leslie, Shane 242
Listener 179
Lloyd George, David 134
Local Government Act (1888) 90
London Gazette 148
London Illustrated News 53
Long, Walter 87
Lovat, Laura 241
Lowndes Square 137, 159, 165, 180, 194, 236–7, 238–9
Lowther, Toupie 128
Lubbock, John 28
Lunatics Act (1845) 58
Lytton, Earl of 244–5

Mahon, Viscount 129
'Major' 177, 178
Manningford Bruce manor 7, 27
Many and Various – A Ballet Revue 245
Marlborough Lodge 48, *48*, *110*, 192, *216*
Marne, Battle of the (1914) 140
Married Women's Property Act (1870) 67
Married Women's Property Act (1882) 67
Marsh, Sir Edward 245
Matthews, Capt. Robert J. 30
Megiddo, Battle of (1918) 149
Menin Road, Battle of (1917) 149

Mercure de France 236
Mitford, Nancy 240, 241
Moore, Daphne 111, 119,
    211–12
Morland, George 33
Morning Post 65, 144, 163, 213
Mortimer, Raymond 179
Murray, Amelia 237
Murray, Col. Charles Gostling
    52, 59, 62, 77–8
Murray, George (father of
    Louisa Murray) 52, 57
Murray, Rt. Rev. Lord George
    (grandfather of Louisa
    Murray) 52, 57
Murray, J. H. 166
Murray, Lady George 237
Murray, Nina 198
Murray, Ruperta Catherine 52,
    57, 59
Music and the Ordinary Listener
    238
My Ancestress, Charlotte de la
    Trémoille 236
My Life in Domestic Service at
    Padworth House 168

Napoleon/Napoleonic Wars 29,
    30, 38, 43, 64, 106, 244
Nash, John 20
National Trust 200
Nelson, Lord 169
Neuve-Chapelle, Battle of
    (1915) 142
New Statesman 179
Newlands 55–7, 56, 58, 71, 146
Nicholas, Edward 8
North Staffordshire Militia
    112–13, 115–18
Nulli Secundus Club 156

Oliver, Mrs 114, 129–30
Osborne, Agnes 239
Osmund, Bishop of Salisbury 3
Ovington Square 180, 182, 213,
    238, 240, 244, 246–7

Owen, David 171–2

Padworth House 58, 61, 61,
    62, 168–70, 168, 169, 186,
    193–4, 215, 267
Palmer, Lynwood 198
Palmerston, Lord 62
Parr, Katherine 7
Passchendaele, Battle of (1917)
    147–8
Peacock's Polite Repository 18
Pearson, Mr 174
People's Budget (1909) 134
Percival, Spencer 32
Peterborough Harrier Show
    119, 119
Phillips, David 202
Phillips, John 216
Phillips, Sarah 216
Phipps, Veronica 241
Pictorial Record 121
Pitt the Elder, William 6–7
Pitt the Younger, William 6–7,
    17–18, 28–9, 28
Platt, Stephen R. 64
Poems from Paul Verlaine 236
Pollitt, Dora 193, 215
Poor Law Board 32
Pope-Hennessy, James 240
'Poussin landscape' 198
Powell, Anthony 179
Pratt, Auriol 193, 194
Pratt, Beatrix 161, 215
Primrose League 87
Princess 234
Pritchett, V. S. 179
Pugin, Augustus 76
Pythouse 213, 215

Quakers Walk ix, 8, 8, 19, 20,
    23, 23, 30–1, 58, 80, 164,
    172, 174, 204, 211, 216,
    217–18, 218
Quakers Walk Lodge 48, 48, 50,
    50, 111, 134, 188, 193, 204,
    204, 211, 211

Queen Anne house 6, 8, 10,
    10–11, 15, 16–17

Rambridge, Mary 164
Rebecca, Biagio 16
Recollections of the Early Years of the
    Present Century 237
Red Book 3, 17, 18, 19, 20,
    21–6, 31, 31
Reform Act (1832) 6, 34
Reform Act (1867) 62
Regan, Joan 171, 176
Renton, Dr 189, 190
Repton, Humphry ix, 3, 11, 15,
    17–26, 31
    Red Book 3, 17, 18, 19, 20,
        21–6, 31, 31
Return of Owners of Land 77
Richardson, Sir Albert 209
Richardson, Jonathan 231
Richardson, Richard 27
Richmond, Duke of 240
R.M.S. Osterley 136
Robinson, Henry 17, 111, 146,
    164, 174, 176, 193
    death of 111, 211, 212
    half-century of service
        celebrations 183–4
    hound breeding x, 111–12,
        119, 158–9, 176–8, 212
    photographs 111, 118, 119
    retirement of 196, 211–12
    Roundway Harriers 111, 112,
        118–19, 158–9, 176–7,
        212
    and Ted Colston 111, 112,
        113–14, 115–18, 189–91
Robinson, John Martin 83, 208
Roger of Caen, Bishop of
    Salisbury 7
Rose, Joseph 15–16
Roundway Park (formerly New
    Park)
    billiard room 94, 94
    building of ix, 3, 8, 10,
        14–17, 26

cabinet room 106, *107*, 109

circular room *71*, *87*, *100*, 106, *150*, *199*, 214

close links to Devizes ix, x, 58–9, 66–7, 71, 83–4, 131, 144, 167, 170, 178, 217–18

conservatory 15, 66, *66*, *86*, 122

courtyard 13–14, *14*, *45*, *94*, 97, *97*, 104–5, *105*

day in the life of 101–10

design of ix, 3, 7, 8, 10, 11, 13–17, 122

dining room 15–16, 46, 107–8, *199*

dome chamber 17, *17*

drawing room 15–16, *16*, 46–7, *46*, 107, 108–9, *109*, *199*

drives 18–19, 21, 31, *217*

entrance hall 10, 15, 122, 208

fireplaces *11*, 15, 46, *122*, 122, 206, *206*, 210, 220

greenhouse of x

hunts and shooting 48, 71, 88–9, *110*, 112, *112*, 118–19, *118*, 121, 158, 178, 186,

illustrations and photographs *xii*, *13*, *32*, *71*, *73*, *91*, *94*, *100*, *121*, *123*, *201–2*, *204*, *210*, *211*, *220*

improvements and renovations 35, 45–6, 48, 93–4, 121–2, 204–6, 210–11

kennels *110*, 169, 176–8, 186, 193

kitchen 16–17, 174–5, 210

kitchen garden 14, 19, 48, 205

landscaping of ix, 3, 11, 17–26, 30–1, 48, 49

library 15, 46, 101, 103, 122, *122*

maps and plans of 8, *9*, *12*, *19*, *36*, 47–8, *82*, *120*, *123*

modern residential properties 205–6, *205*, *206*, *216*, *218*

paintings and sculptures at 33, 46, 47, 108, 169–70, 198

Palladian style of ix, 3, 13, 122

panelling 10–11, *11*, 122

parkland ix, 18, 45, 48, *71*, 83–4, *84*, *87*, *110*, 133

partial demolition of ix, 204, 208, 209, 210–11

planting schemes 19–20, *20*, 30

plasterwork ceilings 10, *11*, 15–16, *16*, 17, *17*, *150*, *199*

pleasure gardens 19, 31, *49*, 50–1

portico *12*, *45*, *94*, *104*

proposed use as educational establishment ix, 201, 203

purchased by Alan Frank 215

purchased by Derek Alsop 212

purchased by Edward Francis Colston 35, 37

purchased and sold by George Charles Holford 34, 35

purchased by Peter White 203–5

renamed from New Park 35, 45

sale of contents, fixtures and fittings 197–8, 205, 206–8

servants and staff x, 17, 55, 72, 131, 164, 171–8, 188, 193–4

servants' quarters 17, 174, 176

sold by Gladys Colston 195, 196–200, 214

sold for demolition ix, 203

staircases 10, *11*, *17*

valuations 30, 33–4, 164,

193, 197, 199–200, 212

views and vistas 11, 13, 18, 20–6, *21–6*

walled garden 18, 19, 31, *31*, 122, *122*

water gardens 49, *49*, 216

Roundway Harriers 111, 112, *112*, 118–19, *118*, *119*, 158–9, 176–7, *177*, 212

Royal African Company 37, 227

Rupert of the Rhine, Prince 52

Russell, Dr 235

Rysbrack, John Michael 231

Sackville-West, Eddy 240, 242

Samuels, Freddie 209

Sartin, Jack 174

Savage, John 102, 105–6, 127, 143, 164, 189

Schlieffen Plan 140

Sheep Wash Dell 48

Shepherd, R. P. 170

Sheppard, Henry *202*

Slade School of Fine Art 235

slave trade 37, 226, 227, 232

Sloper, George 28

Society of Merchant Venturers ix, 197, 199–200, 215, 230

Somme, Battle of the (1916) 146–7

Sotheron, Admiral Frank 32, 34

Sotheron, Lucy 32, 34

Spectator 179

St James's Church (Devizes) 56, *57*, 60, 124, 166, 170

St Joseph of Arimathea – The Glastonbury Legend 241

St Leger, William 147–8

St Peters Church (West Lydford) 51, *51*

Stanton Drew and Wells Harriers 158

Stringer, Selborne 203

Strong, Phyllis 174, 176

Stuart, Daniel 65

Sutton, Charlotte ('Sarah') 7,

30, 34
Sutton, Edward 4
Sutton, Eleanor 7, 20, 30, 32, 34
Sutton, George 30
Sutton, James (grandfather of James Sutton) 4
Sutton, James 3, 4–6, 7–8, 19, 27, 28–30
  design and building of New Park 3, 7, 8, 10, 11, 14, 16
  landscaping of New Park 17–19, 26
Sutton, James (cousin of James Sutton) 7
Sutton, James (son of James Sutton) 30
Sutton, Mary 30
Sutton, Prince 4–6, 7
Sutton, William 6
Swiss Cottage 48–9, 49, 58, 71, 88, 121, 195, 200, 214, 217

Tebbutt, Lt. Colonel 141
Thatched cottage 20, 87, 216
The Beauties of Wiltshire 26
The Blind Fiddler 65
The Clown of Paradise 235
The Decline and Fall of the British Aristocracy 145
The Destruction of the Country House 1875–1975 x
The Forsyte Saga 65
The Great Landowners of Great Britain and Ireland 77
The Man of Property 65
The Regent and his Daughter 237–8
The Stag Hunt 198
The Youthful Queen Victoria 213

Thomas, Bill 183, 187–8, 195, 196, 197, 200, 214
Thomas, Eileen x, 187–8, 195, 200, 214
Thompson, F. M. L. 156
Thrupp, Mr 58
Thynne, Angela 129
Times 119, 131, 155, 163, 164, 215
Times Literary Review / Supplement 237, 240
'Togo' 181, 186, 187
Town and County Planning Act (1947) 198–9
Town Hall (Devizes) 4

Uphill Castle 76, 76

van Wittel, Caspar 47
Verdun, Battle of (1916) 146, 147
Verelst, Simon 198
Verlaine, Paul 236
Victoria, Queen 72, 124, 237, 245, 246
View of the Seats of Noblemen and Gentlemen in England, Wales, Scotland and Ireland 32
Villa Aldobrandini 47, 47

Wadham Locke family 30, 99, 214
Wages During Sickness 180
Wainwright, C 76
Wales, Princess of 72
Wall Street Crash (1929–31) 168, 169, 170
Ward, John 27
Ward, Stephen 247
Way, R. P. 198

White, Peter ix, 203–6, 207–11, 212
Whitton Park 59, 77, 77, 122, 196, 208
Wilhelm II, Kaiser 149
Wilkie, Sir David 65
Wilkinson, Brian 210
Willats, Ione 114, 182, 184
Willats (later Crofton), Julia Ruperta 92, 92, 182, 182–3, 184, 187
Willats, Ruperta 92, 114, 128, 129, 182, 184, 186, 195
Willats, William 92, 182
Willy the elder, George (grandfather of James Sutton) 5, 6, 8
Willy the younger, George (uncle of James Sutton) 5, 6
Willy, Mary 4–6
Willy, William 5, 6, 8
Wilson, Woodrow 147
Wiltshire Advertiser 163–4
Wiltshire County Lunatic Asylum 58
Wiltshire Friendly Society 35
Wiltshire Gazette 90, 128, 140, 154, 178, 181, 192
Wiltshire Telegraph 131–3
Wiltshire Volunteers 84, 84–5, 88, 145
Wiltshire Yeomanry 88, 88, 93, 145
Witherington, Miss 109
Worsley, Giles 209
Wyatt, James ix, 3, 7, 8, 10, 11, 13, 14–17, 26, 122

Zucchi, Antonio 16

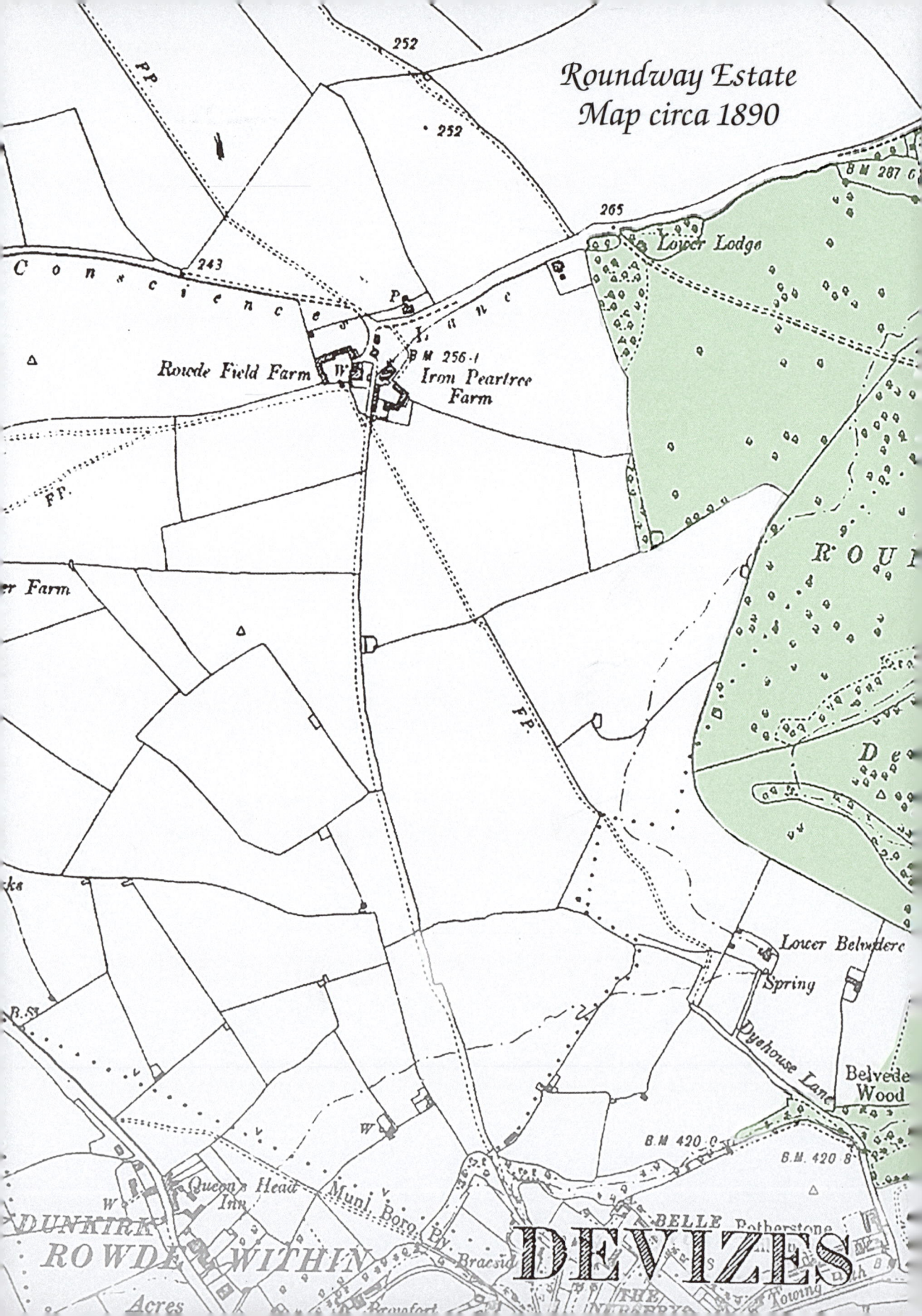

Roundway Estate
Map circa 1890